Race and Education in North Carolina

MAKING THE MODERN SOUTH

David Goldfield, *Series Editor*

Race and Education in North Carolina

From Segregation to Desegregation

John E. Batchelor

Louisiana State University Press
Baton Rouge

Published by Louisiana State University Press

Manufactured in the United States of America
First printing

Designer: Laura Roubique Gleason
Typeface: Corda
Printer and binder: Maple Press

Library of Congress Cataloging-in-Publication Data

Batchelor, John E.
Race and education in North Carolina : from segregation to desegregation / John E. Batchelor.
pages cm. — (Making the modern South)
Includes bibliographical references and index.
ISBN 978-0-8071-6136-4 (cloth : alk. paper) — ISBN 978-0-8071-6137-1 (pdf) — ISBN 978-0-8071-6138-8 (epub) — ISBN 978-0-8071-6139-5 (mobi) 1. School integration—North Carolina—History—20th century. 2. African Americans—Education—North Carolina—History—20th century. I. Title.
LC214.22.N66B38 2015
379.2'6309756—dc23

2015008667

The paper in this book meets the guidelines for permanence and durability of the Committee on Production Guidelines for Book Longevity of the Council on Library Resources. ♾

For
H. G. Jones
and
Dallas Herring

Contents

Preface

North Carolina has been regarded as a bellwether state in race relations, school desegregation, school reform, and politics. *Race and Education in North Carolina* is a history of school desegregation in North Carolina, framed in a national context. It traces the evolution of case law and the interaction of law with policy, within constraints established by political and social history, along with the decisions, actions, and motivations of state leaders.

As documented by A. Leon Higginbotham Jr., retired chief judge of the U.S. Court of Appeals for the Third Circuit, the American legal process has substantiated, perpetuated, and legitimized the precept of racial inferiority while also providing the mechanism for ameliorating the conditions which the legal system helped to establish and maintain.[1] To a significant extent, the judicial reasoning examined was conceived within the context of making decisions that "accorded with broadly held social values."[2] Written legal opinions as well as statutes, in the words of G. Edward White, "reflect to some degree the changing patterns of American civilization and may fruitfully be viewed as indices of the general tone of American culture at various points in time."[3] Case law, therefore, not only furnishes the historian with sets of well-tested facts, but also provides a powerful measure of ideas and attitudes that predominated in particular periods. I have, therefore, at various points considered case law and legislation as cultural artifacts. Case law shows the slow but inexorable movement toward court-mandated school desegregation as well as providing a strong measure of attitudes and beliefs regarding race. I believe the utilization of case law in this multilayered manner is unique to the writing of North Carolina history.

My research utilized several types of sources. A synthesis of relevant secondary works establishes the political framework for North Carolina. As a former school-system superintendent, I am familiar with State Department of Public Instruction Reports. Those documents provided data that describe the actual conditions of education from approximately 1900 to 1950. In addition, major daily newspapers constantly covered the news of school desegregation. I supplemented these major dailies with articles from some smaller, local newspapers. Such coverage, however, flowed from a predominantly mainstream, white perspective. Those newspapers, therefore, were counterbalanced by two weeklies, *The Carolinian* and *The Carolina Times,* which were circulated statewide and devoted to black readership.

In my efforts to identify primary sources, I found the papers of the Umstead, Hodges, Sanford, Moore, and Scott administrations, housed in the North Carolina State Archives, to be voluminous. They contain not only correspondence but extensive internal memoranda circulated within the highest levels of those administrations. The papers of William Dallas Herring constitute one of the largest private collections in the archives. Dallas Herring was a member of the first committee appointed by the governor of North Carolina to study how the state should respond to school desegregation orders; he later chaired the State Board of Education for approximately twenty-five years. The Thomas Pearsall Papers are housed in the Southern Historical Collection in Chapel Hill. Pearsall chaired the governor's Special Advisory Committee on Education, which developed North Carolina's policies related to early desegregation.

In order to understand the stimulus for change, I have reviewed the papers of black leaders in North Carolina who were associated with the civil rights movement. The Kelly Alexander and Frederick Alexander Papers are housed at the University of North Carolina–Charlotte. Kelly Alexander was state president of the National Association for the Advancement of Colored People. Frederick Alexander, his brother, was one of the first black men in twentieth-century North Carolina to hold elected public office. Kelly Alexander was more the activist, working in cooperation with the national NAACP office to raise issues and instigate lawsuits. Frederick Alexander worked more quietly, behind the scenes and within the system.

Much civil rights litigation in North Carolina came about in the early years through the efforts of attorney Conrad Pearson of Durham. Later, Charlotte attorney Julius Chambers took over the initiative. Chambers eventually became chief legal counsel to the NAACP Legal Defense and Educational Fund. He left that position to return to North Carolina as chancellor of North Carolina Central University, at the invitation of C. D. Spangler Jr., who by that time was president of the University of North Carolina system. Spangler was the former chair of the Charlotte-Mecklenburg Board of Education, whom Chambers had sued. Chancellor Chambers provided advice regarding my case law interpretations as well as explaining his own goals and intentions. I have also reviewed the Chambers Papers at UNC-Charlotte.

To provide a supplement to archival materials, I have conducted interviews with surviving individuals who participated in the decisions that produced North Carolina's response to the U.S. Supreme Court's historic 1954 *Brown v. Board of Education of Topeka* case, as well as individuals who constantly pushed for greater movement toward school desegregation. These interviews focused on what the individuals involved believed, why they acted as they did, and what they thought about other individuals, especially those who held public office. Former governor and U.S. senator Terry Sanford cooperated in an interview during the research phase of the work. During the final months of his life, he also read the portion of the manuscript that applied to his administration, and he provided me with additional advice.

In order to understand the conservative point of view, I attempted to interview Dr. I. Beverly Lake. But Dr. Lake's hearing had become impaired, and he could not understand me over the telephone. He was cooperative and amenable to an in-person interview, but I failed to recognize the urgency of the situation, and he died before I could arrange a meeting. I met briefly with Thomas Ellis, but he declined to be interviewed, based on responsibilities of attorney-client confidentiality. I did interview W. W. Taylor. We did not discuss specifics that might have infringed on attorney-client confidentiality, but he helped me understand the points of view that have prevailed among conservatives in North Carolina. I came away with an appreciation for the sincerity of his beliefs as well as his honesty and expertise. He was a founder and principal of one of the largest and most influential law firms in the state, and his abilities speak for themselves.

Acknowledgments

I would like to thank Bettye MacPhail-Wilcox, Burton Beers, Barbara Parramore, and Bruce Beezer of North Carolina State University for their guidance. James Mulholland and James Crisp of North Carolina State, plus Allen Trelease and Robert Calhoon of the University of North Carolina–Greensboro, as well as William Link, then at UNC-Greensboro, now at the University of Florida, reviewed and criticized earlier, narrower phases of the research. Dallas Herring's candor in response to my questions and his willingness to allow me access to his papers reflects his devotion to history.

Robin Brabham, special collections librarian, and Randy Penninger, manuscript curator, at the University of North Carolina at Charlotte, provided valuable assistance regarding the Alexander Papers. Cathy Martin of the North Carolina Legislative Library assisted me in tracking down some details. Linda Cox, of the North Carolina Attorney General's Office, answered inquiries concerning the tenure of several attorneys general. Richard Lankford and the staff of the North Carolina State Archives cooperated with my lengthy stay there while I researched the governors' papers. The study could not have been completed without the assistance and resources of H. G. Jones and Alice Cotten, as well as other members of the staff at the North Carolina Collection, plus Dorothy Grant and the Law Library staff, at the University of North Carolina at Chapel Hill Libraries. Stephen Fletcher, Robert Anthony, and Jason Tomberlin provided assistance in the Photo Archives of the North Carolina Collection.

Dale Batchelor, my wife, and Robert Holmes provided valuable criticisms with regard to the conception of the work as well as its readability. Although I sought to document the book to the standards of legal scholarship, I also hope I have produced a work that is readily accessible to the general reading public.

Additional appreciation goes to attorneys who reviewed portions of draft manuscripts and helped me avoid blunders in reporting, citing, and analyzing case law, as well assisting me in tracking down obscure cases: Jerry Weston in particular, plus Fred Johnson, Richard Schwartz, William Womble, Mark Lowe, Winburne King, Nick Sojka, and Andrew Vanore Jr. Rick Pinto helped me comprehend legal logic in several casual conversations. Nick Sojka, in particular, encouraged me to incorporate the experiences and point of view of a school superintendent as I thought about these issues.

I especially appreciate the advice and expertise of Rand Dotson and the staff at Louisiana State University Press and the anonymous reviewers who provided critiques of the manuscript. Copyeditor Stan Ivester earned gratitude as well as sympathy for the level of detail involved in his work.

I have not merely researched these events from the distant point of view of the scholar. I have lived them. I attended segregated elementary and junior high schools in Greensboro, North Carolina, as well as two years in segregated private schools, before graduation from Page High School in 1964. My class was one of the first to include black students. I began my career as a teacher in the Guilford County Schools in 1969, during the early years of desegregation. Since 1985, I have served two school districts as an assistant superintendent, two as superintendent. In both of the districts where I was superintendent, white students were in the minority, and the districts were categorized by the state as high poverty/low wealth. They were among the 12 (out of 117) lowest in academic achievement in North Carolina when I went there. The year I retired, every school in the district was rated "Exemplary" on academic achievement, based on the state accountability model in effect at the time.

Obviously, my approximately thirty years as a public school educator in North Carolina exerted a powerful force in the development of my interpretations and conclusions. I gained additional insights over the next ten years, when I worked in over thirty states as a leadership consultant for the Success for All Foundation and the Center for Data Driven Reform in Education at Johns Hopkins University. I modified my outlook on education continuously during that period as I saw aspects of the United States that I never knew existed and realized how naive I had been all my life. I was able to devote the concentrated, extended time necessary to complete the book after I re-retired.

I hope I have accurately represented the points of view of all parties in this complex range of developments related to education, politics, and race. My own overriding point of view will be obvious to the reader: I believe in equal educational opportunity for all children, and I believe that if people get to know each other, they will be able to make informed perceptions based on individual qualities, rather than generalizations that are culturally ingrained. That requires spending time, preferably during formative years, in settings that are diverse, to include people of other races and cultures. I believe that strong evidence supports the conclusion that, whenever students are isolated in high concentrations of race and poverty, that condition inherently handicaps the school's capacity to teach and students' capacity to learn. I believe, therefore, that schools that are integrated on the basis of race, culture, and socioeconomic family levels, are good for students, good for North Carolina, and good for the United States.

Race and Education in North Carolina

1
Education, Race, and Politics

What is education? The eminent historian Bernard Bailyn defined education not only as pedagogy but "the entire process by which a culture transmits itself across the generations."[1] That is a grand vision, couched in the origins of the new American nation.

The history of education, as formal schooling actually developed in the nineteenth and twentieth centuries, forces a somewhat different perspective, more narrowly defined. Education became the process by which members of each generation acquire the knowledge and skills that enable them to become responsible citizens and gain access to desired levels of earning, power, and socioeconomic status, or whatever they believe will enhance the quality of their lives.

In the modern era, access to education has been controlled by governments, or entities functioning in the capacity of governments.[2] Such control flows along a continuum. Thus, governments prohibit, restrict, allow, provide, or ensure education. In this context, providing or ensuring education can pave pathways to greater freedoms. Restricting or prohibiting education can constitute a mechanism for subordination.

For most of history, in most countries, education has been widely prohibited. Access to education has tended to be restricted to the elite. The United States, over time, has broken with that tradition. Thomas Jefferson voiced the view that the new nation ought to provide free public education, although, in the context of the times, that meant restricted to white males. But Jefferson's vision was rejected as radical. The word "education" never appeared in the U.S. Constitution, thus deferring control of education to state governments. In 1893, the Committee of Ten, a task force established by the National Education Association, made up largely of scholars and headed by Charles W. Eliot, president of Harvard University, envisioned a role for education that was far from universal: to identify and select young men of proper family background and high intelligence and prepare them to assume their roles as leaders.[3]

North Carolina has prided itself on an early commitment to higher education. The University of North Carolina at Chapel Hill was the first state university to admit and graduate students. But North Carolina began providing education to young children reluctantly. Educational opportunities were provided to white children before the Civil War, but on a highly restricted basis. North Carolina and other southern states prohibited education for blacks by law until after the Civil War, provided education to blacks on a widespread basis during Reconstruction, but restricted access thereafter, and maintained such restrictions into the 1970s. States in the North and West restricted access to education by black children, but by custom rather than by law.

Educational opportunities have occupied a multitiered structure, stratified along lines identifiable not only on the basis of race but also by gender, geography, and socioeconomic levels. Through the mid-twentieth century, states expanded educational opportunities, but restrictions continued to conform to widespread notions about academic abilities and adult roles and occupations that followed lines defined by race, gender, geography, and socioeconomic level, conditions determined by circumstances of birth.

Young women were gradually incorporated into the educational system, albeit within a framework centering on training for family roles; clerical or other work at lower levels of business, but not management; seldom academia; nurses, but rarely doctors, and even then probably restricted to the specialty of pediatrics; teachers, but not administrators above the elementary level. Children from lower socioeconomic strata of all races and children who were born in or lived in locations that were historically poor have been underserved by educational systems throughout the history of the states and the nation.

Restrictions based on race have been strongest. Racial segregation and systematic subordination were elaborately interwoven not only into the nation's culture, but also into its legislative and judicial code, operating not merely as custom but as law. In addition to restrictions on elementary and secondary education, access to higher education, especially graduate and professional schooling—historic gateways to upper echelons of political and socioeconomic status—was restricted or prohibited, by law in the South, by custom elsewhere, on the basis of race, and by custom on the basis of gender.

Ensuring equal educational opportunity to all children regardless of race, gender, geography, or family socioeconomic level did not become a goal for educational and political systems in the United States until the 1970s and 1980s. Discrimination, therefore, has been a core element of education through most of U.S. history, as the system that policy makers designed parsed out schooling in varying degrees of quantity and quality. Discrimination in the educational system has been constructed on a foundation of beliefs that adults hold about the potentials inherent in children, beliefs clustered according to race, gender, geography, and family socioeconomic level. Educational systems, perfectly aligned to produce the results they in fact produce,[4] have generated patterns of achievement that conform to adult belief systems, because the discriminatory aspect of the system itself is a self-fulfilling prophecy.

At various points in history, different political entities have sought to expand or to restrict access to education, especially on the basis of race. Republican rule ensued in North Carolina during Reconstruction, and in some localities during this period more educational opportunities were provided to blacks than to whites. Conservative Democrats regained control thereafter, and restrictions were imposed on blacks, both in education and in voting, that remained in effect for more than half a century.

The Democratic Party continued to control government in North Carolina for over seventy years. Within the party, factions ranged from strong conservatives to moderates. True liberals seldom appear, at least not among elected officeholders. Conservatives tended to favor limited government, low taxes, and maintaining the existing social order, which included strong support for racial segregation. Conservatives spanned the entire spectrum of socioeconomic levels, from lower and poorly educated to upper and well educated. Moderates supported broader access to educational opportunity as well as improving the quality of education within existing schools. They were willing to consider higher taxes to support more government services, including expanding education. They were proud of what they perceived as harmony and cooperation between the races. In the face of challenges to the existing order, they considered obeying the law and following a moral voice more important than maintaining segregation. Moderate leaders tended to be better educated than most of the population and were more likely to be business owners and managers or lawyers, as well as professional educators and members of the clergy.

Throughout the twentieth century, the primary impetus for social change, especially in matters related to race, came from the judicial system, responding to lawsuits initiated at the local level. Often, such suits originated within organizations that were able to garner resources sufficient to sustain legal challenges through multiple levels of appeal. The National Association for the Advancement of Colored People (NAACP) was by far the most important of these organizations. Litigation related to segregation and desegregation filed during the twentieth century thus creates the structure of change as well as providing deep insights into the tenor of the times and the range and depth of belief systems related to race.

Change occurred slowly, propelled by court decisions that created identifiable inflection points. These points would force changes in the nature of what constituted political moderation and moderate civic leadership. Political positions that appear to be conservative from a twenty-first-century point of view amounted to reasonable, moderate accommodations to dramatic cultural shifts in the context of the mid-twentieth century. Accommodations that would have been unimaginable before 1950 became moderate responses to demands for change that at the time appeared radical.

The legal and political systems thus created the framework that drove the educational system. Over approximately seventy-five years, the legal system shifted from sanctioning to outlawing segregation. Opposing polarities in the political system sought to balance obeying the law, as the law changed, versus maintaining social structures that had constituted the normal way of life, rarely examined, hardly ever challenged. The educational system would have to find ways to transition from entrenched assumptions of inferiority that logically supported a pattern of practices producing stratified outcomes to a goal of equal educational opportunity for all children, without regard to race, gender, geography, or family socioeconomic level.

2

Segregation

SEPARATE AND UNEQUAL, THROUGH THE 1950S

North Carolina in the twentieth century enjoyed a reputation for moderation with regard to race relations. It was a relatively peaceful state. Other states in the South witnessed higher levels of intimidation, violence, and restrictions on freedom, as well as greater restrictions on educational opportunities for blacks. But all southern states required racial segregation in schools and public accommodations, and segregation existed in the North and the West as well. Segregation functioned within a system of subordination that not only included race but also extended to gender, geography, and the socioeconomic status of families.

What pattern of practices related to this system operated in the United States through the mid-1950s? How did North Carolina and the South fit into this pattern? What forces began to overcome discrimination in education and move nation and state toward equal educational opportunities for all children?

The National Framework: Separate but Equal

Prior to the mid-1950s, every state practiced racial segregation in schools, based either on law—*de jure* segregation—or on custom—*de facto* segregation. *De facto* segregation tended to be based on patterns of residence, which closely followed family socioeconomic levels.

In 1896, the U.S. Supreme Court decision in *Plessy v. Ferguson*[1] established the practice of racial segregation in law. The court upheld a Louisiana statute requiring separate but equal seating for white and black railway passengers. Albion W. Tourgée, a white[2] carpetbagger attorney who had lived in Greensboro and served as a judge in North Carolina during Reconstruction, argued on behalf of Homer A. Plessy, noted by the court to be of "seven-eighths Caucasian and one-eighth African blood."[3] Plessy had been imprisoned for boarding a railroad car designated for whites.[4] The court concluded that laws separating the races were justifiable as part of the regulatory powers of the state.

Three years later, the court applied the concept of separate but equal to public schools in *Cumming v. Board of Education*.[5] The court held that, although black students in Richmond County, Georgia, had not been provided a tax-supported, tuition-free high school, the Board of Education had the discretion to decide what types of schools to establish. Separate schools were permitted, and the legal obligation of equality had been met, since elementary schools were provided for black students. Almost a decade later, the court validated racial separation in higher education in *Berea College v. Kentucky*.[6]

Over the next twenty-five years, legal determinations of equality would become a judicial chimera that obscured layers of discrimination. For black Americans, reality was separate and unequal. The NAACP was founded in 1909, based on the mission of eliminating racial subordination. The organization promptly began sponsoring lawsuits seeking to overturn the doctrine of separate but equal.[7]

Early cases in education targeted the graduate and professional level, especially law schools. This strategy grew out of several considerations.[8] Of greatest importance was the fact that most southern states provided no graduate or professional education for blacks. Such absence obviated the burden of proving inequality. The NAACP also sought to promote the development of an educated black leadership class that would probably lead to the expansion of the organization's membership. Furthermore, NAACP leaders thought that judges would be sympathetic to men seeking legal education. Women did not occupy seats in the nation's law schools at that time. Focusing on law schools thus allowed the NAACP to avoid prejudice regarding social contacts between black men and white women.[9] In addition, the organization's leaders believed that white society might not feel as intimidated by desegregation among students old enough for graduate school, whereas the image of young black and white children in school together, or of white elementary children being taught and disciplined by black teachers, could spawn a backlash.[10]

Through the 1930s, litigation focused on whether equal facilities had been provided to blacks. If some measure of similarity existed, the Supreme Court consistently held that racial segregation created no conflict with basic constitutional rights. Around 1940, however, the court began to look at the implications of school segregation in the broader constitutional context of equal opportunity under law. Precedents in higher education cases thus paved the way for litigation in public school education.[11]

In *Brown v. Board of Education*,[12] the Supreme Court reached the conclusion in 1954 that segregation was inherently discriminatory, and that segregation had no place in the scheme of public education at the elementary and secondary level. The justices acknowledged, however, that the consideration of appropriate relief "presents problems of considerable complexity."[13] The court realized that it was outlawing a way of life in the South and invited those states that practiced *de jure* segregation to return to the court to answer questions about implementation.

Brown II,[14] the implementation phase of the decision, was argued and decided in 1955. The southern states complained that ending segregation was all but impossible. If the practice had to end, however, the states needed time to develop strategies to comply. The court granted time when it directed that schools be desegregated "with all deliberate speed,"[15] terminology indicating that the South had a period of time, as yet unspecified, to adjust. Such time was necessary because over six million students were assigned to schools on a segregated basis. The sheer magnitude of reassignments would demand time for logistical considerations.

Generations of Americans, especially in the South, were accustomed to a pattern of racial segregation deeply embedded in their culture and enforced by legislative and judicial systems. Litigation leading to a Supreme Court order to desegregate thus became the initial force redirecting the pattern of discriminatory practices that had been in place for generations. Although *Brown* reversed the direction of judicial rulings in school segregation, racial attitudes and political practices would continue to represent a barrier to change.

Swift and smooth desegregation was not likely. Samuel Lubell, one of the nation's most astute judges of public opinion, predicted, "Probably no other single issue would stir as violent an emotional storm in the South as to outlaw segregation in elementary schools."[16] The history of school desegregation in North Carolina and in the nation would prove Lubell's prophecy correct.

The "Separate" Aspect of Separate but Equal in North Carolina

North Carolina initially provided little education for any of its young people. The North Carolina Constitution of 1776 included the establishment of public schools, but the legislature appropriated no funds for schools below the university level for over fifty years.[17] In the 1830–31 session of the legislature, a joint House and Senate committee reported, "One source of great evil which suggests itself . . . is, the teaching of slaves to read and write; thereby affording them facilities of intelligence and communication, inconsistent with their condition, destructive of their contentment and happiness, and dangerous to the community."[18] The state had never provided education to blacks at that time, but representatives were aware that individuals might undertake such initiatives. The legislature thus prohibited education for slaves, making teaching a slave to read or write a crime.

After the Civil War, the state's new constitution directed the General Assembly to provide a system of public schools supported by taxes. Conservative Democrats initially tried to insert a requirement for racially segregated schools, but carpetbagger delegates, led by Albion Tourgée, who would later argue *Plessy*, and State Superintendent of Public Instruction Samuel S. Ashley, beat down the effort. Legislation passed the following year nevertheless established schools on a segregated basis. Fears among whites of racially mixed schools remained strong and undermined efforts to reestablish schools during Reconstruction.[19]

Education for blacks during this period received support from the Freedmen's Bureau and from associations affiliated with religious groups that had opposed slavery.[20] The Peabody Fund provided additional help for the education of both races.[21] Freedmen's Bureau schools for blacks met significant opposition among whites. For example, Captain A. W. Bolenius, a federal officer occupying Guilford County, reported to his superiors in Washington, "The want of public schools throughout the county is most deplorably felt."[22] Freedmen's Bureau agent Hugo Hillebrandt advised that the freedmen in Guilford County were too poor to provide for their own education and that no help from the state could be expected. Some white citizens favored educating freedmen and poor whites, Hillebrandt went on, but most were antagonistic, and some threatened to burn any schools that were erected.[23]

In larger cities, however, more educational opportunity was being provided to blacks than to whites during the period immediately after the Civil War. Only 275 of 600 white children in Raleigh were attending school in 1868, compared to 700 of nearly 900 black children. Similar figures appeared in Charlotte and New Bern.[24] This circumstance fed resentment among whites. Bitterness over education for black children simmered throughout Reconstruction and the period of Republican rule. In 1877, conservative Democrats regained power. They succeeded in the promotion and ratification of an amendment to the state constitution requiring black and white children to attend separate schools, although no discrimination "in favor of, or to the prejudice of, either race"[25] was to be allowed.

For the rest of the century, schools for white children made little progress, and educational opportunities for blacks seriously deteriorated.[26] In Guilford County, for example, white schools did not return to the status achieved before the Civil War until after 1900.[27] Restricted educational opportunities combined with hatred of taxation received judicial reinforcement throughout the latter 1800s.[28] The state constitution of 1868 conferred upon townships the power to levy taxes for necessary purposes. But in *Lane v. Stanly*,[29] the North Carolina Supreme Court held in 1871 that schools did not constitute a necessary purpose. Taxation, therefore, could not exceed mandated limitations.

Subsequent legislation revised the limitations, but in 1885 the North Carolina Supreme Court again held in *Barksdale v. Commissioners of Sampson County*[30] that commissioners could not levy taxes exceeding rate limitations, even if schools could not be operated within existing appropriations for the four-month term mandated by the state constitution. Dr. Barnas Sears, general agent for the Peabody Fund, acidly remarked that North Carolina law seemed to permit tax funds dedicated to preventing pigs from running in the streets, but the same sort of appropriation to take children off the streets and put them into schools was deemed unconstitutional.[31]

Moreover, at that time any registered voter who failed to cast a ballot was counted as a negative vote, so supplemental school taxes were seldom approved. Only such larger cities as Greensboro, Raleigh, Salisbury, Goldsboro, Wilmington, Fayetteville, Durham, and Charlotte passed referenda creating local administrative units with special taxes in support of schools. These systems maintained school terms of approximately 180 days per year, while the rural areas of the state maintained terms of less than 60 days.[32] A pattern of significantly differentiating educational terms thus emerged on the basis of geography, in addition to race.

On top of the generally restricted condition of education statewide, attempts to apportion tax monies on the basis of race further handicapped the education of black children.[33] Whites generally opposed the appropriation of monies collected from whites to support schools for blacks. The Raleigh *Observer*, for example, editorialized, "We do not hesitate to say that we fear to place in the hands of a non-tax-paying negro constituency, the power to levy without limit money to purchase building sites and to erect buildings thereon."[34]

Subsequently, the General Assembly of 1880, with conservative Democrats in control, authorized the creation of a special tax district in Goldsboro, where the people could approve special school taxes devoted exclusively to each race. A coalition of blacks and poor whites initially defeated the measure, but subsequent renewed efforts driven by Julius Bonitz, editor of the *Goldsboro Messenger*, produced passage.[35] Over the next five years Goldsboro's example inspired Durham, Wilson, Statesville, New Bern, Fayetteville, Monroe, Edenton, Tarboro, Lenoir, Shoe Heel, Lumberton, Rocky Mount, Washington, Smithfield, and Magnolia to follow suit.[36] Division of taxes on the basis of race played an important role in securing passage of special tax districts. Whites had to be convinced that expanded schooling would not result in "educating negroes over-much."[37]

In the late 1880s, however, the North Carolina Supreme Court, in *Puitt v. Gaston County Commissioners*,[38] found "no countenance in the Constitution" for tax discrimination resting upon race. *Riggsbee v. Town of Durham*[39] affirmed that principle in similar language. The towns of Wilson and Kinston, among others, consequently abandoned their white graded schools rather than allow special taxes to support schools for black children. The schools were eventually restored, however.[40]

Duke v. Brown,[41] a case originating in Durham, repeated such prohibition of discrimination, while ruling on the additional question of whether a majority of qualified voters, as opposed to a majority of the qualified voters who actually cast ballots, was necessary to enable a municipality to issue bonds. The court affirmed that a majority of the qualified voters was necessary.[42] Anyone not voting, therefore, continued to count as a negative ballot.

In each case, the permissibility of separate schools based on race seemed beyond question. *Puitt* included a statement that prohibition of discrimination between the races did not extend "to the law requiring the children of the two races to be educated in separate schools when the advantages are equal."[43] Neither federal law nor the Fourteenth Amendment appeared relevant. The discrimination inherent in race-based apportionment of tax monies constituted only a violation of state tax laws.[44]

The 1890s witnessed a brief burst of liberalism, followed by a period of reaction. Conservative Democrats had held a firm grip on power since the end of Reconstruction. Black males, after they acquired the vote,[45] tended to affiliate with the Republican Party. By the early 1890s, a new party, the Populists, began to attract many of the state's more liberal voters.[46] In 1894 and 1896 Populists and Republicans, with black male support, combined forces (termed "Fusion"), backed the same candidates, and defeated Democrats. The resulting legislature instituted sweeping changes, raising appropriations for education, taxing railroads and businesses, and providing for increased participation by black males in the electoral process.

A backlash ensued from Democrats, based on white supremacy and marked by intimidation and corruption. Conservative white Democrats swept Republicans and Populists alike out of office across the state in the election of 1898. Democrats claimed that the overwhelming victory of white supremacy mandated disfranchising black voters. Many whites considered ridding the electoral process of black voters to be a constructive reform.

The General Assembly of 1899 thus repealed the Fusionist electoral measures, changed town charters, and instituted an appointive system of local offices that gave conservative Democrats in the legislature widespread control over state and local governments. A new school law instituted a higher pay scale for white than black teachers. Railroads and steamboats were required to provide separate but equal accommodations for white and black passengers, similar to the Louisiana legislation contested in *Plessy*.[47]

Most significantly, the General Assembly approved a constitutional amendment requiring a literacy test and poll tax in order to vote, and scheduled the amendment for a referendum. The measure would effectively disfranchise black voters, since it allowed great latitude on the part of local officials. Descendants of individuals who had voted before January 1, 1867, however, would retain the right to vote. That provision, often referred to as the "grandfather clause,"[48] protected illiterate whites. All new voters would have to pass the literacy test after 1908.

The initiative to disfranchise black voters in North Carolina occurred within the context of a national trend. State legislatures controlled by the Democratic Party enacted complex requirements for voting as well as poll taxes and literacy tests.[49] The U.S. Supreme Court allowed these practices in an Alabama case, *Giles v. Harris*.[50]

North Carolina's amendment disfranchising black males garnered overwhelming support from conservative Democrats, but one of the state's most important leaders of the Populist Party, State Superintendent of Public Instruction Charles H. Mebane, supported it as well. Mebane argued that the institution of a literacy test would force white parents to send more children to school.[51] Indeed, support for public education and support for disfranchisement tended to go hand-in-hand.[52] Clarence Poe, editor of *The Progressive Farmer*, secretly supported disfranchisement and the Democratic campaign as well, although he was ostensibly a spokesman for the Populists.[53]

Charles B. Aycock, the Democratic nominee for governor in 1900, became the hero of the Democrats. Aycock and the Democratic candidates traveled the state together in a procession that included hundreds of men clad in blood-red shirts, the symbol of a defiant Confederacy, followed by women in pure white dresses. This symbolism operated in concert with Aycock's standard speech, emphasizing white supremacy and disfranchisement of blacks. Wiping out illiteracy was added to the litany after Republicans and Populists began to convince poor whites that their children would be disfranchised along with blacks.[54]

Aycock won, 186,650 to 126,296. The constitutional amendment requiring a literacy test passed along parallel lines, 182,217 to 128,285. Counties in the western part of the state, where the black population was small, voted against the amendment, but it carried overwhelmingly in the East. The eastern counties contained the state's heaviest black population, though, and blacks were still eligible to vote in 1900. This condition has led Richard L. Watson Jr. to observe, "The overwhelming victory for the amendment in 1900, and . . . for Aycock . . . , was achieved, as in 1898, by fraud and intimidation and by calling for the unity of white men against the Negro domination allegedly brought about by the fusion of Republicans and Populists."[55]

William S. Powell, the dean of North Carolina historians, offers a more positive appraisal. Aycock's goal was not so much disfranchisement of blacks as education for all children, so that illiterate whites and blacks could participate intelligently in the electoral process in the future.[56] Aycock convinced the legislature to make significant appropriations for education. During the Aycock era illiteracy among blacks decreased by over 15 percent, due largely to increased educational opportunities for black children.

In 1902 the North Carolina Supreme Court, with a majority of the justices appointed during the Fusion era, ruled in *Hooker v. Town of Greenville* that black students must receive the same per capita share of school appropriations as white students. *Lowery v. School Trustees of Kernersville*, decided three years later, with a new majority appointed under the Aycock administration, struck down the equal appropriations requirement, however.[57]

Improved appropriations for education received additional impetus after Aycock left office, when the North Carolina Supreme Court reversed itself on the local taxation issue. *Collie v. Commissioners of Franklin County*[58] overturned *Barksdale*,[59] removing the judicially imposed cap on county education appropriations. Subsequent revision of state statutes expanded the taxing power of county and municipal governments to support schools.[60]

In addition to taxation in support of education, another issue recurring in the courts around the turn of the century centered on how to classify pupils according to race.[61] Since blacks and whites were required to attend separate schools, how were school officials to determine who was black and who was white? The legislature sought to clarify the question in 1889 with a measure specifying that anyone who had a black ancestor within three generations was considered black under the law.[62]

Four years later the North Carolina Supreme Court held in *Hare v. Board of Education of Gates County*[63] that a child with a black great grandfather could not attend a school for white children. The legislature adopted a more strenuous definition in 1903, prohibiting any child "with Negro blood, or what is known as Croatan Indian blood, in his veins, however remote,"[64] from attending a school for white children. Legislators seemed to think that making the schools more racially pure would improve education, and white newspaper editors tended to agree.[65]

Several cases are illustrative. In *Gilliland v. Board of Education*,[66] Mrs. Gilliland's children had been denied admission to a white school due to allegations that their great grandfather, who lived in Buncombe County, was part black. The North Carolina Supreme Court accepted as sufficient evidence of pure white ancestry the testimony of a neighbor who remembered that the great grandfather had voted. Having passed the test of racial purity, Mrs. Gilliland's children were allowed to enroll in white schools.

Johnson v. Board of Education[67] upheld the assignment of a child in Wilson County who had distant black ancestry to a black school, holding that, although the marriage of a white man and a one-eighth black woman made their children legitimate, "by no subtle alchemy known to the laboratory of logic can it be claimed [that an otherwise legal marriage] extracted the negro element from the blood . . . of [the] offspring and made it pure."[68] *Medlin v. County Board of Education*[69] cited *Johnson* as precedent. In *Medlin* the issue hinged on proper procedures to determine a child's race. The trial court, trying to resolve conflicting testimony about the lineage of a Wake County child's grandparents, allowed the jury to look at the child. The jury decided the child was white. The North Carolina Supreme Court, on appeal, held that, when the race of a child had been determined by a "jury of twelve white men, . . . there can be little doubt of the correctness of their conclusion."[70]

According to Bruce Beezer, these and other cases provide a strong foundation for an inference regarding North Carolina's rationale for maintaining racially segregated schools: the courts assumed that nature had ordained separation of the races. The assumed natural antagonism of the races "assured trouble," and failure to keep the races separate "would result in the breakdown of discipline."[71] This belief was so ingrained that the North Carolina Supreme Court never had to consider another school segregation case from 1922 until after *Brown*.

Clearly, North Carolina maintained the "separate" side of the "separate but equal" equation. But what of equality?

The "Equal" Aspect of Separate but Equal in North Carolina

Not long after the turn of the century, State Superintendent J. Y. Joyner complained bitterly that, while most white citizens in North Carolina had accepted some obligation to provide an education to their own children, "there are those who deny these [obligations] in their application to the negro race, who are unwilling for the white race that pays the greatest part of the taxes to assume the burden of the education of the negro."[72]

The following tables detail varieties of inequality that existed during the period 1901–50.

Comparing data for whites and blacks in table 1 shows a near parity in enrollment and attendance around the turn of the century. But for both races, more than one-third of children were not enrolled in school at all. Patterns of disparity emerged following disfranchisement of blacks and the racial backlash of the early 1900s. Increasing enrollment and attendance in later decades grew out of compulsory attendance laws adopted in 1907.[73] White enrollment increased for twenty years, then held steady for another twenty. Enrollment levels are lower for blacks, but not dramatically so. Attendance levels for blacks, however, are quite lower until the 1940s. The data thus show significantly lower levels of education being provided to black children.

Table 1 Enrollment and Attendance, 1900–1951

WHITE					
Year	Census	Enrolled	% Enrolled	Average Attendance	% Enrolled Attending
1900–1901	448,304	290,178	64.7	172,272	59.4
1910–11	504,519	367,682	72.9	247,019	67.1
1920–21	589,731	492,857	83.5	356,606	72.4
1930–31	724,142	602,512	83.2	498,745	82.8
1940–41	772,963	633,697	82.0	555,870	87.7
1950–51	773,003	677,014	87.6	576,117	85.1
BLACK					
Year	Census	Enrolled	% Enrolled	Average Attendance	% Enrolled Attending
1900–1901	219,677	141,180	64.3	80,747	58.0
1910–11	245,078	160,731	65.6	97,412	60.6
1920–21	270,597	214,905	79.4	138,281	64.3
1930–31	321,088	257,970	80.3	193.250	74.9
1940–41	352,711	273,341	77.5	230,504	84.3
1950–51	345,280	286,035	82.8	238,919	83.5

Source: Biennial Report of the Superintendent of Public Instruction (Raleigh: Edwards and Broughton (1900–1902), 96–97; (1910–12), 36–37; (1920–1922), 50–51; (1930–1932), 3, 15; (1940–1942), 5, 16; (1950–1952), 14–16. Later editions of these reports were published by the Department of Public Instruction.

Table 2 shows significant and consistent differences in the value of school property for white and black students. Schooling for black children received impetus from the Jeanes, Slater, and Rosenwald funds, northern philanthropic sources. Often, however, white school boards

Table 2 Value of School Property and School Term, 1900–1951

WHITE				
Year	Value of School Property	Number of Schools	Avg. Value of School	Avg. Term/Days
1900–1901	$885,298	5,411	$163	75.3
1910–11	$5,698,944	5,379	$1,059	107.2
1920–21	$25,306,295	5,475	$4,622	137.6
1930–31	$100,920,973	3,305	$30,536	160.4
1940–41	$105,658,494	2,077	$50,871	164.7
1950–51	$235,852,975	1,937	$121,761	179.0

BLACK				
Year	Value of School Property	Number of Schools	Avg. Value of School	Avg. Term/Days
1900–1901	$266,018	2,418	$110	72.5
1910–11	$797,048	2,296	$349	96.2
1920–21	$2,896,055	2,426	$1,194	130.2
1930–31	$12,009,398	2,359	$5,091	141.6
1940–41	$15,580,743	2,025	$7,694	164.4
1950–51	$46,705,140	1,519	$30,747	179.0

Source: Biennial Report of the Superintendent of Public Instruction (1900–1902), 104–5; (1910–12), 43, 49, 50; (1920–22), 70–71, 87; (1930–32), 30, 59; (1940–42), 5, 34, 65; (1950–52), 17, 69.

submitted plans for new schools to serve blacks, but used the funds to improve white schools. The state agent for Negro rural schools, Nathan Carter Newbold, was white. In his state-funded position, he labored to improve education for black children, albeit within a paternalistic framework. Donations from the North Carolina Teachers Association, the organization of black educators, and from black businessmen, paid the salary of his black assistant, Charles Moore. When Moore protested about inequities and criticized the conduct of white boards and superintendents, Newbold secured his resignation.[74]

Geography accounts for even more dramatic variations than race, however. From the 1870s well into the twentieth century, towns and cities in North Carolina often made their boundaries coterminous with school districts and voted in supplemental school taxes to improve funding for the resulting city school systems. By 1905–6, the average value for white, rural schools was $319 versus $13,029 for white, city schools; for black, rural schools the average value was $136 versus $3,177 for black, city schools.[75] These variations are attributable to the number of one- and two-teacher schools, many of which were log cabins, that still prevailed in rural areas. Far more blacks attended such schools than whites. On the other hand, city schools for blacks generally occupied better facilities than those provided for rural whites.

These differences fit into a geographic pattern found nationwide. Southern schools, in general, were inferior to schools in the Northeast and Midwest. This was due to greater economic prosperity in these regions, a function of industrialization, compared to the relatively lower level of living in the South, an effect of rural, agricultural economies. Northeastern and midwestern schools during the first half of the twentieth century followed an agenda that centered on acculturating immigrants and training for manufacturing, whereas schools in the South tended to prepare students for agricultural roles within patterns of racial segregation. The most significant fiscal dividing line, especially in the South, lay between rural and urban schools. Southern, rural blacks were the most subordinated, followed by the poor in general, working-class immigrants, children with disabilities, and females. Other disparities existed due to family socioeconomic status, a function of occupation, handicapping conditions, and place of residence. In 1940, about two-thirds of blacks lived in rural areas, overwhelmingly in the South. About half of black teachers had no more than a high-school education, compared to only 7 percent at that level among white teachers. Whites who lived in cities were the most educationally favored group. Even within cities and within race, socioeconomic class still shaped educational opportunity. In the Northeast, only 56 percent of low-income children entered high school in 1935–36, versus almost 90 percent from prosperous families.[76]

In North Carolina, black and white students went to school for similar terms at the turn of the century. By 1910, however, discrepancies had developed. By 1940 the gap had narrowed, and by 1950 comparable terms existed once again. City and rural school terms, however, exhibited wide variations throughout the first half of the century. To a significant extent, school terms for both black and white students in rural areas reflected the predominance of child labor in the South's agrarian economy. Schooling was considered a waste of time for children who would live their lives working on farms. Even if they left the farm, they most likely would go to work in textile mills, where education conveyed little, if any, benefit.

Cross-referencing school-term data for race and geography reinforces geographic discrepancies. In 1905–6 the average term for white, city schools was 170 days, versus 86 days for white, rural schools. The average term for black, city schools was 167 days, versus 82 days for black, rural schools.[77] Black, city school students, therefore, were provided with almost twice the number of school days than white, rural students. A statewide twelfth grade was added in 1942–43; a ninth month in the school year was added in 1943, for both races.[78]

Table 3 Average Monthly Teacher Salaries, 1900–1951

Year	White Salary	Black Salary
1900–1901	$25.39	$22.06
1910–11	$42.43	$24.74
1920–21	$96.60	$56.47
1930–31	$177.79	$78.59
1940–41	$118.36	$93.69
1950–51	$311.97	$323.36

Source: Biennial Report of the Superintendent of Public Instruction (1942–44), 102–4; (1900–1902), 104–5; (1910–12), 43; (1920–22), 70–71; (1930–32), 33, 141; (1940–42), 163; (1950–52), 161.

Salaries were lower for black teachers through the period 1910–41 for two reasons: the state maintained a lower rate of pay for blacks until the early 1940s, and fewer black teachers prior to the 1940s held higher-level certificates, which at that time meant a certificate based on the baccalaureate degree.[79] The state assumed the overall responsibility for education during the Great Depression.[80] Teacher pay was reduced during this period, but more for blacks than for whites. Some movement toward parity in black and white teacher salaries began in the 1940s. The state appropriated funds in 1941–42 and 1942–43 specifically for the purpose of equalizing black and white teacher pay scales.[81] Salaries for black and white teachers were eventually equalized during the administration of Governor J. Melville Broughton,[82] which ended in 1945, and the state's leadership subsequently emphasized with pride that equalization measures were passed voluntarily. On the other hand, lawsuits challenging separate salary scales based on race were underway, and knowledge of those suits was widespread among state leaders.[83] In the 1950s, average salaries for black teachers exceeded those of white teachers due to a higher percentage of blacks who had earned "A" certificates by the mid-1940s. Fully qualified white teachers were in short supply during and after the Second World War.[84]

These tables support the conclusion that elementary and secondary schools for black children never approached equality with schools for white children during the era of separate but equal. Layers of discrimination followed geographic lines and crossed racial boundaries, but within those layers, blacks were always subordinated to whites. With regard to the separate but equal doctrine in North Carolina, therefore, the schools were separate, but they were never equal. A North Carolina court finally recognized this inequality in 1951, in *Blue v. Durham Public School District*.[85]

Nationally, *Plessy* left a bitter legacy. Former federal judge A. Leon Higginbotham Jr. has remarked, "Many more millions of African Americans were denied the benefits of first-class citizenship by the Supreme Court's opinions in *Plessy v. Ferguson* and other related . . . cases than by all the machinations of the Ku Klux Klan."[86]

Higher Education Precedents in North Carolina

In a manner similar to litigation at the national level leading up to *Brown,* lawsuits in North Carolina challenging segregation in higher education laid a foundation for subsequent actions at the elementary and secondary level. Each of the major cases received support from the NAACP.

In 1933, Thomas Raymond Hocutt, an undergraduate at North Carolina College in Durham, sought admission to the University of North Carolina School of Pharmacy.[87] Dr. James E. Shepard, president of North Carolina College, was so opposed to Hocutt's application that he refused to allow his institution to provide a transcript. Dr. F. D. Bluford, president of North Carolina Agricultural and Technical College in Greensboro, expressed alarm over the involvement of the NAACP.[88] Both of these black educators feared that efforts to desegregate institutions of higher education would generate outrage among whites that would ultimately hurt blacks. Shepard also wanted to expand course offerings at black institutions.[89] Desegregation of the University of North Carolina would reduce such a need.

UNC denied admission solely on the basis of race. With the assistance of NAACP attorney William Henry Hastie, along with two black Durham attorneys, Conrad Pearson and Cecil Aubrey, Hocutt challenged the denial.[90] Attorney General Dennis G. Brummit told the court that Hocutt was simply being used by outsiders who wanted to promote social equality and racial intermarriage. Judge M. V. Barnhill ruled that Hocutt had not met UNC's admissions criteria because he had not presented an undergraduate transcript. The Hocutt initiative was thus lost. The case, however, bore portent for school desegregation litigation at the national level. It was the first case the NAACP instituted on the long road to *Brown*.[91]

President Shepard used the Hocutt matter to generate pressure on North Carolina's white political leadership to enhance North Carolina's black institutions of higher education. Governor Clyde Hoey urged the legislature to establish new programs in the state's black colleges. "North Carolina does not believe in social equality between the races," Hoey told members of the General Assembly, "but we do believe in equality of opportunity in their respective fields of service, and the white race cannot afford to do less than simple justice to the Negro."[92] The legislature provided significant appropriations to North Carolina College, with authorization to institute master's degree programs in liberal arts and the professions, plus the establishment of a law school for blacks, as well as authorization to North Carolina Agricultural and Technical College (A&T) for master's programs in agriculture and technology.[93]

Over the next decade, however, a level of support comparable to that provided to the state's white graduate and professional schools never emerged.[94] According to the *Raleigh News and Observer,* expanded postgraduate programs for blacks "simply testified to the resolve of North Carolinians to maintain racial segregation regardless of the cost."[95] Some measure of progress did develop, however. In 1942 the Association of American Universities made North Carolina College the fourth black school in the nation to be placed on its list of approved universities and colleges.

The state's effort to maintain segregation in higher education eventually died in concert with the NAACP-sponsored higher-education cases that had been working their way through the courts during the late 1940s and early 1950s.[96] In 1948 Harold T. Epps and James R. Walker, already enrolled in law school at North Carolina College, sought admission to the University of North Carolina law school. James E. Thomas and James H. Henderson applied to the UNC medical school. The university found them otherwise qualified, except for their race, and denied admission. Epps sued.[97]

Attorney General Harry McMullan assembled a team of distinguished white attorneys to prepare North Carolina's case. The attorney general's staff received assistance from J. C. B. Ehringhaus Jr. of Raleigh, L. P. McLendon of Greensboro, and William B. Umstead of

Durham.[98] With keen awareness of the "equal" aspect of "separate but equal" generated by the higher education victories in other states, feverish efforts ensued to upgrade the law school at North Carolina College. Attorney General McMullan enlisted the aid of Raleigh attorney Willis Smith, a former president of the American Bar Association, in an effort to gain bar association accreditation for the North Carolina College law school.[99] Judge Johnson J. Hayes of U.S. Middle District Court subsequently held that North Carolina had provided equal opportunities.[100]

While Epps's case had been pending, several other students were permitted to intervene as plaintiffs. Epps graduated, and the case was appealed under the name of another student, Floyd B. McKissick. Meanwhile, UNC president Gordon Gray appointed a committee of trustees to review the university's admissions policies. Some of UNC's trustees did not take kindly to the idea. John Sprunt Hill denounced the committee as "a big scheme to bring about social equality in the South."[101]

The committee subsequently recommended, and the university adopted, a revised policy to consider applications without regard to race in programs not already available in black schools in the state.[102] While the new applications policy appeared progressive on its face, the latter phrase was very significant, in that it would still deny the admission of blacks to the UNC law school, and in effect constituted a minimal compromise that precluded the admission of blacks to all undergraduate programs and to most graduate programs.

Judge Morris Ames Soper's decision in the U.S. Court of Appeals overturned the trial court in the *Epps* case, now entitled *McKissick v. Carmichael.*[103] McKissick's attorneys were Thurgood Marshall, Robert L. Carter, Frank D. Reeves, and Spottswood W. Robinson III. Judge Soper ordered the university to cease discrimination on the basis of race in its graduate admissions, holding further that the law schools at North Carolina College and the University of North Carolina were clearly not equal.[104] The state, with additional counsel from Kenneth C. Royall, appealed, but the U.S. Supreme Court denied certiorari.[105] Attorney General McMullan, bitter over the outcome, complained about the court's "dictatorial power."[106]

By 1951, therefore, university cases in North Carolina had set the stage for further school desegregation, in a pattern reflecting the national trend. Some measure of progress had occurred in higher education, with expanded programs for black graduate schools and a revised policy governing the state's university system that would prohibit denial on the basis of race to certain graduate programs.

But state government had given only as much ground as the judicial system demanded. North Carolina was not moving willingly toward widespread desegregation of its institutions of higher education. Several of the individuals involved in the higher education cases would play significant roles in the near future. Floyd McKissick would become one of the nation's most prominent civil rights leaders. Harry McMullan and Gordon Gray would be directly involved in formulating the state's response to *Brown*. Willis Smith's impact would be more indirect, but his role would help establish the overall racial climate in North Carolina on the eve of the *Brown* decision.

Race and Politics in North Carolina through the 1950s

Whereas the most significant period of racial turmoil in the South occurred during and after Reconstruction, the early twentieth century saw considerable distress in the North, the West, and the Midwest, including numerous outright race riots. In Chicago, 38 people were killed and more than 500 injured. Membership in the Ku Klux Klan has been estimated at more than 100,000 during this time, and Klan members dominated state governments in Indiana and Oregon. White rioters burned the homes of black residents in Tulsa, Oklahoma, killing more than 250.[107]

In contrast, North Carolina enjoyed a reputation as a moderate state with regard to race relations during the first half of the twentieth century.[108] Comparing North Carolina to other southern states, V. O. Key Jr. concluded, "No where had cooperation between white and Negro leadership been more effective. No where, except perhaps in Virginia, have over-all relations, year in and year out, been more harmonious."[109] John Hope Franklin, one of the most prestigious black voices among historians, expressed the opinion that North Carolina had given more attention to educating its black children than most other southern states.[110] In 1948 *The Carolinian*, one of two newspapers with statewide circulation devoted to black readers, considered the state's educational record with regard to black students "better in recent years than that of most Southern states."[111]

Violence against blacks occurred with less frequency in North Carolina than in any other southern state.[112] The sadism that characterized such actions in the Deep South was absent from North Carolina as well.[113] North Carolina was one of the few southern states that actually passed laws dealing with lynching.[114]

The Ku Klux Klan was active in the state, however.[115] W. Horace Carter, editor of the *Tabor City Tribune*, and Willard Cole, editor of the Whiteville *News Reporter*, won a Pulitzer Prize in 1953 for editorials and coverage of the Klan in Columbus County.[116] Dargan Frierson, who directed the Greensboro office of the Federal Bureau of Investigation from 1951 to 1971, estimates that the Klan had 8,000 to 10,000 members in North Carolina during the 1950s and 1960s. The FBI considered the potential for violence "very serious,"[117] especially as the civil rights movement developed.

Some political developments in the decade prior to *Brown* support North Carolina's moderate-to-progressive image regarding race relations, but others contradict it. In the early 1940s, North Carolina ranked second only to Tennessee in percentage of voting-age blacks who were registered to vote. Other southern states made much more rapid progress over the next ten years, however, and by 1952 the state held the dubious distinction of exceeding only Virginia, Alabama, and Mississippi on this criterion. North Carolina, along with South Carolina, Louisiana, and Georgia, continued to require a literacy test for voter registration until well after *Brown*. Arkansas and Texas required a poll tax but no literacy test, while Mississippi, Virginia, and Alabama required both a poll tax and a literacy test.[118] With regard to voting opportunities for blacks, therefore, North Carolina represented neither the best nor the worst of the South, instead occupying the middle range.

North Carolina showed some measure of progressivism regarding race at the 1948 Democratic National Convention. President Harry S. Truman had made civil liberties a central point in his administration, appointing a Civil Rights Commission that called for a federal antilynching law, a permanent Fair Employment Practices Act, and an end to racial segregation and poll taxes. At the urging of Hubert H. Humphrey, the 1948 convention adopted a civil rights plank in its platform.[119] A southern revolt ensued, spawning a third party, the Dixiecrats. But North Carolina cast 13 of its 32 votes for Truman, providing the only support he received from a southern state at the convention. In the general election, North Carolina awarded Truman 459,000 votes compared to 259,000 for Republican Thomas E. Dewey. Strom

Thurmond, the strong conservative Dixiecrat candidate, drew only 70,000 votes in North Carolina, although the Dixiecrats carried Alabama, Louisiana, Mississippi, and South Carolina.[120]

Another development in 1948 also affirmed North Carolina's tilt toward progressivism: the state elected Kerr Scott governor. Scott, a farmer and former commissioner of agriculture, was the first nonlawyer elected since before the turn of the century.[121] A year after the election, Governor Scott faced a difficult decision that would eventually exert a profound effect on the state's racial climate.

J. Melville Broughton, the former governor, had been elected to the U.S. Senate in 1948. Broughton enjoyed substantial support among blacks, who favored him over the incumbent, Senator William B. Umstead.[122] Umstead tried to appeal to white voters in the latter days of the campaign by opposing President Truman's civil rights program, but his statements failed to generate enough support to win the election.[123] Then, less than a year after his election, Senator Broughton died.

The state constitution authorized the governor to appoint a successor to serve until the next regularly scheduled election, to be held in November 1950. Governor Scott shocked the state with his choice: Frank Porter Graham, often termed North Carolina's "best known liberal."[124] A member of President Truman's Civil Rights Commission, Graham's nineteen years as president of the University of North Carolina had earned him a distinguished national reputation. He had served in several New Deal agencies and as a United Nations mediator. According to Samuel Lubell, Graham epitomized "the enlightened South."[125] His father had been superintendent of the Charlotte and Fayetteville school systems.[126]

Governor Scott followed Graham's appointment with two more that broke new ground. In April 1949 Governor Scott appointed Dr. Harold Trigg to the State Board of Education, the first black to serve in such a capacity.[127] Dr. Trigg, president of St. Augustine's College in Raleigh,[128] was former state inspector of Negro high schools.[129] In June, Scott appointed Susie Sharp to a Superior Court bench, the highest state judicial appointment to that date for a woman. That same month, in an address delivered on his behalf at North Carolina College in Durham, Governor Scott pledged "the state's acceptance of the responsibility for providing educational facilities for Negroes equal to those made available to other citizens."[130]

North Carolina appeared to be entering its most progressive era. But as in the early 1900s, race became a significant intervening variable.

In the Democratic Primary of May 1950, Senator Graham, the appointed incumbent, faced three challengers. The most prominent was Willis Smith, a Raleigh attorney, former Speaker of the State House of Representatives. He chaired the Board of Trustees of Duke University.[131] He had also helped to promote Bar Association accreditation of the North Carolina College law school.

Just before the election, postcards bearing the name and address of a fictitious organization which could have been easily misconstrued as the NAACP flooded North Carolina. The cards sought to lead voters into believing that the national office of the NAACP was supporting Frank Porter Graham.[132] The Smith campaign vigorously denied any knowledge of the cards.

Graham led the first primary with 303,605 votes (48.9 percent) to Smith's 250,222 (40.5 percent), short of a majority. Graham's election had seemed certain, and Smith did not believe that any further campaign would have much chance of success. But three days before the deadline for requesting a runoff, a young news reporter named Jesse Helms helped organize a rally on Smith's behalf.[133] The crowd that showed up heard Godfrey Cheshire, a Raleigh business leader, warn that Supreme Court decisions[134] issued the day before would threaten segregation in North Carolina. Smith's supporters urged him to continue the campaign, pointing to Graham's vulnerability on the race issue. The next day Smith requested a second primary.[135]

The campaign turned bitter, with race in the forefront. Posters appeared, screaming, "White People Wake Up," "The South Under Attack," and "End of Racial Segregation Proposed."[136] Leaflets listed black men who had married white women. A whispering campaign circulated: "Vote for Graham if you want your children sitting in Negro schools."[137] Hecklers cursed Graham's campaign workers, hollering that they worked for a "nigger lover."[138] Campaigners against Graham flashed a photograph showing black soldiers dancing with white women; it had been altered to include Frank Porter Graham's wife. A campaign phrase attributed to but never acknowledged by Jesse Helms labeled UNC the "University of Negroes and Communists."[139]

Smith won 281,114 votes to Graham's 261,789. The eastern section of the state, with the highest proportion of the black population, voted for Graham in the first primary but for Smith in the second. Significant intimidation of prospective black voters occurred in the East prior to the first primary, resulting in an overall low black voter turnout in both elections.[140] Majorities in prosperous white neighborhoods such as Charlotte's Myers Park, Greensboro's Irving Park, and the precinct containing Woman's College in Greensboro (now UNC-Greensboro), however, voted for Smith as well.[141]

The historiography surrounding the Smith-Graham campaign could constitute a significant study in itself. Suffice it to say that race is consistently identified as a factor of great importance, although observers point to other factors as well,[142] including Samuel Lubell's recognition of the appeal of economic conservatism to white middle and upper classes, a point supported by Paul Luebke.[143] To Julian M. Pleasants and Augustus M. Burns, in their excellent book about the campaign, the predominant factor was not race per se, but Graham's failure to respond to race-related attacks effectively. Race had not entered into North Carolina's political contests since the early 1900s because so few white North Carolinians had any idea that segregation was being challenged. Once they perceived a threat to segregation, racial concerns became volatile. To the campaign issues of race and economic conservatism, therefore, Pleasants and Burns add Graham's own political ineptitude,[144] a factor further explained in more positive terms by John Egerton.[145]

William Chafe acknowledges race as significant in Graham's defeat but downplays its importance.[146] Chafe draws a picture of a North Carolina society preoccupied with jobs, families, and other concerns, not seriously concerned about race, ready to respond to responsible leadership. Instead of providing such leadership, Chafe believes the state's political elite used traditions of civility, capitalizing on North Carolina's cherished reputation for moderation in race relations, to block desegregation due to their own preference for segregation.[147]

Chafe's de-emphasis of the race issue hinges on the powerlessness of supposedly racist lower classes: "Without question, most poor white farmers and workers harbored anti-black attitudes. But there were no redneck hordes in power, nor was there any likelihood of their coming to power. Instead, a diffuse political constituency existed that could be manipulated by those who did hold power."[148] In his focus on "redneck hordes," therefore, Chafe treats uneducated, lower-class whites as if that segment of the population were the principal element in North Carolina supporting segregation. Was that the case?

Beliefs in North Carolina Related to Race

Public opinion polling and related social science research received a stimulus from the *Brown* decisions, as scholars sought to gauge the prospects for social change in the South. Guilford County was the subject of a pioneering study, conducted in the mid-1950s by a research team from Princeton University led by Melvin M. Tumin.[149] This study provides a measure of racial attitudes prevalent in North Carolina at the time of the *Brown* decision.

Tumin selected Guilford County because he believed it contained as wide a variety of living conditions as could be found anywhere in North Carolina and perhaps anywhere in the South. He considered Guilford County to be representative of other counties in the state and of the South. If Tumin erred, he probably overestimated similarities. Residents in Guilford County's central Piedmont location probably would have tended to be more receptive to change than North Carolina's eastern counties, where the black population approached or exceeded 50 percent.[150]

Table 4 summarizes the views of white respondents.

Table 4 Views of White North Carolinians Regarding Racial Issues in the Mid-1950s

Blacks are inferior to whites with regard to:	
"Responsibility"	72.8 percent agree
"Morality"	69.0 percent agree
"Ambition"	66.5 percent agree
"Intelligence"	59.2 percent agree
Prefer segregated schools:	75.61 percent
Favor a constitutional amendment if faced with the "threat" of desegregation:	77.30 percent
Favor withholding State funds from schools in order to maintain segregation:	55.55 percent
Favor closing the public schools in order to avoid desegregation:	43.46 percent
Support the use of force in order to preserve segregation:	24.82 percent

Source: Tumin, *Desegregation*, 34, 36, 37, 45.

Most white respondents considered blacks inferior to whites with regard to responsibility, morality, ambition, and intelligence. Levels of education did not seem to affect attitudes significantly, except for those with some college education. Less than 25 percent of those surveyed, however, had attained such educational levels. Social and economic class variables indicated that, the higher one stood on the ladder of education, occupation, and income, the more favorable the image of blacks and the greater the readiness to accept school desegregation. High levels in all three categories had to appear, however, in order to predict such readiness.[151] Such consistently high levels appeared only among a small segment of the population. The overall picture, therefore, suggests broad and deep racial prejudice, as well as strong support for continued segregation, predominant not merely among lower class, poorly educated people, but among middle and upper classes as well.

The Tumin study weighs heavily in the Chafe thesis. Citing Tumin as his source, Chafe asserts, "18 percent [of the population] wished to push ahead much faster with integration."[152] A careful reading of Tumin, however, actually shows that significantly less than 18 percent of the individuals in his sample were willing to pursue desegregation. Tumin states, "Almost 18 percent of the sample disapproved of all four techniques," that is, the means of resistance to desegregation cited in table 4. Tumin does not indicate what percentage of the sample would take positive steps to implement desegregation, but it is clear that the number is contained within the 18 percent, not the whole 18 percent.[153] Tumin's study, therefore, shows little support for desegregation, along with a great deal of support for continued segregation.

Racial attitudes in North Carolina thus appear definitely pro-segregationist, with strong beliefs related to black inferiority, a point of view nevertheless relatively moderate in the context of the South in the mid-1950s. Segregationist sentiment was not universal. Some individuals, associated primarily with the Episcopal, Methodist, and Presbyterian churches, would initiate efforts to promote racial justice. Charlotte newspaper editor C. A. "Pete" McKnight editorialized, "Segregation, as an abstract moral principle, cannot be defended by any intellectually or spiritually honest person."[154] But initiatives to end segregation were rare, they met with strong resistance, and they did not spread.[155]

* * *

In the nineteenth century, North Carolina provided education on a very limited basis to white children, within variations that were primarily a function of gender and geography. Education for black children was prohibited before the Civil War, provided for many during Reconstruction, but restricted after the turn of the century.

Racism strongly influenced North Carolina politics from Reconstruction through the early 1900s, but the issue subsided through the first half of the twentieth century. Overt racism lay dormant as long as segregation remained deeply ingrained, unquestioned, and unchallenged in the culture of the state. Once segregation appeared threatened in the latter 1940s and early 1950s, racial prejudice and support for continued segregation appeared in an overwhelmingly wide spectrum of the population—not just among the lower, uneducated classes—and began to exert strong influence on state politics.

Racism is institutional in nature, intricately threaded through the structure of society, of law, of the economy, and of educational systems. Racist beliefs supported segregation, a pattern of practices and policies that caused North Carolina to maintain separate school systems, based on race. Although laws required equality within segregation, no measure of educational services ever showed anything even approaching equality. Considering law as cultural artifact, both legislation and case law show that separation of the races and subordination of blacks was believed to be normal, part of the natural order.

State leaders would formulate adaptations to the *Brown* decisions within a social and political framework that initially assumed the continuation of segregation. Another generation of litigation would bring that assumption to an end. How would North Carolina and its citizens adjust to a new way of life?

3

North Carolina's Response to *Brown*

THE PEARSALL PLAN, 1952 TO 1956

In 1952, William B. Umstead succeeded Kerr Scott as governor. Umstead had served in the U.S. House of Representatives and the U.S. Senate.[1] He voiced strong support for public schools in his inaugural address.[2] Umstead's political positions were more associated with the preservation of segregation than the relative racial liberalism of Kerr Scott and Frank Porter Graham. Umstead had to a significant extent based his senatorial campaign against Melville Broughton on support for segregation. He had also assisted in the preparation of the state's defense of segregation in the *Epps* case. During his gubernatorial campaign, Umstead vigorously supported segregation.[3]

Developing a policy that would enable North Carolina to cope with the changes implied by *Brown* would have constituted a huge challenge for a strong man. But Governor Umstead was not physically well. He suffered a heart attack two days after his inauguration and remained hospitalized or bedridden for as long as he remained in office. He died about eighteen months after taking office.

What kind of response would North Carolina's leaders formulate to the demands of *Brown*? How would North Carolina's response compare to other states in the South?

Brown Shocks the State

When the Supreme Court announced its decision on May 17, 1954, "North Carolina and the other Southern states were stunned."[4] Politicians all over the South thundered out against the court and its ruling. Virginia's governor, Thomas B. Stanley, initially received the *Brown* decision calmly, promising that the views of both races would be considered as the state planned its course of action. That attitude soon shifted to "massive resistance," however, under prodding from the commonwealth's political machines and the influential editor of the Richmond *News Leader,* James J. Kilpatrick.[5] The Virginia, South Carolina, Alabama, and Mississippi legislatures passed resolutions of "interposition and nullification,"[6] stating that the court's decision could not be applied in their states. Several southern states enacted penalties for anyone who attempted to desegregate schools. Compulsory attendance laws were repealed, and procedures were developed to close public schools if segregation were outlawed.

The reaction in North Carolina was quieter, in keeping with the state's reputation for moderation. The North Carolina Democratic Convention had been scheduled to meet on May 20, 1954, just a few days after the *Brown* decision was announced. Senator Clyde R. Hoey had died earlier in the spring, and Governor Umstead had asked Winston-Salem attorney Irving Carlyle, a former legislator, to take Hoey's place as the convention's keynote speaker.[7] Political observers speculated that Umstead was about to appoint Carlyle to fill Hoey's seat.

Carlyle was associated with the more progressive wing of the Democratic Party. The night before he was to speak, his wife, Mary Belo Carlyle, addressed the Parent-Teacher Association of Reynolds High School, marking the end of her term as president. Referring to the *Brown* decision, she told the audience, "For us to try to evade the law would be to invite anarchy."[8] Irving Carlyle added that sentiment to his convention speech, urging North Carolina to obey the court's decision. The audience applauded, but a friend warned him, "That's not approval of what you said. They're just admiring your stinkin' courage."[9] Carlyle received support for his comments from Frank Porter Graham and from Edward Hudgins, a prominent attorney who chaired the Greensboro Board of Education.[10] But most who contacted him denounced his stand.[11]

Governor Umstead withheld comment concerning *Brown* until he had met with Attorney General Harry McMullan, State Superintendent Charles F. Carroll, and State Supreme Court Chief Justice M. V. Barnhill.[12] After the convention, Umstead made no public statement regarding Carlyle's speech.[13] The Senate appointment went to Morganton attorney Samuel J. Ervin Jr., a staunch segregationist.[14]

Umstead issued his first statement regarding *Brown* on May 27. He pointed out the state's efforts "to equalize . . . the school buildings available to both races"[15] and the actual equalization of black and white teachers' salaries. Umstead acknowledged *Brown* without defiance. But neither he nor any other southern governor took a public stance in the mid-1950s that promised desegregation.[16]

Advice and Decisions

Governor Umstead sought advice from the Institute of Government at the University of North Carolina. Assistant Director James C. N. Paul pointed out that the Supreme Court had not set any deadline for school desegregation. He warned that state aid to segregated private schools was legally risky. A statewide pupil assignment plan could use only valid criteria and maintain segregation only for a limited period. Allowing parents to choose schools might be sanctioned during a transitional period, but such a plan would be judged invalid if its purpose was to preserve segregation. Finally, Paul suggested a system of administrative appeals to review pupil assignments.[17] Director Albert Coates urged, "Play for time."[18]

Historian William Chafe believes Umstead was moving the state toward desegregation.[19] Actually, internal correspondence within the Umstead administration shows that he intended to keep schools segregated, although he resolved not to defy the court.[20] He decided to appoint a committee to consider the state's response to *Brown*. Holt McPherson, editor of the *High Point Enterprise,* and Charles F. Carroll, state superintendent,[21] urged the inclusion of black members. But Umstead received bitter criticism from individuals close to him when the consideration of blacks became public.[22]

The First Pearsall Committee

On August 4, 1954, Governor Umstead announced the appointment of the Governors' Special Advisory Committee on Education.[23] Membership was diversified. It included four attorneys. Thomas J. Pearsall of Rocky Mount, chair, had been a member of the Rocky Mount school board and Speaker of the North Carolina House of Representatives. William T. Joyner of Raleigh had headed the state's Board of Elections. Fred B. Helms of Charlotte was former president of the North Carolina Bar. L. R. Varser of Lumberton once held a seat on the North Carolina Supreme Court. Five members were business executives with experience in public service. Arthur D. Williams of Wilson chaired the Wilson County Board of Commissioners. R. O. Huffman of Morganton, the committee's sole Republican, was president of Drexel Furniture. Dallas Herring of Rose Hill, a casket manufacturer and former mayor, chaired the Duplin County Board of Education. J. H. Clark of Elizabethtown was a banker, former member of the State Senate, and held the chair of the North Carolina Medical Care Commission. Helen S. Kafer of New Bern was a hospital administrator and a member of the New Bern School Board. Two other female members, Hazel S. Parker of Tarboro and Ruth Current of Raleigh, were home economists. Two members were school superintendents: I. E. Ready of Roanoke Rapids and James C. Manning of Martin County. Four were university presidents: Dr. Paul A. Reid of Western Carolina, Dr. Gordon Gray of the University of North Carolina,[24] Dr. F. D. Bluford of Agricultural and Technical College, and Dr. J. W. Seabrook of Fayetteville State Teachers' College. Two were journalists: Clarence Poe, editor of *The Progressive Farmer,* and Holt McPherson, editor of *The High Point Enterprise.*

Several additional characteristics of the committee's membership could play a role in its decisions. Three members were black: Dr. Bluford, Dr. Seabrook, and Mrs. Parker. But all three were state employees,[25] which concerned some black leaders.[26] A majority of the members, fourteen of nineteen, including both school superintendents, lived in the East, where the black population was heaviest, the political orientation most conservative. In the 1950 senatorial campaign, Pearsall and Helms had supported Frank Porter Graham, whereas Joyner had been a Willis Smith ally.[27]

Among the whites, Poe was the most outspoken. He had championed segregation based on the apartheid model of South Africa.[28] Gordon Gray, seemingly the most liberal, nevertheless supported segregation: "I hope that the Supreme Court does not outlaw segregation in the public schools or at the undergraduate level. . . . I suppose that [desegregation] will come about eventually, but not necessarily through court action. I also suppose that eventually may be a long time away."[29]

Chairman Pearsall began to receive communications and petitions from concerned citizens soon after appointment of the committee. By far, most correspondence supported continued segregation. Many letters included signed petitions, sometimes with twenty to thirty signatures, often in the hundreds.[30] Fear of miscegenation became a recurring theme in public and private comment.[31]

The committee met on August 11, 1954. Governor Umstead shared the Institute of Government *Report,* emphasizing the gradual approach the report recommended. The governor charged the committee with developing "a policy . . . which will preserve the State's public school system by having the support of the people."[32]

Chairman Pearsall designated the attorneys to serve as a subcommittee to consult with Attorney General McMullan regarding the state's brief in the upcoming Supreme Court implementation hearings. Pearsall told the press that the committee hoped to have recommendations for the General Assembly in January.[33]

Early Challenges to Segregation

During the period surrounding *Brown,* while state officials were contemplating official responses, they were also making plans to provide legal assistance to local school boards.[34] Attorney General McMullan expressed alarm over the NAACP's new approach, directly attacking segregation, as opposed to seeking equal facilities within racially segregated settings.[35]

In June 1954, the State Board of Education announced its intention to continue segregation in the forthcoming term.[36] This spawned a protest from Kelly Alexander, president of the North Carolina Conference of NAACP Branches, demanding that the state desegregate without delay.[37] Governor Umstead replied that he supported the board.[38]

On advice from Thurgood Marshall,[39] the NAACP began to challenge segregation immediately. Harnett County Schools superintendent Glenn T. Profitt reported he had received a letter from local black leaders, urging immediate desegregation. Profitt suspected the communication was part of a statewide effort since it was written on a preprinted form. The NAACP was indeed circulating forms[40] seeking "law abiding citizens . . . to translate this decision into a program of action to eradicate racial segregation in public education as speedily as possible."[41] A blank contract provided for representation by attorneys T. H. Wyche, C. E. Bell, and Conrad Pearson, of Durham.[42] NAACP branches sent petitions to at least a dozen school boards. Some invited representatives to meet with them, but all added that the state had directed them to maintain segregation for 1954–55, and they intended to comply.[43]

On August 13, black school administrators attending a conference at North Carolina College voted unanimously for a resolution of "wholehearted support"[44] for the *Brown* decision, and they sent copies to the Pearsall Committee.[45]

The Emergence of a Moral Voice

Some white civic and religious organizations sought to assist the process of change. Mrs. Carl A. Plonk of Asheville, president of the North Carolina Division of the American Association of University Women, urged members to work quietly with local school boards toward a positive plan to reduce racial tension.[46] Leaders of religious groups urged North Carolinians to think about racial change in a moral context. The Episcopal Diocese of North Carolina urged people to accept the *Brown* decision in the spirit of Christian brotherhood; the North Carolina Conference of Methodist Youth resolved that segregation did not follow Christian principles; and the governing bodies of the Baptist, Presbyterian, and Methodist churches—the largest Protestant denominations in the South—issued statements supporting desegregation, as did southern Catholics and the National Council of Churches of Christ and the North Carolina Council of Churches.[47] The Young Women's Christian Association (YWCA), whose mission included the phrase, "Eliminating Racism, Empowering Women," initiated biracial church services, although blacks and whites sat in separate sections.[48]

Dr. Edwin McNeil Poteat—white pastor of Pullen Memorial Baptist Church in Raleigh, who was also a trustee of Shaw University, a black institution—proposed that business and professional groups of both races study ways in which the community could respond to the *Brown* decision. The proposal grew out of a meeting of the interracial, interdenominational Fellowship of Southern Churchmen. Dr. Poteat was also a member of the NAACP Committee of 100, "a group of responsible white persons"[49] who provided support for the organization.

Rev. Frank C. Smathers, pastor of Grace Methodist Church, a white congregation in Greensboro, announced that local black and white ministers would begin meeting.[50] The superintendent of Durham City Schools, Stacy Weaver, arranged to teach a Sunday School class at Saint Joseph's A.M.E. Church, a black congregation. Several members of Weaver's church accompanied him.[51] Rev. Billy Graham, the most prominent evangelist in North Carolina, probably in the nation, insisted that blacks as well as whites be admitted to his crusades, and he called for a nationwide "baptism of Christian love, tolerance, and understanding."[52] But he also held, at least during the early years of the civil rights movement, that blacks really did not want to mingle with whites, they just wanted legal constraints removed.[53]

Other steps of a secular nature were underway as well, with moral principles often expressed as a primary guiding force. In Lenoir County, an interracial committee had been operating for two years,[54] and local advisory committees to study the *Brown* decision were established in several other counties.[55] Among educators, Superintendent Ben L. Smith of Greensboro wrote to Attorney General McMullan, "With acceptance of the Judeo-Christian principle of the dignity and worth of the individual, and with acceptance of the principle in democratic government of 'equal protection of the law' [the *Brown*] decision has been inevitable."[56] The Greensboro Board of Education passed a resolution declaring its intent to abide by the *Brown* decisions, as did the Charlotte and Asheville school boards.[57]

Support for Segregation

Early initiatives to accommodate desegregation were heavily overshadowed, however, by support for segregation. Governor Umstead received hundreds of pro-segregation petitions.[58] Arguments that separation of the races had been ordained by God appeared frequently. Although many national and some state governing bodies of religious denominations had endorsed the concept of desegregation, local ministers and congregations seldom followed suit.[59]

One of the most prominent segregationists was Dr. W. C. George, former chair of the Department of Anatomy at the University of North Carolina.[60] He circulated a pamphlet asserting, "[T]he Negro race is inferior to the white race in capacity to develop and maintain a civilization," basing his arguments on his interpretations of genetics.[61] Many attorneys numbered themselves among the pro-segregationists.[62] William T. Joyner's communications show his support for maintaining segregated schools.[63] William B. Rodman Jr., of Washington, a member of the UNC Board of Trustees, felt bitter about the work of Dr. William S. Jenkins, a UNC professor who was assisting the Department of Justice.[64] Among the press, one voice in particular stood out in support of segregation. Radio news commentator Jesse Helms told his audience that North Carolina's only choice was between "integrated public schools and free choice private schools."[65]

The Folger Commission

Prior to the establishment of the Pearsall Committee, the General Assembly had created a Commission on Codification of Education Laws, chaired by Fred Folger of Mount Airy.[66] Stacy Weaver, superintendent of Durham City Schools, and Henry M. Marrow of Smithfield, former superintendent of Johnston County Schools, were members.[67] Weaver acted as informal consultant to the Pearsall Committee.[68]

The Folger Commission had prepared recommendations for rewriting public school laws, removing conflicts and obsolete provisions. Following the announcement of *Brown,* commission members added additional proposals, eliminating provisions mandating segregation, shifting pupil assignment authority from the State Board of Education to local boards, and subjecting teacher contracts to annual renewal.[69]

Transition to the Hodges Administration

Governor Umstead died on November 7, 1954. Umstead had not moved toward compliance with *Brown* since the Supreme Court had not issued any implementation orders. Neither had the state moved to defy the court in the manner of many other southern states.[70] The governor had walked a quiet, middle path.

Lieutenant Governor Luther H. Hodges succeeded Umstead. Hodges's father had been a tenant farmer, his mother a cotton mill worker. Hodges had worked his way through the University of North Carolina. After a career with Marshall Field's stores in Chicago, he returned to North Carolina, where he served on the State Board of Education. Hodges ran for lieutenant governor in 1952, driving eleven thousand miles and buying a small amount of gas at numerous stops. He told people, "My name is Luther Hodges. I'm not a politician and I've never run for office before. I'd appreciate your vote."[71]

Succession following a governor's death would have been difficult under any circumstances. But Hodges and Umstead had never been close.[72] Hodges complained in his memoirs that he had been treated as an outsider.[73] The black press regarded him an "unknown quantity."[74]

Deliberations

Hodges soon found that he agreed with the deliberative approach Umstead had taken with regard to *Brown.* He directed the Pearsall Committee to continue.

About this time, Robert E. Giles, formerly of the Institute of Government, now in the attorney general's office, asked Attorney General Rodman and colleagues to identify the most emotionally charged issue the State had faced in the twentieth century. A consensus identified prohibition. Giles pointed out that the state had allowed localities to decide that issue themselves. Thus the idea of local control regarding school desegregation was subsequently conveyed to Governor Hodges.[75]

Meanwhile, members of the committee were left on their own. Dallas Herring communicated extensively with educational and political leaders.[76] He prepared a proposal, entitled "Save Our Schools," and circulated it widely. Any adaptation to *Brown,* Herring asserted, must not conflict with the court's decision, must have widespread public approval, must have the support of local school boards, must "preserve unimpaired and uninterrupted the educational opportunities of *all* children" (Herring's emphasis), and "must stand without the support of extremists."[77] He suggested a pupil assignment plan based on test scores, believing that would help academic progress.[78] He warned that in conversations with members of the legislature, those who had been supporters of education "do not sound like friends now."[79]

Pearsall and a few other members of the committee met with a delegation from the NAACP.[80] When asked how the NAACP proposed to deal with the growing threat of closing schools, the delegation replied that desegregation had to be undertaken, no matter what the consequences. Committee members could not accept that position. After that meeting, white members of the committee did not seek any more input from blacks outside the committee. The central question became how the state could preserve public schools in the face of its segregationist temper. Members of the committee feared whites would abandon public schools and move their children to segregated private schools.[81]

Assistant Attorney General I. Beverly Lake advocated to Pearsall that the state make plans to close public schools and pay tuition to private, segregated schools, following a model based on the G.I. Bill that paid college tuition for soldiers.[82] Neither Pearsall nor any other member of the committee supported closing schools.

Pearsall called another committee meeting for November 23, 1954, to look at the Folger Commission report.[83] Governor Hodges's notes at the time read, "[D]ecentralization. [P]ower to assign pupils to local boards if not done by race. Wait for court actions! Teacher contracts. Don't abolish. Don't defy. But in time and patience."[84] At that meeting, the committee discussed pupil assignment plans. Dr. Seabrook favored freedom of choice, gradual desegregation beginning with the first grade, segregation by gender in high school, and grouping pupils on the basis of intelligence tests.[85] I. E. Ready suggested student transfers in the first grade, adding a grade each year.[86] Discussion appears to have produced agreement favoring local control of pupil assignments.[87] Pearsall appointed committee members Bluford, Joyner, Kafer, Manning, McPherson, and Parker as well as Chairman Pearsall himself to study proposals. They subsequently met with the State Board of Education on December 1, 1954.[88]

Report of the First Pearsall Committee

The Pearsall Committee met for the third time on December 30, 1954. Chairman Pearsall presented members with a completed report that resembled earlier discussions in only the most general way.[89] The draft stated as its two main objectives, "Preservation of public education . . . [and] Preservation of the peace," urging North Carolinians "to act cooly, exercise restraint, exhibit tolerance, and display wisdom." The report held categorically, "[T]he mixing of the races in the public schools . . . cannot be accomplished and should not be attempted."[90]

That phrase outraged Dr. Seabrook. He demanded an unequivocal statement regarding whether North Carolina intended to obey the Supreme Court. Pearsall compromised by inserting the word "forthwith,"[91] implying that, although desegregation at the present was not practical, it might occur in the future. Additional dissent came from Holt McPherson, who believed the tone sounded defiant. Instead, he urged a report that made clear the state's intent to obey the law: "We ought to say that we want to comply; . . . [but] we'll have to have time."[92]

The committee's slightly revised report recommended that North Carolina try to meet the *Brown* decision within the framework of the public schools. But "abandoning or materially altering" the system might be necessary. The General Assembly should enact legislation transferring pupil assignment authority to local boards. Finally, the legislature should create a new committee to study problems that would be created by forthcoming implementation decrees.[93]

Dallas Herring left the meeting, refusing to sign even the revised version. When he arrived home, the telephone was ringing. Tom

Pearsall was calling. Governor Hodges wanted that report to be unanimous. "He put me under quite a lot of pressure,"[94] Herring recalled. After extracting assurance that Hodges did not intend to close schools, Herring agreed to sign. Chairman Pearsall carried copies of the committee report, now unanimous, to the governor.[95]

Why did the draft report sound more defiant than member discussions had suggested? Under Hodges's directive, Pearsall also had been working with the Attorney General's Office to prepare a pupil assignment bill. Attorney General McMullan constantly deferred to Assistant Attorney General I. Beverly Lake, who was developing North Carolina's arguments in the upcoming implementation hearings. Pearsall asked Lake to draft a bill modeled after a statute from Alabama, but deleting race as a basis for pupil assignment. Lake refused, stating that he would only prepare a bill that maintained segregation. According to Pearsall, both McMullan and Lake "felt desegregation was absolutely impossible, and as the committee refused to go along with their radical views, they gave no aid to it."[96] Pearsall noted that McMullan had already prepared a draft pupil assignment bill prior to their meeting.[97] McMullan's bill shifted pupil assignment authority from the state to local boards and based school assignments on a series of non-racial criteria.[98] Parents could appeal assignment to superior court, and that ruling could be appealed to the State Supreme Court.

McMullan had sent a draft pupil assignment bill to Umstead on July 29, 1954.[99] The draft had grown out of a communication from Senator Lunsford Crew of Roanoke Rapids.[100] Crew had been part of the group that developed the study commission idea in mid-summer, leading to the establishment of the Pearsall Committee. McMullan had used a Mississippi bill provided by Crew as his model.[101]

Pearsall also met with members of the General Assembly. Governor Hodges asked Larry Moore Jr., Speaker of the House, and Luther Barnhardt, President of the Senate, to appoint a committee to advise Pearsall. The legislators who met with Pearsall included W. W. Taylor Jr. of Warren County, William Rodman Jr. of Beaufort County, Lunsford Crew of Halifax County, and Paul Jones of Pitt County.[102] These legislators would play significant roles over the next two years.

Thomas Pearsall worked out a draft in cooperation with Attorney General McMullan, Assistant Attorneys General Claude Love and I. Beverly Lake, plus Henry Marrow and Stacy Weaver of the Folger Commission, legislators W. W. Taylor Jr. and Paul Jones, along with State Superintendent Charles F. Carroll.[103] It followed the lines drawn by McMullan back in July. I. Beverly Lake exerted heavy influence. Pearsall reviewed it with John Pritchett, chairman of the State Board of Education's Committee on Segregation, who secured the state board's approval.[104]

Thus North Carolina, the state that prided itself on moderation in race relations, initially modeled its response to *Brown* after Alabama and Mississippi, the states that arguably maintained the worst race relations in the nation. The development came about, not on the basis of deliberations within the biracial committee appointed by the governor, but as a function of strong conservatives in the Attorney General's Office and the legislature, working behind the scenes, outside public scrutiny.

The Pupil Assignment Act, 1954–1955

Hodges had concluded by fall 1954 that some response to *Brown* was necessary, without waiting for further court orders, in order to head off strong segregationists in the legislature who were making plans to close the state's public schools.[105] Governor Hodges and his aides arranged to have the new Pupil Assignment Bill introduced immediately after the Governor's Biennial Address on January 6, 1955.[106] Senator Paul Jones of Pitt County and Representative George Uzzell of Rowan County introduced it.[107] Hodges called it "the first of several steps."[108] But the bill did not satisfy the segregationist faction in the General Assembly. Representatives Sam Worthington of Pitt County and Byrd Satterfield of Person County introduced a constitutional amendment providing for state grants to parents "in discharge of all obligations of the State to provide . . . education for its citizens."[109]

Robert Carr, Duplin County's representative in the legislature, warned Dallas Herring that Worthington had secured commitments from 80 percent of the representatives to close schools rather than desegregate. Herring urged Carr to try to "have this reactionary legislation withdrawn."[110] The amendment's sponsors agreed to let the measure die in committee in return for a promise from the governor that he would call a special session of the General Assembly after the Supreme Court issued its implementation decrees.[111]

During public hearings in 1955, a black delegation led by John H. Wheeler, a lawyer and banker from Durham, warned that the proposed legislation appeared to be designed to avoid obeying *Brown*.[112] Nevertheless, the all-white[113] General Assembly passed the Pupil Assignment Act on March 30, 1955,[114] and authorized the appointment of a new committee to study additional responses to *Brown*.[115] In a related measure, introduced by Representative C. Gordon Maddrey of Hertford County,[116] the legislature terminated all teacher contracts and substituted a system of annual renewals.[117] Hodges and his supporters in the General Assembly further placated the segregationist faction by supporting a resolution vowing that desegregation of the schools could not be accomplished and should not be attempted.[118]

The Pupil Assignment Act thus ensured a lengthy period for transition. By shifting pupil assignment authority from the state to local boards, the statute eliminated the possibility that a single lawsuit could direct desegregation of all schools in North Carolina. Fear of a strong backlash from white citizens dominated discussions among the state's leaders. Even those political leaders who found saving the schools more important than maintaining segregation feared violence and disruption if schools were desegregated. Their principal concern, however, centered on gradual abandonment of the public schools by middle- and upper-class white parents who might initially withdraw financial support, and ultimately might withdraw their children.

North Carolina's Arguments in *Brown II*

Assistant Attorney General I. Beverly Lake presented the state's oral arguments before the U.S. Supreme Court in April 1955. Lake wielded a powerful intellect; his legal skills were appreciated even by those who disagreed with his positions. North Carolina's brief urged the court to allow the "greatest possible latitude to District judges in conducting . . . hearings and in drafting . . . decrees." Any attempt to compel immediate integration would result in "such violent opposition as to endanger the continued existence of the schools."[119] Allowing federal district courts to frame local decrees could lead to a drawn-out period of litigation, but that would be "preferable to a generation of bitterness and strife . . . , chaos inside the schoolroom, or a generation with no public schools at all."[120] When Lake touched on the latter point, Justice Frankfurter commented that North Carolina "could bring up its children in ignorance if it wanted to." Lake countered, defiantly, "The State could abolish the public school system."[121]

North Carolina's white leaders reacted very positively to Lake's performance. Attorney Fred B. Helms considered Lake's argument "superb." The justices seemed to listen more intently to North Carolina's presentation than they did to those of the other states, including the litigants. Lake was "clear-cut, frank, unequivocal, and unapologetic," Helms reported with satisfaction.[122]

Initial Reactions to *Brown II* in North Carolina

The Supreme Court issued its implementation decree on May 31, 1955. Throughout the South, prominent business and professional leaders organized White Citizens Councils, lending support from the middle and upper socioeconomic classes to continued segregation. Race-related violence emerged in many locations during the summer. In Mississippi, Emmett Till, a young teenager from Chicago who was visiting relatives, was murdered after allegedly flirting with a white woman.[123]

In contrast, a period of calm reflection ensued in North Carolina. William F. Womble of Winston-Salem, one of the state's most prominent attorneys and a law partner of Irving Carlyle, wrote an interpretation concluding that *Brown II* had abandoned the word "segregation," instead prohibiting "discrimination." Local school authorities had time to "elucidate, assess and solve" local conditions and eliminate discrimination. The Pupil Assignment Act of 1955 was appropriate, therefore.[124]

Dallas Herring urged the governor to ensure some degree of uniformity among the state's school systems. Herring had assumed that his initial refusal to sign the first Pearsall Committee's report and his subsequent critical letters to the governor and to Pearsall had offended Hodges. He did not expect to be given any role in the future.[125] In late June 1955, however, Hodges appointed Herring to the State Board of Education.

State Superintendent Carroll believed that, for the vast majority of North Carolinians, compliance with the Supreme Court decision would represent a profound change in a social pattern older than public education itself. Heretofore social change had been viewed as an evolutionary process, and nature could not be rushed. All parties concerned could lose "by confusing emotion and opportunism with reason."[126]

Greensboro superintendent of schools Ben L. Smith warned that the situation was "extremely explosive and could erupt . . . without much notice." But Smith advised that the *Brown* decisions had been made with great deliberation, and counseled that the order to desegregate would not be reversed. Smith acknowledged his belief, however, that most people, white and black, preferred separate schools. If integration were coerced, "friction, conflict, and violence" would result.[127]

Governor Hodges made his own response to *Brown II* in late June 1955. "[W]e must keep the peace if we are going to keep the schools," he told the state. "This is a time for calmness and courage. We need wise counsel rather than inflammatory headlines."[128] Hodges urged citizens to maintain segregated schools on a voluntary basis for 1955–56.[129] He expressed additional concern that most people in the state did not realize the full implication of the court's opinion.[130] The court had required a prompt and reasonable start toward compliance. But some move toward desegregation had to come soon, and when that occurred, he feared what would happen next.

The Second Pearsall Committee

Soon after the announcement of *Brown II,* Governor Hodges and his staff began thinking about another committee to consider the court's implementation orders.[131] Hodges considered appointing blacks.[132] Holt McPherson, in particular, urged black participation.[133] Hodges came under considerable pressure to keep blacks off the committee, though. State Senator John Kerr Jr. of Warren County warned, "[T]his commission should be composed of . . . men who are opposed to integration and should not contain . . . anyone who is willing to compromise."[134] Hodges concluded that black members would be too susceptible to pressure from the NAACP.[135]

On June 21, 1955, Governor Hodges announced the appointment of a new committee, all white and all male, again chaired by Thomas Pearsall. The second Pearsall Committee included two members from the first, William T. Joyner of Raleigh and R. O. Huffman of Morganton. Two members were chosen from the State House of Representatives: Cloyd Philpott of Davidson County, a furniture executive, and Edward Yarborough of Franklin County, an attorney. Two other attorneys, members of the State Senate, completed the membership: William Medford of Haywood County and Lunsford Crew of Halifax County.[136] Three members came from counties with black populations of over 40 percent.[137] The makeup of the second Pearsall Committee thus appeared predisposed toward maintaining segregation.

The second Pearsall Committee met on June 23, 1955. The committee recommended that school systems operate during school term 1955–56 on the same segregated basis as in the past and appoint local committees to consider how to deal with the segregation issue.[138]

Attorney General Harry McMullan died on June 24, 1955, at age seventy-one.[139] He had held the office since 1938, maintaining a segregationist stance throughout his tenure. Hodges persuaded a reluctant William B. Rodman Jr., a member of the House of Representatives from Beaufort County, to serve as attorney general following McMullan's death by telling Rodman that he was needed due to the critical situation regarding school desegregation.[140]

Chairman Pearsall asked the black members from the first Pearsall Committee to "invite three Negroes each, other than public officials,"[141] to meet with the new committee.[142] The black delegation protested the all-white nature of the second committee and affirmed that desegregation must proceed forthwith. The committee refused to consider such a position, and members concluded that further attempts to find cooperative blacks would be useless.[143] The committee was convinced that few blacks wanted desegregation, and that the NAACP spoke for only a small minority. The committee thus made no further effort to solicit the views of blacks.

Later in July, the second Pearsall Committee acquired a full-time, professional staff. W. W. Taylor Jr., a Warren County attorney and legislator, became executive secretary.[144] Warren County contained a black population of approximately 66 percent.[145] Taylor had attended law school at Wake Forest, where he had studied under Professor I. Beverly Lake.[146] Thomas F. Ellis, a Raleigh attorney, was appointed Taylor's assistant.[147] Ellis had practiced in the firm of J. C. B. Ehringhaus Jr., and he had served as assistant U.S. attorney for the Eastern District of North Carolina.[148] He had also been part of the inner circle of Willis Smith's supporters.[149]

Pearsall advised Taylor and Ellis that the committee was operating under two clear directives from the legislature. First, that "mixing of the races forthwith in the public schools throughout the state cannot be accomplished and should not be attempted," and second, "that North Carolina try to find means of meeting the requirements of the Supreme Court's Decision within our present school system before consideration is given to abandoning or materially altering it."[150]

Early Accommodations

Educators and school board members were worried about *Brown II*. The Duplin County school board adopted a policy that eliminated race but included academic aptitude as a basis for pupil assignment. Dallas Herring supplied a copy of the policy to Fred Smith, assistant superintendent of the Wake County schools. Smith suggested a similar policy to Superintendent Randolph Benton, but Benton considered it too liberal.[151]

The Wake County Board of Education, however, following complaints from the Raleigh Citizens Association, a black organization led by Rev. G. A. Fisher,[152] subsequently adopted a similar pupil assignment policy.[153] Students could apply for new school assignments. Appeals followed the steps prescribed in the Pupil Assignment Act. Following these actions and the advice of the Pearsall Committee, school systems in Asheville, Charlotte, Winston-Salem, Guilford County, Bertie County, Lee County, and Burlington appointed committees to consider revised pupil assignment policies. The Winston-Salem, Bertie, and Lee committees included black members.[154] Other, unidentified systems probably took similar steps.

Litigation, 1955

The NAACP was advising state and local branches that *Brown II* had declared all school segregation invalid.[155] NAACP branches should file petitions with local boards seeking a commitment to desegregate and initiate litigation in the absence of cooperation.[156] Kelly Alexander subsequently charged that Wake County's pupil assignment plan constituted an effort to evade the district's responsibility to integrate at once, and announced that a suit would be filed seeking an immediate, statewide integration order.[157]

Two relevant North Carolina cases were decided in 1955. *Carson v. Board of Education of McDowell County*[158] had been filed prior to *Brown*. The board had required Lionel C. Carson, a black student, to attend school in Burke County instead of McDowell County. Plaintiffs sought equal facilities in McDowell County as well as injunctive relief against discrimination. Judge Wilson Warlick of U.S. Western District Court dismissed the case on grounds that *Brown* had made equalization of facilities inappropriate. On appeal, Judges John J. Parker, Morris Ames Soper, and Armistead M. Dobie held that the children were entitled to have discrimination removed and their rights declared, even though equalization of facilities was not an appropriate relief. The court added, however, that federal courts should not intervene until state-provided remedies had been exhausted.[159] Thus the appeals procedures in the Pupil Assignment Act must be followed before federal action would be considered.

In the Matter of Assignment of the School Children in the Stella Community of Carteret County[160] had also been filed prior to *Brown*. Plaintiffs asked the State Board of Education to assign black children to the Onslow County schools since Carteret had no accessible facilities. The State Supreme Court held that the board no longer had the authority to make such assignments, thus validating pupil assignment by local boards.

The most important court decision in 1955 came from South Carolina. *Briggs v. Elliott*,[161] one of the original cases clustered into the *Brown* decisions, had been heard on remand. Judge John J. Parker, a University of North Carolina Law School graduate who had previously been nominated for the U.S. Supreme Court,[162] held that the court had not ordered states to mix persons of different races in the schools. The court had only decided that a state could not deny to any person on account of race the right to attend any school that the state maintained. "The Constitution . . . does not require integration. It merely forbids discrimination,"[163] Parker wrote.

Judge Parker's ruling was warmly received in North Carolina.[164] In the opinion of North Carolina Assistant Attorney General I. Beverly Lake, however, not enough was being done to defend segregation.

I. Beverly Lake's Split with the Hodges Administration

In July, Lake addressed the Asheboro Rotary Club, advocating state financial support for segregated, private schools. In a subsequent speech to the Gastonia Civitan Club, Lake urged citizens to begin making preparations for such a system. Lake spoke at the invitation of Gaston County's state senator, Frank Patton Cooke.[165] These clubs numbered among their members the business and civic leaders of their communities. Lake's presentations were widely reported in the press.

Governor Hodges attempted to remain neutral. He issued a statement that Lake was speaking as a private citizen.[166] Hodges refused to join Lake's call for public support for private schools.[167] But Lake later acknowledged that his comments had been read and approved by Attorney General Rodman. Rodman subsequently agreed that the private school approach might have to be considered, if the NAACP kept pushing for integration.[168] In summer 1955 some prominent white citizens began to act on Lake's suggestions. Raleigh Private Schools, Inc., obtained a charter to operate private educational institutions. Among the company's officers were attorney Vaughn S. Winborne, the son of Stanley Winborne, who chaired the State Utilities Commission.[169]

Lake's speeches outraged the NAACP. Kelly Alexander demanded that Lake either resign or be fired. Governor Hodges replied that he had no such intention.[170] The governor accused the NAACP of operating on the basis of policies sent from New York that were "designed to split North Carolina citizens into racial camps."[171] The NAACP, Hodges continued to believe, did not represent the state's black population.

Governor Hodges's mail grew heavy following Lake's speeches, overwhelmingly favoring segregation.[172] Lake's position also generated sympathy among powerful elements in the General Assembly.[173] By the end of the summer, Governor Hodges and his advisors perceived Lake as a serious threat to the position, moderate in the context of the times, that Hodges was trying to maintain. Edwin L. Rankin Jr., Hodges's advisor, termed Lake a "strictly negative influence,"[174] but also an extremely strong possible political opponent. Hodges, therefore, tried to keep Lake within his political circle, taking care not to criticize him in a way that would generate sympathy. Lake continued to make presentations promoting state support for segregated, private schools.[175] But his break with the Hodges administration would soon be complete.

Trying to Win Black Support

By fall 1955, Hodges and his staff were convinced that any move toward desegregation would hand the state over to extreme conservatives who would abandon the public school system.[176] Central to Hodges's concern was the perception that the public did not understand that segregation was threatened.[177] Hodges expected the situation to remain dormant until spring, when blacks would begin requesting reassignment. This would focus attention on segregation during the height of the 1956 election, when Hodges would be running for his own full term. He hoped to keep segregation out of the campaign.[178]

Hodges stood firm on voluntary segregation.[179] In a radio and television broadcast on August 8, 1955, he warned, "[I]f we are not able to succeed in a program of voluntary separate school attendance, the state within the next year or so will . . . face . . . deciding the issue of whether it shall have some form of integrated public schools or . . . abandon its public schools." Losing public schools would be the fault of the NAACP: "Organizations that attempt to force us into deciding this issue will . . . have done North Carolina the greatest disservice . . . in the 180 years of its existence." By voluntarily continuing segregated schools, black children would continue to receive a good education. Black schools would probably become even better. But if schools were forcibly integrated, "nobody knows how much education the children of either race will get."[180]

Governor Hodges reported that the response to his address was extremely positive.[181] Among professional educators, the North Carolina Education Association's Division of Superintendents passed a resolution of support.[182] Senator Sam Ervin voiced his approval.[183] The Young Democrats endorsed the plan, but they also wanted the people to be given the opportunity to vote on whether to eliminate the state's constitutional requirement for public schools.[184] *The Carolinian,* however, wrote in scorn, "Hodges came up with the same old harangue . . . about keeping the races pure, keeping outside agitators away . . . , and how sincere white people are when they attempt to deny Negro citizens the things that white people have enjoyed all these years."[185]

Hodges and his advisers were convinced that blacks supported the governor. They could not conceive that the NAACP represented the views of any meaningful proportion of the state's black population. Actually, Governor Hodges did not know much about black people or their views. His papers contain virtually no direct communications from individuals identifiable as black, except for an occasional letter from Kelly Alexander, whose ideas were invariably rejected. Advice Hodges received regarding black points of view came from white political allies.[186]

Late in summer 1955, Hodges began to take his message directly to some of the state's black leaders. He addressed officers of the North Carolina Teachers Association, the professional organization for black educators.[187] The audience applauded politely, but clearly they had not been won over.[188] The NCTA went on record opposing voluntary segregation.[189] W. I. Morris, executive secretary of the organization, wrote Hodges a polite note of thanks for his "clarifications."[190]

Hodges addressed another black audience in the fall at Agricultural and Technical College in Greensboro.[191] Most of Hodges's address praised the achievements of A&T's professors and graduates. Late in the speech, members of the audience interrupted the governor with a "discourteous snicker."[192] A few moments later, the audience began rustling and talking loudly. Hodges turned to Dr. F. D. Bluford and asked if he should continue. Dr. Bluford replied, "Suit yourself."[193]

Hodges paused until the commotion subsided, then completed his address.

Subsequent explanations focused on Hodges's pronunciation of the word "Negro." Some members of the audience perceived "nigra,"[194] or, according to *The Carolina Times,* "something that rhymed with 'trigger.'"[195] Hodges denied mispronouncing the word, and he resented what he termed Dr. Bluford's "lack of courage."[196] Dr. Bluford, a number of A&T students and faculty members, and several student organizations wrote letters of apology. Hodges responded tersely: "I hereby acknowledge receipt of your communication . . . regarding the unfortunate incident at A&T College."[197] Hodges continued to believe that disapproval from black audiences did not represent the opinions of most black citizens.[198] He remained confident that blacks supported voluntary segregation, estimating the proportion at 85 to 90 percent.[199]

The Patriots of North Carolina

Meanwhile, strong segregationists were mobilizing. In a development similar to the establishment of White Citizens Councils elsewhere in the South, the Patriots of North Carolina obtained a charter in August 1955.[200] Membership listed 356 prominent citizens in 59 of the State's 100 counties.[201] The Patriots cited as their goals the preservation of "the purity and culture of the white race" as well as encouraging "friendly race relations and racial peace and good will."[202] They circulated literature claiming that integration was the goal of communists and that the NAACP sought "amalgamation"[203] of the races.

Dr. W. C. George of the University of North Carolina was president. The board of directors included Senators Sam Worthington of Pitt County and John H. Kerr Jr. of Warren County, plus Representative Fred H. Holcombe of Madison County.[204] Former legislator Julian Allsbrook of Roanoke Rapids, Dr. Spencer P. Bass of Tarboro, prominent industrialist Stark S. Dillard and former mayor Fielding L. Fry, both of Greensboro, were listed as well. Attorney C. L. Shuping of Greensboro was general counsel. John W. Clark of Greensboro, a UNC trustee, had been one of the state's most vocal supporters of continuing segregation for undergraduates. Former Speakers of the House John G. Dawson of Kinston and W. F. Taylor of Goldsboro were among the Patriots' charter members, along with Senator Dennis S. Cook of Lenoir, Representative Thomas J. White of Kinston, Representative J. Paul Wallace of Troy, and McDaniel Lewis of Greensboro, who chaired the State Board of Archives and History.[205]

These were not the "redneck hordes"[206] to which Professor Chafe has alluded. On the contrary, the Patriots were members of the state's socioeconomic and political elite; indeed, they constituted the state's white leadership class.

Hodges attempted to maintain a congenial tone with the Patriots.[207] He assured them he would do everything he could to maintain segregation.[208] By winter, though, Dr. George was accusing Hodges of not fighting hard enough: "You have not said you will use all the authority of your office and mobilize the resources of the State to prevent it."[209] Hodges's notes read, "Legally impractical!" But his reply to George was courteous: "We are working on the matter very diligently. . . . I hope you will be pleased with what we bring forth."[210] Hodges did not want to alienate the Patriots. He thought they were signing up members "by the thousands," yet he hoped to avoid "terrible extremes, developing . . . rapidly."[211]

Work of the Second Pearsall Committee

The potential for "extremes" was weighing heavily on the governor by fall 1955. He continued to consider himself a moderate, trying to balance on a tightrope between extremists: blacks who wanted immediate integration versus whites who wanted to abolish public schools. His primary goal was saving the schools. That was the context within which the second Pearsall Committee operated.

Members of the Committee met with officials from Mississippi to discuss how that state was preserving segregation.[212] Committee attorneys Taylor and Ellis plus Attorney General Rodman began providing assistance to school systems that might be faced with desegregation litigation.[213]

Early in fall 1955, based on advice from Rodman, the Hodges administration began considering a state constitutional amendment allowing localities to discontinue public schools.[214] Hodges, Rodman, and members of the committee studied legislation from Georgia, Louisiana, and Mississippi.[215] The Mississippi legislature, in particular, had worked out a plan using tax funds to support private schools.[216]

In September, Hodges issued a statement that, if voluntary segregation were not accepted, then the state would have to resort to other defenses, such as local option school closings. Attorney General

Rodman lamented, "Abolition of the public schools and their replacement to a most uncertain extent by private ones, is a last-ditch and double-edged weapon. If the weapon is ever used in North Carolina, its results will be appalling in ignorance, poverty and bitterness."[217] Rodman also acknowledged, however, that local boards had the authority to admit black students. The Raleigh *News and Observer* denounced the idea of local option school closings as "the most tragic proposal ever made in a presumably intelligent land, . . . a secession from civilization," and a step that "would turn back the clock a century."[218] In the meantime, Hodges was meeting with legislators to discuss the idea in depth.[219]

Taylor and Ellis attended a hearing in a Montgomery County case, *Covington v. Edwards,*[220] for the purpose of ascertaining the sort of attack that could be expected in the future. Their report reveals a great deal about their frame of reference. They found themselves "shocked at the arrogance, rudeness, and complete self-confidence of the Negro attorneys. . . . Equally as shocking to us was the fact that they have been permitted to get away with it, both by Judge Hayes and the Special Master [Rufus Reynolds, who was presiding over the taking of depositions], neither of whom has called them down or censured them."[221]

They were observing Conrad Pearson of Durham. The testimony of black witnesses also appalled Taylor and Ellis. Blacks who had told "reputable white persons" that they did not believe in race mixing and had not employed counsel testified under oath that they had employed an attorney and that they now desired integration. Taylor and Ellis left the hearing "with the very depressing feeling that any appeal to reason will be wasted on Negroes . . . and that we had seen an indication of action which can reasonably be expected in practically every county in this state."[222]

Taylor and Ellis thus advised Governor Hodges to go forward with repeal of the sections of the North Carolina Constitution requiring public schools, along with enactment of a local option school closing plan and the elimination of compulsory attendance. They also investigated procedures in other states for punishing schools that desegregated. They devoted additional inquiries to other states regarding suspected communist influences in the NAACP, as well as disciplinary measures that might be taken against black teachers who attempted to promote integration.[223]

By December 1955, outlines for the second Pearsall Committee's report had been completed.[224] Signatures from Taylor and Ellis indicate they were the principal authors. Outlines indicated that the state should assure parents that no child would be compelled to attend an integrated school. Provisions should be developed for state grants to pay private school tuition. Compulsory attendance should be repealed. Constitutional amendments should eliminate requirements for public schools. The state should provide legal assistance to school systems defending integration lawsuits.[225]

The committee prepared a draft in early January 1956. The report concluded that the Supreme Court had destroyed the foundation of North Carolina's school system. Segregation was that foundation. White people would not accept integrated schools. The rest of the report, however, followed a more moderate tone. The decision of the Supreme Court was the law of the land, and defiance of the court would be "foolhardy." The report concluded, "So, we think . . . that our problem *is to . . . go forward under the Supreme Court decision; to refrain from defying the Court or the Federal Government; and to build a new school system, regretfully acknowledging the invalidity of law compelled segregation*" (emphasis in original).[226]

The report was developed and issued during a period of continuing turmoil at the national level. In December 1955, Rosa Parks refused to give up her seat on a Montgomery, Alabama, bus to a white person. The Montgomery bus boycott ensued through the winter and spring, led by Martin Luther King Jr. Autherine Lucy, a black student, was almost lynched by a mob when she attempted to enroll at the University of Alabama in February 1956.[227]

In spring 1956 representatives from southern states in the U.S. Congress issued "The Southern Manifesto," written largely by North Carolina Senator Sam Ervin, denouncing the Supreme Court for substituting "naked power for established principle."[228] A total of ninety-six representatives and senators, including most of North Carolina's delegation, signed. Representatives Harold Cooley, Thurmond Chatham, Charles Deane, and Charles Jonas did not sign, however.

In March, Luther Hodges announced that he would seek a full term as governor. He emphasized support for segregation and the success of voluntary segregation, promising that, if events warranted, he was prepared to propose a policy declaring that no children would be forced to attend a school of mixed races. Legislation authorizing tuition grants to private schools was being prepared.[229]

With an election year underway, W. W. Taylor Jr. resigned as executive secretary and returned to Warren County to run for the State House of Representatives.[230] Ellis succeeded Taylor.[231] He made an unsuccessful effort to place the committee on record more strongly in favor of segregation.[232] The second Pearsall Committee filed its report on April 5, 1956.[233] Its recommendations followed the interim report and urged a special session of the legislature.[234] Chairman Pearsall explained the contents of the report to a statewide radio and television audience. He strongly criticized the "belligerence" of black leaders, vowing that public education could survive only with continued white support.[235]

Constitutional Amendments, 1956

Hodges called the legislature into special session on July 23, 1956. Assistant Attorney General Robert Giles bore the primary responsibility for drafting proposed legislation.[236] Pearsall made arrangements with William Friday, acting president of the University of North Carolina, to have WUNC television broadcast the session.[237] Pearsall, Ellis, and Hodges secured advance support for the proposals from the State Board of Education, the PTA, and the North Carolina Education Association.[238] Staff solicited small groups of legislators.[239]

One of the bills amended the North Carolina Constitution to authorize suspending the operation of local public schools and paying tuition to private schools in order to enable children to avoid attending school with another race.[240] Another authorized local boards to call a special election if 15 percent of the voters signed a petition requesting that schools be closed. If a majority so voted, the schools would be closed. The schools would reopen if 15 percent petitioned for an election and a majority voted favorably. Whenever schools were closed, principals and teachers were to continue to receive their salaries for the duration of their contracts, unless they secured other employment.[241] Another bill eliminated compulsory attendance for any child assigned to a school that included members of another race.[242]

Senators Lunsford Crew and William Medford, along with Representatives Edward Yarborough of Franklin County and H. Cloyd Philpott of Davidson County, introduced a joint resolution "of condemnation and protest against oppressive usurpation of power by the Supreme Court of the United States."[243] The resolution had the backing of Governor Hodges.[244]

Some legislators wanted a more powerful defense of segregation.

Senators Robert Morgan of Harnett County, Adam Whitley of Johnston County, B. C. Brock of Davie County, and Mitchell Britt of Duplin County, along with Representative Byrd Satterfield of Person County, sponsored a constitutional amendment allowing the state to provide educational expense grants to parents of children enrolled in private schools[245] and making closing public schools much easier than the Hodges legislation would have required.[246] Many observers believed that I. Beverly Lake, a close associate of Morgan, had prepared the Morgan bill.[247]

Two other bills introduced by J. A. Speight of Bertie County were obviously retaliatory. One directed the immediate closing of all the state's colleges for blacks upon the admission of one or more black students to colleges and universities previously attended only by whites.[248] The other would have required all black teachers and principals to take special examinations prior to the opening of school in 1956–57 and provided that certificates of black teachers be graded according to the results.[249] Those bills received unfavorable reports from committees, and action was postponed indefinitely.[250]

All the administration's bills were enacted. Representative William Womble of Forsyth County, one of the most progressive members of the House, concluded, "If segregation as a matter of law is wrong, forced integration as a matter of law is also wrong."[251] A more moderate course existed, and Womble believed that the Hodges legislation represented that moderate course, especially in comparison to actions being taken in some other southern states.

The State Board of Elections scheduled a referendum on the proposed constitutional amendments for September 8.[252] A massive campaign promoted the amendments, now known as the Pearsall Plan. Holt McPherson, editor of the *High Point Enterprise,* chaired the initiative.[253] Early supporters included the Patriots.[254] Support among the press was widespread.[255] Additional endorsements came from the North Carolina School Boards Association, the Junior Chamber of Commerce, the State Association of School Superintendents, the State Association of County Commissioners, and the white North Carolina Education Association, but not the black North Carolina Teachers Association.[256] Much of the state's delegation to the U.S. Congress endorsed the plan as well.[257] Senator Sam Ervin made a television appearance on its behalf.[258] Not many blacks favored the amendments, but the Hodges administration listed John W. Parker of Fayetteville State College and Dr. Reginald L. French of St. Augustine's College as supporters.[259] Few organizations opposed the Pearsall Plan at the outset, but the state PTA was among them. Irving Carlyle publicly opposed the plan, as did Greensboro superintendent Ben L. Smith.[260]

Governor Hodges made personal appearances and a statewide radio and television broadcast, assuring the people that the school closing provisions and tuition grants represented only "safety valves" in case local conditions became intolerable. The goal of the plan was to ensure the preservation of the public schools, providing an "orderly and lawful" means to meet problems.[261]

Voter turnout on September 8, 1957, was the largest for a special election in the state's history.[262] All one hundred counties voted in favor of the Pearsall Plan by a margin exceeding four to one.[263] The only significant opposition came from a few precincts in large cities where blacks constituted a majority.[264]

North Carolina's history of segregation as well as its pattern of moderation in race relations weighed heavily in its response to the *Brown* decisions. The state had been providing education to all its children, black as well as white, albeit within a segregated, highly discriminatory framework. North Carolina's legal representatives defended segregation on the grounds that it had been legal throughout the school system's development. If schools had to be integrated immediately, then the public schools would probably be abolished, and the state would stop providing education to large numbers of students. Black children and black educators would be hurt most. But the state would obey the law. A lengthy period of time would be essential, however, in order to adjust.

After the court issued implementation orders, reaction was mixed. Some of the state's white leaders counseled a gradual approach. Some school systems adopted policies that eliminated race as a basis for pupil assignment. A voice emerged from within civic and religious organizations supporting desegregation on moral grounds. But segregationist sentiment permeated the public and the legislature, especially among legislators from the East. Segregationist sentiment was strong across all socioeconomic levels, including the white elite. One mechanism favored by strong segregationists centered on providing state expense grants to pay for attendance at segregated, private schools.

The Hodges administration tried to avoid the two alternatives that seemed to foretell disaster: integration or abolition of the public schools. Instead, Hodges sought what he considered moderate steps.

He tried to enlist black support for his ideas, without success. The governor concluded that the only way to save the schools was to keep them segregated for the time being. Consequently, the second Pearsall Committee developed legislation providing a school closing mechanism that localities could use in order to avoid integration. Hodges termed these measures a "safety valve," and expressed hope they would never be used.

The legislature passed the program, termed the Pearsall Plan. In the largest voter turnout for a special election in the state's history, the Pearsall Plan received overwhelming approval in all one hundred North Carolina counties. Thus procedures were put in place that could either shut the schools or save them.

4

Tokenism

FROM 1956 TO 1960

The Pupil Assignment Act of 1955 placed sole authority for pupil assignment to schools with local boards of education. The second phase of North Carolina's adaptation to the *Brown* decisions, the Pearsall Plan, allowed communities to vote to close schools in order to avoid desegregation and established a mechanism allowing parents to apply for tuition grants to enable students to attend segregated, private schools. Because implementation of these measures hinged on local board-of-education action, local decision makers began to carry the burden of response to local school desegregation initiatives during the latter 1950s. State officials took a step back, allowing implementation of the process.

How did this approach actually operate in practice? What sort of desegregation initiatives did the NAACP maintain during this period? How did local and state decision makers respond? To what extent did North Carolina actually desegregate schools during the five years following the *Brown* decisions?

Early Desegregation Initiatives

During the 1956–57 school year, the state's public schools continued to operate on a racially segregated basis, just as the second Pearsall Committee and Governor Hodges had urged. Segregation continued in spite of NAACP-backed petitions seeking integration submitted to local boards in at least twenty-six school systems. Steps toward possible accommodation to desegregation, however, emerged as well. At least sixty-seven school systems appointed committees to study desegregation.[1]

During fall 1956, William T. Joyner and Holt McPherson, both of whom had been members of the first Pearsall Committee, began to discuss publicly the idea that some measure of school desegregation ought to occur, soon, on a voluntary basis.[2] Joyner's position as a well-connected, politically powerful Raleigh attorney and member of the second Pearsall Committee, combined with the fact that he was the son of J. Y. Joyner, state superintendent of public instruction during the Aycock era, generated a lot of attention. McPherson, editor of the *High Point Enterprise,* had chaired the campaign to pass the constitutional amendment that formed the foundation of the Pearsall Plan. In addition, Fred B. Helms, a prominent Charlotte attorney who had served on the first Pearsall Committee, urged the establishment of biracial community councils as a step toward improving race relations.[3]

Because of the prominence of these individuals, some newspapers speculated that their ideas represented the thoughts of the state's highest officials. Governor Hodges, however, refused public comment, in spite of pointed inquiries from the press, especially Reed Sarratt, editor of the *Winston-Salem Journal.*[4] Hodges simply stated that pupil assignment was a matter for local boards to decide. Hodges and his advisors believed that validation of the Pearsall Plan by the courts would hinge on recognition that local boards of education were, in truth, free to make local decisions.[5] State officials, therefore, maintained a strict "hands off" posture with regard to school desegregation after passage of the Pearsall Plan. The state's adaptations to *Brown* had to be allowed to function in practice.[6]

In March 1957, Kelly Alexander and Dr. Reginald Hawkins led a delegation of black parents who met with the administration and board of the Charlotte City Schools.[7] Superintendent Elmer Garinger subsequently told board members, "Desegregation is not only the law, it is also right."[8] That summer, superintendents and board chairs Garinger and Bishop Herbert Spaugh of Charlotte, Craig Phillips and E. T. Pullen of Winston-Salem, along with Ben L. Smith and Edward Hudgins of Greensboro, met quietly to discuss the admission of black students into formerly all-white schools in their respective systems. They received behind-the-scenes encouragement from Thomas Pearsall, who also attended the meetings.[9]

The Hodges administration was aware of the meetings, but the State Attorney General's Office warned that no state official should attend. Pearsall could be present because he was acting as a private citizen, the work of the second Pearsall Committee having been completed the year before. Guy B. Phillips, dean of the School of Education at the University of North Carolina, founder of the State School Boards

Association, and a member of the State Board of Education, reported the contents of the meetings to Dallas Herring, recently selected to chair the State Board of Education. Guy Phillips was Craig Phillips's father. From the outset, the admission of blacks to white schools in these three school systems was considered not an isolated experiment but as the beginning of a freedom-of-choice approach to school desegregation that would be replicated elsewhere.[10]

The initial enrollment of black students into previously all-white schools was scheduled for fall 1957.[11] Charlotte admitted four black students to previously all-white schools: Dorothy Counts to Harding High, Gus Roberts to Central High, Delores Huntley to Alexander Graham Junior High, and Girvaude Roberts to Piedmont Junior High.[12] Greensboro admitted six: Josephine Boyd to Greensboro Senior High; Harold Davis, Elijah Herring Jr., and Russell Herring to Gillespie Junior High; plus Brenda Kay Florence and Jimmie B. Florence to Gillespie Elementary.[13] Winston-Salem admitted one black student, Gwendolyn Bailey, to Reynolds High.[14] The boards denied another thirty-nine transfer applications.[15] Raleigh City and Mecklenburg County also considered a series of transfer requests but either deferred or denied all of them. The boards did not release specific reasons for the decisions, other than stating that each application for transfer had been considered on its individual merits and that the decisions had been made so as to promote orderly administration and effective instruction in the schools, as well as the health, safety, and welfare of students.[16]

Following public announcement of the admissions, Governor Hodges held fast to his position supporting segregation: "My personal view against mixing of the races is well known. Without judging whether recent actions by some local school boards are right or wrong in accepting or rejecting negro applicants, I want to emphasize that the State and the people of North Carolina will not tolerate any lawlessness or violence in connection with this problem."[17] Hodges made no move to intervene, however.

The reference to lawlessness grew out of Hodges's continued belief that the people of North Carolina would not accept anything more than token desegregation, if that. In preparation for anticipated outbursts, he had his staff review existing laws and advise him regarding the authority of the governor to utilize state militia and law enforcement officers to quell domestic disturbances.[18] In political and legal terms, Hodges's staff felt confident that the Pearsall Plan provided the safety valve that would head off violent reaction. But they felt the need to be prepared in case violent protests occurred.[19]

When the students actually enrolled in school during September 3–10, 1957, the situation was tense. Undercover police officers and State Highway Patrol troopers were stationed in the vicinity of all the schools involved. The troopers called in reports to headquarters which were relayed to Governor Hodges on an almost hourly basis.[20]

In Greensboro and Winston-Salem, no serious incidents occurred the first two days. On September 4, at Charlotte's Central High and Piedmont Elementary, a crowd taunted black students entering school.[21] At Charlotte Harding High, according to a Highway Patrol report, a "Mr. and Mrs. Warlick, the couple who entertained segregationist Casper on his visit to Charlotte,"[22] took up a position near the school. The Warlicks began agitating students and anybody else who would listen. The individual referred to as "Casper" was John Kasper, who also visited Winston-Salem and Greensboro, urging white students to make life miserable for black students through insults, elbowing, or any other means.[23]

Harding principal James R. Hawkins reported to detectives on the scene that the Warlicks were stirring up trouble.[24] A crowd of over two hundred students and forty adults gathered. A teenaged white girl spit at Counts, and others in the crowd threw ice chips at her. Counts's father picked her up at school and took her home. Police made two arrests: an eighteen-year-old white male on a charge of simple assault, and a fifteen-year-old white female on a charge of disorderly conduct.[25] In class, Counts reported that her teachers ignored her. After four days, Counts withdrew. Three months later, Dr. Frank Porter Graham spoke to the Harding student body, exhorting them that, if the United States were to lead the free world, integration would be essential. Moved, the student body applauded.[26] But Dorothy Counts never returned.

Someone set off firecrackers at Reynolds High in Winston-Salem on September 5, and fifteen police officers were ordered to patrol the school. As Gwendolyn Bailey entered the school, two autos drove by and someone yelled, "nigger." "Go home, nigger, you black s.o.b.," was painted on the street in front of the school. Bailey was removed from school for the rest of the day.[27] While she was gone, a group of white students gathered brooms, brushes, and paint remover and scrubbed the words off the pavement. Principal Claude Joyner told the student body in an assembly program that integration "will be better for us, our schools, and our communities."[28]

On the same day, at Charlotte Central High, a group of about fifty white students stopped Gus Roberts as he attempted to enter the school, slapped him, pushed him, and generally roughed him up. The principal personally escorted Roberts into school. Police surveillance was intensified at Gillespie Junior High in Greensboro, but no incidents occurred.[29] White students heckled Josephine Boyd as she entered Greensboro Senior High.[30] On September 6, in Charlotte, an improvised coffin appeared on the steps of Central High School, and a human replica was found hanging from the school's flagpole. For the remainder of the week, conditions stayed relatively quiet and peaceful in the schools of all three cities.[31]

During the week of September 17, however, white students at Greensboro Senior High hit black student Josephine Boyd with thrown eggs. She went home, changed her clothes, and returned to school. Rankin School experienced minor vandalism. Several crosses were burned at schools in Greensboro, plus one on the lawn of Superintendent Ben L. Smith.[32] Special duty police in plain clothes and unmarked cars guarded his home.[33] Eventually, a group of teachers and members of the Student Council arranged to take Boyd's lunch to her in the balcony of the auditorium, where she could eat without interruption.[34] At the end of the year, Josephine Boyd became the first black student to graduate from a formerly all-white high school in North Carolina.[35]

Governor Hodges spoke in Greensboro on September 13, 1957. He repeated his personal preference for segregation, adding that he was sure most people in North Carolina felt the same way. But he praised citizens for suspending their personal desires and concentrating instead on obeying the law. Hodges denounced "outsiders," naming both the NAACP and the Ku Klux Klan and vowing that blacks in segregated states were better off than in states that were integrated.[36]

In October, a bomb exploded at the home of Elijah Herring, whose children were among those attending Gillespie Junior High in Greensboro. Herring gave police the license number of a car seen fleeing the scene. A patrol car located the vehicle and questioned its white male occupants, all residents of Liberty, North Carolina. They denied knowledge of the bombing, claiming they had heard an explosion and drove to the vicinity to see what had happened. The officers released them. The police noted that Herring was believed to be one of the blacks who had played golf at Gillespie Park Golf Course, which resulted in the closing of the course as well as a desegregation suit in federal court. The police advised Governor Hodges that the bombing was probably the work of "the negro element of the NAACP."[37]

Reflecting on the situation in North Carolina later in the fall of 1957, NAACP national executive secretary Roy Wilkins remarked that, although the organization was not satisfied with the "less than token" level of school desegregation that had been achieved so far, he could not condemn the state's approach to pupil assignment completely. If some school boards would move more toward integration, maybe the situation would open up, Wilkins hoped. "North Carolina has had a period of soul-searching which is not yet ended." The state was to be commended for "turning its back" on legislation aimed at repressing the NAACP, Wilkins believed.[38]

State Government's Relationship with the NAACP

Wilkins was referring to repressive measures which had been adopted in other southern states. In Alabama, the NAACP had been prohibited from operating after a state court found the organization had failed to register as an out-of-state corporation.[39] South Carolina had required its teachers to sign a pledge that they were not members of the NAACP and barred members from municipal or state employment.[40] Virginia had passed punitive legislation targeting the NAACP.[41]

Although Wilkins praised the absence of repression in North Carolina, members of the legislature and the Hodges administration had seriously considered the idea. C. L. Shuping, general counsel for the Patriots, had initiated such consideration when he wrote to Secretary of State Thad Eure in November 1955, charging that the NAACP was not registered properly under a 1947 law that applied to any organization seeking to influence public opinion and legislation.[42]

Attorney General William B. Rodman sought to enforce the statute after an exchange of letters with NAACP officers. The NAACP claimed the organization did not do business in the state in the manner the law envisioned.[43] Before Rodman could initiate action, however, NAACP attorneys filed suit against the state, seeking a judgment that the state was without power to require the organization to register. Judge Hamilton Hobgood ruled in favor of the state. In subsequent action, NAACP attorney Conrad Pearson paid a fine of five hundred dollars and filed the requisite papers. The Attorney General's Office later admitted that only six to eight corporations had ever filed prior to the NAACP, and no other action of such nature had ever been brought before.[44]

During the legislative session of 1957, Representatives Byrd Satterfield of Person County and John Kerr Jr. of Warren County filed a bill that would have required organizations concerned with "the advancement of the interests of citizens on the basis of . . . color, race, religion, or national origin" to reveal their membership lists and financial contributors.[45] Satterfield made clear that the measure was intended to apply to the NAACP. Fines of up to $10,000, as well as cancellation of the right to operate in the state, would have been imposed. Governor Hodges indicated that he was considering similar legislation.[46] A Hodges-supported bill, introduced a few days later in the House by Representatives Addison Hewlett Jr. of New Hanover County and W. Reid Thompson of Chatham County, and in the Senate by J. William Copeland of Hertford County,[47] would have prevented the NAACP from paying the costs of legal actions on behalf of clients seeking civil rights injunctions and disbarred attorneys who accepted such payments. Membership disclosures would not have been required, except for officers.[48]

These bills were clearly repressive in intent. The Satterfield bill could have targeted individuals for retaliation through the disclosure requirements, while the Hodges bill would have struck at the heart of the NAACP's strategy of litigation. Neither bill moved forward in the legislature, however, after the Attorney General's Office warned that they were illegal.[49]

Litigation, 1956–1957

Black families, mostly with NAACP support, continued to press for desegregation through the courts. The principal thrust of litigation during the latter 1950s sought to void the individual transfer application and appeals process prescribed in the Pupil Assignment Act and to obtain court orders requiring system-wide integration. Such suits were filed against local school systems, not against the state, although plaintiffs sometimes attempted to make the state a defendant in an effort to expand the scope of a court order the suit was seeking. Conrad Pearson of Durham acted as principal counsel during this period.

The first major challenge to the Pearsall Plan was filed in 1956. Pearson, along with Major S. High, J. Kenneth Lee, and George A. Lawson of Greensboro, represented Helen Covington and others in *Covington v. Montgomery County School Board.*[50] Garland S. Garriss of Troy represented the board. The suit requested that a panel of three judges be convened, as provided by federal law when the constitutionality of a state statute was at issue or where a restraining action was sought against a state officer.[51] This could have resulted in local pupil assignment authority, the essential element of the Pupil Assignment Act of 1955, being struck down, because it would have opened up the possibility of a single judgment ordering statewide integration.

Judge Johnson J. Hayes of U.S. Middle District Court ruled that any requirements for segregation by race were now unconstitutional.[52] Plaintiffs were not, however, entitled to a hearing before a three-judge panel, because the *Brown* decisions had settled the constitutionality issue.

In *Joyner v. McDowell County Board of Education,*[53] filed the same year, plaintiffs Albert Joyner, Lucille Lytle, James Bryson and Thurman Greenlee, represented by Samuel S. Mitchell and Herman L. Taylor of Raleigh, tried to force the Board of Education to admit black students to Old Fort School. The board, represented by Roy W. Davis of Marion, replied that no specific black pupils had sought a transfer to Old Fort, so no such steps could be undertaken. The case reached the North Carolina Supreme Court in the spring of 1956. Plaintiffs were rebuffed on the grounds that the suit was "in reality a class suit . . . requiring the immediate integration of all Negro pupils residing in the administrative unit. . . . Such a procedure is neither contemplated nor authorized by statute,"[54] the court ruled.

Plaintiffs in another McDowell County case, *Carson v. Warlick,*[55] asked for a writ of mandamus ordering the board to allow black pupils to enroll as though the Pupil Assignment Act had never been enacted. The Fourth Circuit Court of Appeals refused, holding that the Pupil Assignment Act could not be considered unconstitutional on its face, reaffirming that students were admitted to schools as individuals, not as a class or group, although they had the right "to be admitted to the schools of North Carolina without discrimination on the ground of race."[56] The U.S. Supreme Court subsequently declined to review the case,[57] thus upholding the appellate decision in *Carson.*

In another 1956 case, the North Carolina Supreme Court held in *Constantian v. Anson County*[58] that the portion of the 1875 amendment to the state constitution which purported to make mandatory the separation of the races in the public schools violated the equal protection clause of the Fourteenth Amendment of the U.S. Constitution. The decision, however, did not regard *Brown* as requiring the elimination of racially segregated schools. School systems were simply required to admit black students to formerly all-white schools, if they requested it, just as Judge Parker had ruled in South Carolina.[59]

In fall 1957 the white parents of J. E. Turner Jr., James A. Strunks, and James W. Cudworth, represented by J. J. Shields, filed suit to block the Greensboro Board of Education's action allowing black students to transfer to formerly all-white schools.[60] Robert F. Mosely and Welch Jordan represented the board. Guilford County Superior Court judge L. Richardson Preyer ruled that the board had clearly acted in good faith after careful deliberation, and that only persons who had been denied application for assignment to a particular school could appeal the board's action to Superior Court.[61] Since the individuals filing suit had not been aggrieved under the terms of the Pupil Assignment Act, they had no grounds to sue. On appeal later in the school year, the North Carolina Supreme Court upheld Preyer's ruling.[62] "To say that the parent of every child has a right to challenge the assignment of another child . . . would . . . make the administration of the public school system an utter impossibility,"[63] the court held.

By the end of 1957, therefore, courts were upholding the Pupil Assignment Act. Black parents had to apply for the reassignment of individual students rather than proceed as a group. Whether boards of education allowed or denied such transfers, the courts affirmed the boards' actions.

North Carolina's early desegregation initiatives, therefore, though highly limited, operated within the framework of law. Developments in North Carolina were orderly and peaceful in contrast to what happened in some other southern states. School administrators consistently sought to protect newly enrolled black students and appealed to white students in a framework of moral responsibility.

North Carolina Compared to Virginia and Arkansas

North Carolina's legislation fared better under federal review than the approach of its neighbor, Virginia. In reviewing that state's pupil assignment act, the U.S. Eastern District Court noted that the Virginia legislature had passed a Resolution of Interposition, vowing that the state was not bound by the *Brown* decisions. Virginia's governor had made speeches clearly indicating his intent to maintain school segregation. Virginia law defined an "efficient" school system as one in which the students were segregated by race and prohibited the use of state funds in support of systems that were not "efficient."[64] The court thus reasoned that Virginia's legislative history showed patent racial discrimination and intent to continue discrimination.[65] The court thus declared Virginia's pupil assignment act unconstitutional on its face.[66]

Events in Little Rock, Arkansas, during 1957–58 showed how serious school desegregation issues could become. The Little Rock Board of Education had adopted a desegregation plan for the entire school system. Arkansas governor Orville Faubus, however, called out the National Guard and ordered its members to block the entrance of black students into the city's high schools.[67] The Eighth Circuit Court of Appeals ruled that the governor could not use the National Guard in order to defy the law. President Eisenhower dispatched a contingent from the 101st Airborne to Little Rock and placed the Arkansas National Guard under federal control.[68]

Governor Hodges and other southern governors were horrified by these developments. Governor Hodges denounced President Eisenhower's action, decrying what he termed "strong armed tactics."[69] The Southern Governors Conference subsequently selected Luther Hodges to chair a delegation to visit the president. Hodges told Eisenhower that the welfare of the nation required some understanding to be reached whereby the use of federal troops could be immediately discontinued.[70] Faubus backed down somewhat, and the president withdrew the troops.[71] But all of Little Rock's high schools were soon closed, and they remained closed for the rest of the school year.[72]

In litigation growing out of the Little Rock matter, the U.S. Supreme Court drew a firm line: "[T]he . . . rights of [children] are not to be sacrificed or yielded to the violence and disorder which have followed upon the actions of the Governor and Legislature, and law and order are not . . . to be preserved by depriving . . . Negro children of their constitutional rights." Local hostility to desegregation was irrelevant, the court warned.[73] Hodges announced to the public that he found nothing in the Little Rock case that directly affected North Carolina.[74] No North Carolina politician sought to exploit Little Rock for political gain.[75] Internally, however, the governor continued to look at North Carolina's response to *Brown* as compared to the situation in other states.[76] The key element in North Carolina's approach, setting it apart from any other southern state, seemed to be the requirement of a local referendum on school closing. Such local decision making appeared to strengthen North Carolina's legal position. Attorney General Seawell warned Hodges, therefore, not to intervene in any litigation.[77]

Hodges's actions in the Little Rock matter shifted North Carolina's position somewhat toward the strong segregationist camp. Hodges did not denounce Faubus for blocking a locally developed plan for desegregation. No indication that Hodges had any such intent appears in his papers. But Faubus's stand had evoked substantial sympathy in North Carolina.[78] Even if Governor Hodges had wanted to take a stance against Faubus's actions, Hodges's closest advisors warned that appearing to undermine Faubus was tantamount to political suicide. Failure to support Faubus would produce a segregationist backlash, Hodges's advisors believed.[79]

The actions of the federal government in the Little Rock matter showed North Carolina and the rest of the South that defiance of desegregation rulings would not be tolerated. The Little Rock incident cast a pall over the South. For strong segregationists as well as for moderates, the specter of federal troops invading and occupying a southern state conjured an image from the previous century that no rational person wanted to see repeated. Such forebodings no doubt caused much soul searching among North Carolina's political leadership. Some probably began to shift more toward accommodation in a sense of the growing inevitability of desegregation. Others, however, became more embittered, and embarked on an even stronger course in defense of segregation.

Developments in Little Rock generated immediate, intense fears in North Carolina. In the fall of 1957, I. Beverly Lake, by then in private practice, warned a WRAL television audience that the policies of the Hodges administration could lead only to race mixing and would destroy the public school system. Lake deplored recent statements by W. T. Joyner, who had described the legal nightmare of trying to defend a school system where not a single black child had ever been admitted to a formerly all-white school. Lake remarked, "What gives me nightmares is the realization that . . . a State administration, primarily concerned with . . . tax concessions to Big Business, has allowed North Carolina to drift into the current of integration which, if we do not assert ourselves strongly and quickly, will sweep us to disaster—to the destruction of our public schools as effective teaching instruments and the bringing to North Carolina of race hatreds and race violence."[80]

The Hodges administration seemed to think that admitting a few Negro children to white schools was a small price to pay in order to preserve the continued operation of the public schools, Lake advised his viewers. Lake saw that view as appeasement, in the spirit of Neville Chamberlain. Just like Hitler, the NAACP could not be appeased, Lake warned. "Its ultimate objective, short of which it will not rest satisfied, is the eventual blending of the white and Negro races into a mixed-blooded whole."[81] Lake continued his commentary through the latter 1950s. By 1959 he was being touted as the gubernatorial candidate to be supported by the strong segregationist wing of the Democratic Party.[82]

Additional Strong Segregationist Activities

Forces far less responsible than Lake, lying well outside the political mainstream, were at work as well. The latter 1950s saw a resurgence of Ku Klux Klan activity in North Carolina, as well as in other states. In a meeting on October 5, 1957, in Robeson County, about 250 people showed up to watch a gathering of Klansmen dressed in purple, scarlet, and white robes. The speaker denounced Ed Sullivan, Ford Motor Company, many area newspapers, and Governor Hodges for not doing enough to block integration.[83] When the Klan returned for another rally in January 1958, however, a group of armed Native Americans broke up the meeting and chased the Klan members out of the county.[84] Governor Hodges telephoned Robeson County sheriff Malcolm McLeod and Mayor J. C. Oxendine of Pembroke to assure them of his support if the situation required further action.[85] Hodges then issued a public statement denouncing the Klan as an organization of intimidation and violence.[86]

The Robeson County incident embarrassed the Klan. Leaders reacted by vowing to each other and to other Klan members that the KKK would become more violent. Klan leaders took up and burned KKK identification cards and assigned members secret numbers. Members claimed they had acquired machine guns and had them stored in Greensboro and Charlotte. In the future, members should expect to fight and shoot, they were told. If they were not willing to fight, they should get out. A few present at a Guilford County meeting told their leaders that the Klan was getting too dangerous, and they were doing exactly that.[87]

Law enforcement agencies took these threats seriously. The license number of a vehicle driven by individuals attending Klan rallies had been traced to Fort Bragg.[88] This piece of evidence lent credence to the Klan's claim of possessing machine guns. Moreover, State Bureau of Investigation agents suspected that some local law enforcement officers were either cooperating with Klan members, or were actually members of the Klan themselves.[89]

In February 1958, the FBI office in Charlotte warned state officials that an informant had advised local police of KKK plans to bomb the Woodland Negro School.[90] On February 15, Charlotte Police stopped a car in the vicinity of the school and found sticks of dynamite with fuses attached.[91] Police stated that one of the men, Lester Francis Caldwell, told them that he and others had burned a cross at the school earlier, but that act had not drawn enough attention. The community needed waking up, and a blast in the yard of the school would have broken some windows and made some noise.[92] Caldwell, along with Jack Ayscue and William Oliver Spencer, received criminal convictions for their acts.[93]

KKK activity expanded to the Piedmont, in addition to eastern portions of the state. Undercover investigators learned of Klaverns in the Glenwood section of Greensboro, as well as Jamestown, Reidsville, and Burlington. By the summer of 1958, the Klan had also increased its activities in Monroe, Concord, Todd, Mount Airy, Salisbury, Mocksville, High Point, Statesville, and Lexington. At a rally on June 7 on Church Street Extension in Greensboro, speakers James W. Cole and Rev. George Dorsett drew a crowd of approximately 75 to 100. They verbally attacked Governor Hodges, Attorney General Malcolm Seawell, Robeson County sheriff Malcolm McLeod, and Greensboro schools superintendent Ben L. Smith. Law enforcement officers considered the Greensboro rally the largest since the Robeson County incident.

Although Klan speakers tended to rail against anyone they thought willing to accommodate any form of desegregation, speakers at public rallies and secret meetings in the Piedmont often addressed school desegregation in particular. At a June 29, 1958, meeting in Jamestown, with 25 to 30 Klansmen present, plans were made to organize and train white children so that they would cause as much trouble as possible for black children who might attend formerly white schools. KKK members planned rallies in Kernersville and Reidsville, to be held in July.[94] In Salisbury, a speaker who identified himself as the Grand Wizard told his audience, "If the Pearsall Plan doesn't work, the Smith and Wesson Plan will."[95]

An August 18, 1958, rally in Davidson County drew 43 robed Klansmen, 25 others not robed, and 250 to 300 spectators.[96] In nearby Forsyth County, undercover agents learned of a gunsmith who was selling guns to Klan members without requiring permits.[97] In late summer of 1958, Klansmen at a Jamestown meeting received a report from Grand Titan J. W. Younger that members of the North Carolina Klan had linked up with John Kasper, the individual who had agitated crowds during the early days of Charlotte school desegregation. Kasper had just been released from prison in Florida. A national organization was being planned.[98]

Accurately assessing the real nature of the Klan threat is difficult.[99] The Anti Defamation League of B'nai B'rith concluded in a report issued in the late 1950s that the Klan was more dangerous than people seemed to realize. B'nai B'rith believed that the success of limited school desegregation had frustrated the Klan and made its members desperate.[100] That conclusion is reinforced by the foregoing narrative, which is based on law enforcement reports. The Klan preached violence, the Klan planned violence, and occasionally, the Klan practiced violence. The threat that the Klan represented in the mid-to-late 1950s should not be dismissed. Moreover, Klan membership would grow in the 1960s.

Litigation, 1958–1959

In spite of any efforts to intimidate them, black parents, through the NAACP, continued to press desegregation litigation. A 1958 case, *Holt v. Raleigh City Board of Education,* yielded additional judicial support for reassignment denials, however. The parents of Joseph Hiram Holt had sought a transfer from Ligon Junior-Senior High, a black school, to Broughton High, a white school of strong academic reputation, on grounds of geographic convenience plus enhanced academic and extracurricular opportunities. The application further accused the board of making the assignment to Ligon solely for the purpose of continuing segregation by race. Acting on the advice of counsel, Samuel S. Mitchell, the Holts did not attend the Board of Education meeting when the application was to be considered, although one of their attorneys, Herman L. Taylor, appeared on their behalf. J. C. B. Ehringhaus Jr. and Thomas Ellis represented the board.

Judge Edwin M. Stanley, sitting in the U.S. Eastern District Court, ruled against the Holts, concluding that they had failed to exhaust the administrative remedy of appeal to the local board of education. Since they had not appeared in person at the board meeting called for the express purpose of considering their request, board members had been denied the opportunity to interview the student and parents personally, he reasoned.[101]

In another NAACP-backed case, *Jeffers v. Whitley,*[102] Conrad Pearson and William A. Marsh of Durham argued on behalf of Mimia and Allene Jeffers and others that the Caswell County Board of Education should be required to submit a comprehensive desegregation plan. Pearson also sought a hearing before a three-judge panel and attempted to make the State Board of Education and State Superintendent of Public Instruction defendants. Yanceyville attorney Robert R. Blackwell represented the board; William T. Joyner of Raleigh provided assistance. Attorney General Malcolm Seawell and Assistant Attorney General Ralph Moody filed a brief seeking dismissal of the claim against the state. U.S. Middle District Court judge Edwin M. Stanley held that state officials had no pupil assignment authority and thus were not appropriate defendants, and reaffirmed that plaintiffs must exhaust local administrative remedies before a case could be heard.

Plaintiffs in *Covington v. Montgomery County School Board,* refiled as *Covington v. Edwards,*[103] contended that exhaustion of administrative remedies should not be necessary, since the lapse in time since *Brown* without widespread desegregation showed that courts could no longer presume that school officials intended to obey the law. Plaintiffs made no claim of having attempted to follow administrative appeals. Conrad Pearson joined Kenneth Lee and Major High from the original case, while Thomas Ellis assisted Montgomery County attorney Garland Garriss. Citing the original *Carson* case, plus *Holt* and *Jeffers* as precedent, along with Judge John J. Parker's holding in remanded *Briggs,* U.S. Middle District Court Judge Edwin M. Stanley ruled that the appeals process prescribed in the Pupil Assignment Act had to be followed.[104] Appeals of *Covington*[105] and *Holt*[106] reaffirmed lower-court requirements that plaintiffs exhaust local administrative remedies before proceeding through the courts. Another attempt to have the courts hear a class action suit, filed on behalf of Joycelyn McKissick of Durham (Floyd McKissick's daughter) and others similarly situated, failed as well.[107]

North Carolina in the Context of Other Southern States

In cases heard throughout 1956 to 1959, the courts had sustained the transfer application and appeals procedures prescribed by the Pupil

Assignment Act. Efforts seeking system-wide desegregation orders uniformly failed during this period, and local board-of-education decisions were consistently upheld. The repeated success in the courts of North Carolina's procedures generated attention in the national press. A *New York Times* article suggested that, although the southern states had been looking to Virginia for a successful anti-integration formula, the pattern set by North Carolina would ultimately prove to be more successful in the long run. Token desegregation started in North Carolina under the Pupil Placement Act had been upheld in federal courts, the article reported, while the Virginia statute had been invalidated on grounds that it was manifestly intended to prevent any integration.

As far as actual integration was concerned, little or none had occurred anywhere in the South. At the beginning of the 1958–59 school term, Louisiana, Mississippi, Alabama, Florida, Georgia, South Carolina, and Virginia had not admitted a single black student to a formerly white school. In North Carolina, 10 of 322,000 blacks were attending formerly white schools. In Tennessee, 117 of 133,740 blacks were enrolled with whites. Arkansas had admitted 98 blacks, of 102,000, to white schools. Kentucky had admitted 117 of 133,740. The only significant numbers of black admissions appeared in border states and in the Southwest: in Delaware, 3,248 of 12,429; in Texas, 3,600 of 258,333; in Oklahoma, 6,633 of 36,390; in West Virginia, 10,000 of 25,834; in Maryland, 25,650 of 116,275; and in Missouri, 62,000 of 67,000, the only majority.[108]

With so few blacks admitted to school with whites anywhere in the South, did any substantive difference really exist among the southern states? All southern states provided for some form of compulsory attendance repeal in the years following *Brown*. South Carolina, Virginia, Georgia, and Arkansas legislation required that their schools be closed in case of integration. Florida, Louisiana, Mississippi, Alabama, and North Carolina authorized school closings but did not require them. Only Florida and North Carolina made such closing a local decision.[109]

Among non-border southern states, only North Carolina had managed to admit blacks to formerly all-white schools while escaping serious disruptions.[110] Admissions had been difficult and extremely limited in number, but they had been accomplished. Whatever difficulties occurred had been contained within the school systems that made the decisions to admit the black students, and no schools had been shut down. Those two criteria, local decision making and actual admissions, however small in number, distinguished North Carolina from the rest of the non-border southern states.

Governor Hodges became quite conscious of this unique status during the latter years of his administration.[111] He tried to make some inroads among black leaders again during 1957. Hodges met quietly with a group from the Durham area in a conversation arranged by A. T. Spaulding,[112] an executive of the North Carolina Mutual Insurance Company, one of the largest black-owned businesses in the United States. What transpired at that meeting is not evident, however.

Hodges's associates within the administration even went so far as to consider some form of negotiations with the NAACP. They proposed the idea of having Albert Coates contact Frank Porter Graham and authorize Graham to tell Thurgood Marshall that high officials in North Carolina were favorably disposed to an agreement with the NAACP. Coates was suggested because Hodges's advisors considered him trustworthy while Graham was considered the best candidate to initiate negotiations due to his well-known support of minority rights. Marshall was thought "to have the most sense" among NAACP leaders.

The idea involved having officials in North Carolina agree to cooperate with the NAACP in selling the idea of desegregation to the people instead of forcing desegregation through litigation. The NAACP, according to the idea, would agree to cease litigation, thus calling the "bluff" of whites who claimed they resented being forced into desegregation, but were not against minority rights. The NAACP might agree because such a move would enhance the status of the organization. If the effort did not succeed, then the old policy could be reinstated with "many times the strength" it previously had. Such proposed negotiations were not carried out, however.[113]

High-level officials within the Hodges administration also changed their tone somewhat in public comments during the latter years of the governor's term. During the early years, pledges to obey the law almost always included a statement of personal preference for segregation. In late 1958, however, Attorney General Malcolm Seawell vowed, "I intend to take my stand on the side of the law. . . . If this is politically inexpedient, dangerous, or fatal, I'll just have to be content with what my future holds for me."[114] Seawell was speaking in the context of school desegregation.

State Board chair Dallas Herring made frequent addresses around the state. With regard to racial matters and the schools, Herring set a tone in 1960 quite different from the tone of his thoughts during service on the first Pearsall Committee: "Is there to be no more room in the great heart of North Carolina for all the people, . . . the . . . children of the rich and of the poor, the black and the white, the tenants as well as the Tories? . . . North Carolina must not face the future with fear and defiance, but with dignity and self-restraint in the confident expectation that that which is just and that which is honest and that which is true will prevail among an educated people whose government is in its own hands."[115]

Herring had become convinced that some level of desegregation must occur. This shift in his perspective grew out of a meeting in the late 1950s with black citizens of Duplin County.[116] In a discussion dealing with the location of a new school, black people that he had known most of his life voiced a preference for integration. Until that time he had assumed that blacks preferred segregation, just as whites did. Such an assumption continued to be widespread among whites. The North Carolina Council on Human Relations, among the state's most liberal organizations that included white people, held that no more than 5 percent of black parents would send their children to school with whites, if given the choice.[117] W. T. Joyner, who by that time publicly favored the voluntary admission of blacks to white schools, assured audiences that, even if school systems allowed transfers across racial lines, racial separation would remain 99 percent complete.[118]

These shifts toward a more moderate tone were not by any means universal. At one point in late 1959, Governor Hodges denounced what he termed the appeasement of minorities.[119] But North Carolina's limited shift toward accommodating desegregation is noteworthy because it occurred at a time when observers tended to think positions were hardening elsewhere.[120] According to Claude Sitton, editor of the Raleigh *News and Observer,* events in Little Rock had shown that precipitous steps toward integration would bring grave social dislocations. Unreasoning animosity toward blacks as well as outbursts of anti-Semitism were increasing throughout the South, Sitton believed. While hope for continued segregation waned, opposition to court-ordered desegregation among southern states had stiffened.

Two polarities had thus been established: the moderation of Florida, Kentucky, Tennessee, and North Carolina, versus the hard-line resistance of Arkansas, Mississippi, Alabama, South Carolina, Georgia, and Virginia. Governor Hodges, who had sought to build his legacy on the foundation of business development, must have been especially sensitive to the negative impact of resistance on the prospects for economic growth.[121] Virginia and Arkansas had seen industrial development decline during the latter 1950s, and in some cases, companies moved out of those states. Industries did not appear to be concerned with the segregation issue itself, but with closing schools. Industry would not relocate or remain where prospects suggested abandoning public education. North Carolina, by contrast, had attracted 250 million dollars in new industry during a comparable period.[122]

Litigation, 1960

The first North Carolina case in which a court ordered the admission of black students to formerly all-white schools occurred in 1960. Plaintiffs in *Griffith v. Board of Education of Yancey County*[123] consisted of virtually the entire black school-age population of the district. Only a single, one-room elementary school existed for blacks in Yancey County. No high school had ever been provided. Black students who wanted to attend high school were transported to Asheville, in Buncombe County, where the board paid their tuition. The trip required approximately three hours per day. In the summer of 1958 the elementary school for blacks had been condemned by building inspectors. The following year, the board transported all black students in the county to Asheville, thus providing no educational facilities of any kind anywhere in the county for black children. The black students requested reassignment to schools within the county, which were all-white, but the board rejected their transfer applications. Then the board constructed a two-room school and assigned all black students in the county to it, regardless of age or grade.

U.S. Western District Court Judge Wilson Warlick held that plaintiffs had complied with all administrative remedies required under North Carolina's Pupil Assignment Act. Moreover, Warlick found the record "replete with evidence that, had plaintiffs not exhausted their administrative remedies, that to have done so would have been . . . futile and vain." Warlick thus ruled that the board had acted on the basis of the students' race in a manner "discriminatory, unlawful, and in violation of the constitutional rights" of the black students.

Plaintiffs in *Griffith* had the backing of the NAACP. Clearly, this was a well-chosen case, one that the organization expected to win. In addition to Ruben J. Dailey of Asheville and Conrad Pearson of Durham, plaintiffs were represented by Thurgood Marshall and Jack Greenberg of the NAACP main office in New York.[124]

Another suit, *McCoy v. Greensboro City Board of Education*,[125] was filed against one of the systems that had voluntarily pioneered desegregation. Valaric McCoy and four other black children attended the Pearson Street branch of Washington School, a black school. The Pearson Street branch was located on the campus of Caldwell School, a white school, but its facilities were inferior. Parents asked the board to assign their children to Caldwell, but their application was denied. They filed suit, but before the case could be heard, the board combined Pearson Street with Caldwell and integrated the student bodies.

Within ten days, however, the parents of every white child enrolled at Caldwell applied for reassignment. All of the white teachers and the principal requested transfers as well. The board granted these requests, moved the students and teachers, and assigned a black faculty and administration to Caldwell School. Although McCoy and her black classmates were thus allowed to attend the school they had requested, the school itself changed from all white to all black. Judge Edwin Stanley, ruling in the U.S. Middle District Court, nevertheless dismissed the McCoys' appeal on grounds that their request to transfer to Caldwell School had been granted.

On appeal, Thurgood Marshall and James Nabrit filed a brief on behalf of plaintiffs. Welch Jordan and Robert Mosely represented the board. The Fourth Circuit Court of Appeals reversed,[126] holding that the board's actions not only violated the spirit of *Brown* but also appeared contrary to the provisions of the Pupil Assignment Act. The case was remanded with instructions for the board to reassign the students.[127]

McCoy was significant, not only because it included court-ordered reassignment of black pupils, but also because, considered as cultural artifact, the case revealed a further measure of popular sentiment with regard to desegregation. As the facts of *McCoy* show, even in one of the most progressive communities in North Carolina, where the board had volunteered to pioneer token reassignments, when small-scale desegregation was attempted six years after *Brown*, the effort met with unanimous rejection not only from the white parents but also from the white professional staff.

Sit-in Demonstrations

During its waning days, the Hodges administration faced the initial thrust of a whole new era in civil rights activities. On February 1, 1960, Franklin McCain, Ezell Blair Jr., David Richmond, and Joseph McNeil, students from North Carolina Agricultural and Technical College in Greensboro, sat down at the lunch counter in Woolworth's, one of the principal retail businesses in the city.[128] At that time, blacks had been served only at the stand-up section. The students' actions helped spawn a movement which rapidly expanded.[129]

Governor Hodges inquired of the Attorney General's Office regarding the governor's authority in large-scale breaches of the peace. Attorney General Wade Bruton, who had just taken office in 1960, advised Hodges that the governor could call out the National Guard as well as utilize the Highway Patrol or the State Bureau of Investigation in order to maintain the peace, but "no constitutional or statutory expression by which the Governor is authorized or empowered to supplant or oust local law enforcement officials" existed.[130]

Although principal responsibility for dealing with the demonstrations thus lay with local officials, Governor Hodges nevertheless contacted managers of the Woolworth's stores and sought their intentions. Woolworth's management maintained that they were just following local custom. They did not want to press trespass charges against the demonstrators, due to the probable negative impact on business. A significant portion of Woolworth's business came from black customers.[131]

Hodges wanted the demonstrations stopped, though, and he wrote to the presidents of all the state-supported colleges and universities to that effect.[132] Furthermore, he warned Woolworth's officials that he did not intend to just sit by and wait for a riot to happen. He intended to preserve law and order, and the tone of his conversations with Woolworth's management strongly suggests he wanted them to press charges against the demonstrators.[133]

Hodges discussed the matter further with Governors Collins of Florida, Almond of Virginia, Hollings of South Carolina, Vandiver of Georgia, Patterson of Alabama, and Ellington of Tennessee, states where demonstrations were also taking place. Governor Collins believed it was not logical to serve blacks in all other phases of store operations while refusing lunch-counter service. The governors of Virginia, Georgia, Alabama, and Tennessee, however, were generally in agreement that stores ought to either have the demonstrators arrested or close down their lunch counters.[134]

Governor Hodges held a press conference on March 10, 1960, to talk about the demonstrations. He stated, "[S]peaking solely for my concern for law and order, I want to make it clear that I have no sympathy whatsoever for any group of people who deliberately engage in activities which any reasonable person can see will result in a breakdown of law and order as well as interference with the normal and proper operation of a private business."[135]

Those demonstrations marked only the beginning of a movement that would sweep the nation over the next five years. The principal responsibility for dealing with the civil rights movement would fall to Hodges's successor.

How are North Carolina's actions through the close of the 1950s to be understood?

The Chafe Thesis

The predominant work on the subject of desegregation in North Carolina has heretofore been William Chafe's *Civilities and Civil Rights.* Professor Chafe contends that the state's leaders used North Carolina's traditions of civility and moderation to block progress due to their own preference for segregation at a time when the people were more willing than their leaders to accept change in racial matters.

My research reinforces Chafe's conclusions in two respects. The state's leaders did prefer segregation, at least initially, and they did appeal to the state's traditions of civility and moderation. In so doing, they preserved the public schools, ensured the uninterrupted education of North Carolina's white and black children, and eventually implemented limited desegregation in the schools with minimal disruption, in comparison to other states. But that accomplishment came about only after the courts had made it clear that school systems had no other choice.

I disagree with Chafe's assessment of the people's willingness to accept desegregation. Segregationist sentiment permeated every facet of North Carolina's population through the 1950s and later. The state's leaders were not eager to move ahead with school desegregation themselves. But neither was any other significant segment of the white population. The issue in North Carolina was not what Chafe termed "redneck hordes."[136] North Carolina was not an extremist, violent state. That aspect of the state's moderate image was justified. But, as Dr. Martin Luther King Jr. wrote, "The Negro's great stumbling block is not . . . the Ku Klux Klanner, but the white moderate who is more devoted to 'order' than to justice."[137] Many members of the state's elite were included among supporters of segregation. Governor Hodges's actions place him within the framework Dr. King envisioned.

The overwhelming majority of the people in North Carolina voted in favor of measures that could have closed the state's schools rather than desegregate them. A minority, but a substantial minority, voiced even stronger support for continued segregation in the most reliable public opinion poll available—their vote. That minority numbered at least a quarter-million through the 1960s, as evidenced by votes cast for gubernatorial candidates who were far more conservative than Governor Hodges.

When school systems in Charlotte, Winston-Salem, and Greensboro voluntarily admitted a small number of black students to formerly all-white schools, some elements of the public reacted in opposition, and some disruptions occurred. These admissions were eventually accomplished, however, and most of the students remained in their new schools. Such voluntary admissions occurred only on an extremely limited basis, though. Given the local decision-making nature of North Carolina's response to *Brown,* if widespread acceptance of desegregation had existed, then it is logical to assume that more systems would have moved to desegregate. The fact that they did not suggests that local decision makers did not favor desegregation themselves and did not believe local school patrons did, either, as well as indicating that support for desegregation among the white population was extremely limited.

Rather than conservative leaders blocking a more liberal populace, as Professor Chafe has interpreted these events, moderate leaders in the political system were walking a tightrope that placated strong conservatives while buying the time needed to accommodate change mandated by the judicial system. Below the governor's level, Thomas Pearsall, Dallas Herring, and some others who served on the Pearsall committees, along with some personnel within the Attorney General's Office, constituted a more progressive element. A majority of the people eventually accepted the rule of law and learned to make accommodations to a new way of life. But multiple manifestations of racial conservatism permeated North Carolina politics and North Carolina schools. A parallel pattern would develop at the national level over the next decade.

School desegregation initiatives during the latter 1950s shifted from the state to local school systems under procedures specified in the Pupil Assignment Act. A small number of school systems admitted a few black students to formerly all-white schools. No attempts were made to invoke the school closing measures provided by the Pearsall Plan, and no students applied for tuition grants. Black parents, with NAACP support, filed suits seeking to compel system-wide desegregation, but the courts sustained the individual transfer procedures established under the Pupil Assignment Act.

Governor Hodges and his advisors believed that the majority of North Carolina's people—black as well as white—supported segregation. The Hodges administration viewed both the NAACP and the Klan as extremist organizations. But, because the schools were not desegregated to any extent beyond tokenism, the public outcry opposing desegregation that Hodges and his advisors feared did not develop. Issues of morality began to surface among prominent political leaders, however. Key members of the state's political and educational elite began to favor some degree of desegregation, and some professional educators stated publicly that segregation itself was morally wrong.

The moderate image in racial matters that North Carolina had established and maintained rested on a substantive foundation. The local decision-making process allowed a degree of flexibility available only in North Carolina and Florida. And only in North Carolina did such local flexibility actually result in some measure of desegregation, even though the actual numbers of black students admitted to formerly all-white schools was miniscule.

5

The Impact of the Civil Rights Movement

FROM 1960 TO THE MID-1960S

As the Hodges era closed, the Pupil Assignment Act and the other elements of the Pearsall Plan remained intact. The only portion of the plan that had been tested in the courts, however, was the Pupil Assignment Act. The tuition grants and local option school closing provisions had not been activated anywhere in the state. Pupil assignment and school desegregation continued to remain a local matter.

During the early 1960s, when state officials became involved in desegregation, it was primarily in the context of initiatives from the civil rights movement. These initiatives dealt more with public accommodations than with schools. The governor, however, still set the general tone for the state, and the election of 1960 was decisive in maintaining and extending the moderate tone that North Carolina had established. The election nevertheless continued to reveal an undercurrent of strong support for segregation in North Carolina.

What do election results reveal about public sentiment regarding race during the early 1960s? What tone did North Carolina's governors maintain regarding civil rights? How did they respond to civil rights initiatives? What sort of progress did school desegregation make during this period? And how did desegregation initiatives affect the quality of education in the state?

Transition to the Sanford Administration

The front-runner in the 1960 Democratic gubernatorial primary was Terry Sanford of Fayetteville. A former FBI agent, past president of the Young Democrats, state senator, and manager of Kerr Scott's successful 1954 campaign for the U.S. Senate, Sanford was associated with the progressive wing of the party.[1] His campaign strategy downplayed race while seeking to make the quality of education the main issue.[2] Opponent John Larkins of Trenton, an attorney and Democratic

National Committee member, stressed economy in government and experienced leadership. Former attorney general Malcolm Seawell of Lumberton emphasized industrialization to increase the incomes of North Carolina's citizens, as well as support for the public schools. Of those three candidates, only Seawall made a point of recognizing the *Brown* decisions as the law of the land.[3]

The fourth candidate in the primary was former assistant attorney general I. Beverly Lake. To Lake, the principal issue was race. While pledging to promote racial friendship, Lake made clear that relations among races had to occur within the context of segregation. Lake vowed to support the owner of any store, restaurant, or café who wanted to choose which customers would be served.[4] North Carolina should adopt segregation as official policy in the operation of public schools. Black children already attending white schools should be returned to segregated schools.[5] Of course, the NAACP vigorously opposed Lake's bid. Kelly Alexander argued that any platform supporting segregation was "a grievous violation of Christian justice." Lake retorted that, if elected, he would dedicate his administration to the defeat of NAACP goals.[6]

Sanford's 269,463 votes led the May 28 Democratic primary, but he did not achieve a majority. Lake came in second with 181,692, Seawell took third with 101,148, and Larkins placed last with 100,757.[7] Lake called for a runoff.[8] Race became the central theme of the second primary. Sanford accused Lake of setting a hard-line segregationist tone that would bring more court-ordered integration to North Carolina schools. Lake vowed that he would do everything possible to keep the public schools operating, but segregated, while fighting the NAACP.[9] He voiced further opposition to Sanford's "free-spending policies," which would require taxes "the likes of which you have never seen in North Carolina."[10] Sanford answered that Lake's references to race were injecting a false issue into the campaign: "[I]t is false because I am, and he knows I am, opposed to integration." He nevertheless told North Carolinians that the *Brown* decisions must be accepted as the law of the land, even if that meant desegregation, a term he chose in order to use softer language.[11]

The candidates attracted the support of many political leaders who had been involved in race-related matters. Dr. W. C. George, now retired from the University of North Carolina, introduced Lake to an audience in Durham. Charles P. Green of Louisburg, a former U.S. district attorney, also endorsed Lake. Green had managed Willis Smith's 1950 campaign for Senate. Attorney and legislator Robert Morgan of Harnett County managed the Lake campaign.[12]

Raleigh attorney and Pearsall Committee member W. T. Joyner endorsed Sanford, as did Thomas Pearsall himself. During the campaign, a public exchange between Pearsall and Lake clarified internal disagreements within the Pearsall Committee. Lake claimed that he had written the Pupil Assignment Act.[13] Pearsall stated that Lake, as assistant attorney general, had been asked to draft a bill according to the Pearsall Committee's instructions, but the bill Lake produced had to be redrafted. This brought a rejoinder in support of Lake from W. W. Taylor Jr., who claimed the law was presented and passed substantially as written and presented by Lake.[14] Pearsall retorted that Taylor had resigned from the Pearsall Committee's service because he was completely out of sympathy with the thinking of the committee. Taylor had filed a signed, written report expressing segregationist views very similar to the ideas of Dr. Lake, Pearsall related, and the committee did not agree with them.[15] The preliminary report that strongly supported segregation, therefore, must have been written by W. W. Taylor, with assistance from Lake. The interim report, issued after Taylor resigned, was more moderate and accommodating in tone. Although unsigned, it reflected the style of Thomas Pearsall, and in the light of this exchange, appears to have been prepared by Pearsall after the second Pearsall Committee members refused to go along with the strong segregationist position of Lake and Taylor.

Late in the campaign, Malcolm Seawell endorsed Sanford, maintaining that the state had to continue its moderate policy regarding school desegregation or face destruction of the public schools.[16] The endorsement split the Seawell camp, however. Armistead Maupin, a Raleigh attorney who had been one of Seawell's most prominent backers in the first primary, had remained neutral out of deference to Seawell. Following Seawell's endorsement of Sanford, however, Maupin issued a statement of support for Lake.[17] Sanford closed the second primary campaign with a classic Democratic charge, reminiscent of the party's hero, Franklin D. Roosevelt: "The only thing [Lake] has to offer is fear itself."[18]

Sanford won the second primary on June 25, 1960, receiving 352,133 votes to Lake's 275,905.[19] The two primaries attracted the largest voter turnout in North Carolina history.[20] Lake's vote in the second Democratic primary indicates a strong segregationist element well in excess of 250,000.[21] In the general election, Sanford defeated Republican candidate Robert Gavin, 735,248 to 613,975.[22] Cloyd Philpott, a member of the second Pearsall Committee, was elected lieutenant governor.[23] Sanford's efforts also carried North Carolina for the presidential candidacy of John F. Kennedy.[24] Kennedy received 52.11 percent of the popular vote (713,136) to Richard Nixon's 47.89 percent (655,420).[25]

Desegregation Early in the Sanford Administration

The Civil Rights Act of 1957 was the first significant federal civil rights legislation since Reconstruction.[26] It dealt primarily with voting rights, although it also showed congressional support for the *Brown* decisions. The act established a federal Civil Rights Commission with advisory committees for each state.

Greensboro attorney McNeill Smith chaired the North Carolina committee, which issued a report on the eve of the Sanford administration.[27] The committee found that North Carolina employed more black teachers than all the thirty-one northern and western states combined. Those North Carolina teachers, however, taught only black students. During the period 1955–60, a total of 983 black students in North Carolina had requested transfers to white schools. Of these, 124 had been granted. During 1960–61, only 77 black students out of 324,234 were attending formerly all-white schools in the state. Most of those, a total of 42, were the children of military personnel, who attended schools in Goldsboro and Havelock, near military bases. One black student attended a formerly white school in Raleigh, two in Charlotte, three in Chapel Hill, three in High Point, five in Greensboro, and nine in Winston-Salem. The largest number not associated with military installations lived in Durham, where 12 blacks attended schools with white students.

North Carolina's voluntary, peaceful admission of blacks to formerly all-white schools affirmed the state's image of moderation in racial matters. Hardly any change regarding racially based school assignments had taken place, though. On the other hand, the state had firmly placed itself on the side of obedience to the law and initiated a course of action, however limited, that looked to the future rather than to the past.[28]

The Chapel Hill–Carrboro Board of Education pioneered systemwide desegregation in North Carolina's public schools. The school system had experienced controversy during the summer of 1959, when the board refused to transfer a black student, Stanley Vickers, to a white school. The decision resulted in the public resignation of one of the board members, Henry Brandis, dean of the University of North Carolina Law School.[29] The Board of Education later admitted three black first graders for the fall of 1960 but rejected nine other requests.[30] The following summer of 1961, however, the board voted to assign first-grade students on an attendance-zone basis, without regard to race.[31] The zones as drawn would redistribute black students to all elementary schools. Carrboro residents opposed the plan, even though the Carrboro zone would receive the smallest number of blacks.

Newly elected board members Dr. Fred Ellis, Dr. Richard Peters, and Mrs. Ross Scroggs supported the plan while incumbent Grey Culbreth, who was employed as manager of the University of North Carolina's utility system, opposed it. Mrs. Judith Farnell, speaking for the League of Women Voters, along with Dr. D. D. Carroll, a local Quaker minister, voiced support. Chapel Hill–Carrboro joined Nashville, Tennessee, and Louisville, Kentucky, as the only school boards in the South assigning black students on the basis of deliberately desegregated attendance zones.[32]

Ironically, the Chapel Hill–Carrboro Board of Education lost a pupil assignment case the same year it pioneered desegregated zones.[33] The family of Stanley Vickers, who had been denied transfer in 1959, filed suit. Judge Edwin Stanley of U.S. Middle District Court ruled in 1961 that Vickers had been denied entry to Chapel Hill Junior High because of race. Judge Stanley remarked that he had no doubt as to the integrity of the board members. The board had based its decision on what it considered the best interest of a minor plaintiff. But that did not alter the fact that Vickers's constitutional rights had been denied.

The board expanded its plan for 1962–63. All elementary students would be assigned on a desegregated, geographic pattern. A few blacks would also be reassigned to white junior or senior highs based on individual application. Elementary redistricting was made possible because of a new school building, Frank Porter Graham Elementary, erected on the fringe of the black community.[34] Chapel Hill–Carrboro was the only system in the state that drew a voluntary, system-wide desegregation plan in the early 1960s.[35]

Desegregation in higher education was proceeding on a parallel course with the public schools, but at a slower pace. Comprehensive desegregation at the undergraduate level in the state's public universities would undergo a lengthy, tortuous process of litigation in a manner similar to public elementary and secondary education. Among private colleges and universities, Duke, Davidson, and Wake Forest decided to admit black undergraduates in 1962.[36] Five black students, Wilhelmina Reuben-Cooke, Mary Mitchell Harris, Gene Kendall, Cassandra Smith, and Nathaniel White Jr., enrolled at Duke in September 1963. Wake Forest and Davidson sidestepped the issue by admitting African students, not African-Americans. Private colleges and universities had possessed full authority to admit black undergraduates earlier, had they so chosen.[37] The fact that these institutions, presumably among the most enlightened in the South and the nation, chose not to desegregate at the undergraduate level constitutes yet another indication of the degree to which white people, including those with high levels of education and socioeconomic status, considered segregation normal and appropriate through the mid-1960s. Their own goals and aspirations notwithstanding, conservative officeholders who sought to block desegregation during this period were representing the views of their constituents.

The Tone of the Sanford Administration

At the outset, Governor Sanford and his advisors believed that issues involving race would constitute a major challenge for the new administration.[38] They thought the state was probably approaching the limits of the period of grace afforded by the Pupil Assignment Act. Nonviolent pressure of the sort seen in the lunch-counter sit-ins would undoubtedly continue. The administration could expect efforts to secure admission of blacks to the National Guard and to professional employment in state government.

Governor Sanford and his staff assumed that changes in race relations were inevitable, and that the tempo of change regarding civil rights would increase. Careful planning and guidance by committees genuinely representing various racial groups would be necessary. Sit-ins had been settled through the efforts of such biracial committees. The governor, therefore, should have counsel devoted particularly to racial matters.[39]

In a personal gesture, Sanford enrolled his own children in a Raleigh public school which was, by the standards of the day, desegregated. One of the Raleigh elementary schools to which black students had been admitted was located near the Governor's Mansion. But the Governor would have to move warily in the area of civil rights, his advisors cautioned, because of the danger of losing political support among whites. Governor Sanford must retain a wide base of support in order to lead effectively. On the other hand, failure to deal with the race problem would be much more dangerous.[40]

Two additional factors influenced Sanford's outlook regarding race. The first, and most important, was the religious-moral conviction that inequitable treatment based on race was unjust, and "segregation in schools, jobs, and elsewhere was wrong and had to go."[41] The second factor centered on economic development. An atmosphere of conflict, especially of a racial nature, was obviously bad for the business climate of the state.[42] Neither Governor Hodges nor Governor Umstead had ever been able to conceive of civil rights leaders, especially those affiliated with the NAACP, as responsible or representative of North Carolina's black citizens. In contrast, the Sanford administration assumed that all black leaders would press for full civil rights, and that such pressure was appropriate for their role.

The predicted call for expanded employment in government came during Sanford's first year as governor. Kelly Alexander and other NAACP representatives met with Sanford to discuss state hiring practices.[43] Although no public announcement was issued, the meeting was cordial. The Sanford administration intended to make hiring practices more equitable, although Alexander and his associates undoubtedly would have preferred more rapid progress. Sanford considered their impatience understandable, but he believed they saw him as an ally.[44]

The summer of 1961 witnessed significant developments in the civil rights movement. During July and August, freedom riders traveled throughout the South, testing local actions regarding black access to public accommodations and transportation. Governor Sanford solicited legal advice about the freedom riders from the Attorney General's Office as well as from Thomas Pearsall. Pearsall advised the governor to contact operators of bus lines and terminals, to get their advice, and to provide instruction regarding the law. He urged Sanford to make a public statement, showing his determination to maintain order. Trouble involving freedom riders in other states had occurred due to the failure of officials to take a firm stand in advance, followed by failure to suppress mob action once it developed, Pearsall advised.[45]

Sanford sent Assistant Attorney General Ralph Moody to various localities where freedom riders were expected. The Highway Patrol monitored their movements. Moody met with local officials in Wilmington and advised them that freedom riders were traveling on interstate tickets, so they had a right to use any rest rooms and eating facilities they chose, and they could ride wherever they wanted on commercial buses.[46] For the most part, freedom riders passed through North Carolina without incident, although some tension occurred in Monroe during August 1961.[47] At the same time events in North Carolina were unfolding in relative peace, however, local officials and citizens in Birmingham, Alabama, were waging war against freedom riders, using attack dogs and high-pressure fire hoses.[48] U.S. marshals and FBI agents were sent to Alabama to preserve order.[49]

Although public accommodations represented the principal focus of civil rights initiatives with which officials at the state level had to deal, the public schools constituted the central focus of the Sanford administration. During the month following his election, before taking office, Sanford addressed an audience at the University of North Carolina at Chapel Hill, pledging improvements in education.[50] He included the statement, "Education is the foundation of democracy. I am concerned with defending the principles of freedom, of individual liberties, of free enterprise, of equality and dignity of man, and therefore I seek the fulfillment of these principles through quality education."[51] Sanford warned that current revenues would not support the level of quality in education he would be proposing for the state.

In his first budget message to the General Assembly, Governor Sanford asked the legislature to cancel all sales tax exemptions, including the exemption on food, provided by state tax laws at that time, in order to generate the revenue needed to support his program of improving education.[52] The "food tax," as it was commonly called, became the source of much controversy for the Sanford administration. In order to generate support for his proposals, Sanford traveled the state, often speaking to as many as ten audiences, black as well as white, in a single day.[53]

Early in his tour, he met with school board members, county commissioners, and other community leaders. But on a visit to Brunswick County, a principal asked him to stop off at a school and address the students. Sanford found the response from young people, in his words, "almost magic."[54] From then on, he arranged to speak as often as possible in schools to student audiences, with adults invited as guests.

The legislature subsequently passed the governor's proposed tax law revisions. The new revenues provided pay increases for currently employed teachers, almost three thousand additional teaching positions, plus specialized training programs, as well as the establishment of a new state agency designed to keep school personnel abreast of pedagogical improvements.[55] Sanford initiated a summer program for academically gifted students, known as the Governor's School, in 1963.[56] The state also established a special school for students with learning difficulties as well as a research center, the Learning Institute of North Carolina. Other initiatives included partial implementation of a kindergarten program as well as state bond issues for school construction to supplement local funding.[57]

Although the higher-quality education program was not specifically designed to assist black students or to promote school desegregation, its effects facilitated general school improvement that benefited all students. Sanford's public addresses frequently included a reference to better educational opportunities for "all" children, or improved schools for "every" child.[58]

Gathering broad public support for educational improvements that focused exclusively on black children would have been difficult, probably impossible, and almost certainly would have been challenged as illegal, since such an initiative would involve decisions based on race. By linking the educational fate of both races, Sanford made significant steps toward establishing the basis for a single, desegregated school system providing better education to all students. Educational improvements could not wait for desegregation to be completed.[59]

A group of prominent citizens organized the North Carolina Citizens Committee for Better Schools, headed by Holt McPherson. Judge L. Richardson Preyer later served as the committee's president. Dallas Herring was prominent among its leaders. The committee worked hand in hand with the Sanford administration to build local support for school improvement.[60]

The goal of school improvement lay at the foundation of Sanford's broader efforts to promote equity. Governor Sanford pointed out to a Methodist Church audience meeting in Polkville that the state's per capita income would rise ten places relative to other states if the income of blacks equaled that of whites.[61] In a 1963 address to the North Carolina Press Association, Sanford warned, "Reluctance to accept the Negro in employment is the greatest single block to his continued progress and to the full use of the human potential of the Nation and its States. The time has come for American citizens to give up this reluctance, to quit unfair discriminations."[62]

That statement marked Governor Sanford's establishment of the Good Neighbor Council. The Good Neighbor Council sought to promote job opportunities in the state without racial discrimination and to develop programs to educate young people who would be better qualified for employment. D. S. Coltrane of Raleigh chaired the council, with James T. Taylor and John R. Larkins assisting. Membership also included Dr. Reginald Hawkins of Charlotte, one of North Carolina's most prominent civil rights leaders.[63]

Litigation, 1961–1962

While efforts to improve the schools emanated from the executive branch, efforts to desegregate the schools continued to flow through the judicial branch. *Morrow v. Mecklenburg County Board of Education* appealed reassignment applications that had originated in 1957.[64] NAACP attorneys Thurgood Marshall and Jack Greenberg assisted Conrad Pearson for the plaintiffs. The board, represented by Benjamin Horack, argued that it did not maintain a policy of continuing segregated schools, but "by custom and choice, students of different races attended different schools."

The Charlotte City and Mecklenburg County boards of education voluntarily merged those two school systems in 1960, creating the largest school system in North Carolina.[65] The board had granted applications for reassignment received in 1960, and members of the current board had voted for those reassignments. U.S. Western District Court held, "there has been no showing that others have been denied reassignment," so the court rejected a class action. The court also rejected additional transfer requests from three other plaintiffs, since the students involved had by that time completed the grades located in the schools to which they had requested reassignment. The court also rejected claims of the remaining students on grounds that racial discrimination had not been shown. In fact, the children were enrolled where their parents had presented them.[66]

In two other cases, combined as *Wheeler v. Durham City Board of Education*,[67] plaintiffs sought declarative judgment on behalf of blacks in the school system for relief of discrimination on account of race. U.S. Middle District Court held that individuals must continue to pursue administrative remedies, maintaining once again that the Supreme Court had "never suggested that mass mixing of the races is required in public schools."[68] The court further ruled, however, that the Durham board had engaged in discriminatory practices during 1959–61. On one occasion, the board had approved only 7 of 205 applications for reassignment.[69] The court therefore ordered the board to reconsider the applications for reassignment of those students named who had appropriately exhausted administrative remedies.[70]

The board subsequently reported to Judge Edwin Stanley that an entire elementary school would be desegregated for the first time in the fall of 1961. Five additional black students, Gloria Jean Morris, Harriet Lou Prince, Marva Maxine Bullock, Brenda Joyce Gunn, and Anita Louise Brame, were assigned to Durham High School, where Brame had already been enrolled. Alex E. Bullock became the first black child assigned to a formerly all-white elementary school in Durham.[71]

The board used academic preparedness as a criterion in rejecting 129 other transfer requests. R. N. Harris, Durham's lone black board member, objected, stating that the board had never used such a criterion before.[72] Durham attorney Floyd McKissick spoke on behalf of the students and as a parent at a subsequent board meeting.[73] The board stood firm on its refusal, however.[74] When the parties to *Wheeler* complained to U.S. Middle District Court that the court's orders had not been adequately followed, the court rejected their request for injunctive relief on grounds that they were actually seeking not individual reassignment but rather court-ordered wholesale integration.[75]

On appeal, however, *Wheeler* was overturned.[76] The Fourth Circuit Court of Appeals held that the board was using attendance zones in effect prior to *Brown* as the basis for pupil assignment. Furthermore, the court found abundant examples of "unfairness and arbitrariness in the procedures imposed upon applicants for transfers to free themselves from . . . initial racial assignments."[77] The court, therefore, ruled that the Pupil Assignment Act was being administered in an unconstitutional manner by the Durham Board and ordered the board to submit a plan that would end discrimination.

Judge Stanley subsequently ordered the transfer of 183 students, effective in the spring semester, 1963.[78] Most, however, asked to remain in the schools they were attending. Many notified the board they would want to transfer at the beginning of next school year, though.[79] The several dozen who did transfer enrolled and attended school without serious incident.[80] Harassment did occur, however. Charmaine McKissick recalls that she was called "nigger" and hit with mashed potatoes in the cafeteria. But she won the spelling bee and was invited to and attended a birthday party. Reflecting on those days, she later commented that few of the individuals involved in those early desegregation assignments want to talk about their experiences. Their ill treatment hurt their feelings deeply.[81]

In spring, the Durham City system announced a desegregation plan in which the graduating classes in black elementary schools would be assigned to formerly white junior highs in fall 1963. The board also announced that it would allow all elementary transfer requests. All first graders were to be assigned on the basis of zones, without regard to race.[82] A freedom-of-choice plan, wherein students could attend a school of their choice without regard to race, was proposed for junior and senior highs. Judge Stanley ruled the plan insufficient.[83] The board's final plan allowed complete freedom of choice, with classroom space the only limiting factor.[84]

A series of events in Caswell County paralleled desegregation developments in Durham, but with an unfortunate side effect. When the parents of Caswell County black students who had filed suit in the *Jeffers* case exhausted administrative remedies with the Caswell County Board, they still were not reassigned to formerly white schools.[85] In fact, when the case was refiled, the Fourth Circuit Court of Appeals found a pattern of invariable denial of interracial transfer requests.[86] Although the court had required the exhaustion of administrative remedies, such a principle "presuppose[d] a fair and lawful conduct of administrative procedures. When, however, administrators . . . consistently employed the administrative processes to frustrate enjoyment of legal rights, there is no longer room for . . . an assumption that the administrative proceedings provide an appropriate method by which recognition and enforcement of those rights may be obtained."[87] The Court of Appeals ordered the admission of plaintiffs to the schools of their choice, therefore, but refused to require full-scale desegregation. The court did order the board not to refuse admission to any pupil on the basis of race, and required the board to either develop a plan to end discrimination or begin notifying parents of their right to choose their child's school.

But the enrollment of black students in Caswell County was not accomplished peacefully. After Jasper Paul Brown, a black farmer, enrolled four of his children in previously all-white schools, a car containing three white men followed him out of town. When the car bumped his truck, Brown got out and shot both occupants. He surrendered to authorities through the cooperation of NAACP field secretary Charles McLean and was taken to an undisclosed jail at his own request. The wounded men were N. L. Oliver, whose father was a member of the Caswell County Board of Education, and James Nixon. They were treated for minor injuries. The driver of the car, Allen Smith, was not injured. Conrad Pearson claimed the incident occurred after a crowd of whites harassed Brown. School officials consequently forbade anyone to enter school grounds unless they were on official business. Sixteen more black students enrolled in Caswell schools without further incident.[88]

Attorney Conrad Pearson complained to Governor Sanford about the local sheriff's failure to provide protection.[89] Later, some name calling arose at Jasper Brown's preliminary hearing, but State Highway Patrol officers kept the situation under control. Pearson personally thanked the Highway Patrol for the way they handled the matter.[90]

The *Wheeler* and *Jeffers* cases signaled a new perspective in the courts. Previously, litigation that had sought to bypass the administrative appeals process at the local board level had failed. Once those administrative appeals had been carried out, however, the courts began to hold that desegregation must occur. When individual students were not reassigned to desegregated schools, the courts ordered more significant steps toward system-wide desegregation. That approach would be put into sweeping effect over the next two years.

Tension and Progress, 1963–1965

Tension in Caswell County paralleled widespread race-related stress throughout the South in the mid-1960s as pressure from the civil rights movement expanded. In the summer of 1963, the student body president of A&T State University, Jesse Jackson, led civil rights marches in Greensboro, with participation sometimes numbering in the thousands.[91] Demonstrations seeking the integration of eating facilities, theaters, transportation, and other public accommodations occurred in every major city in North Carolina and in most small towns as well.[92] In Lexington, one man was killed and another wounded during a demonstration involving over two thousand.[93]

During peaceful marches in Raleigh, Governor Sanford met with some of the demonstrators.[94] They advised Sanford that they sought complete acceptance of blacks as first-class citizens of North Carolina. They called on the governor to institute meetings between government officials and civil rights leaders, to recruit blacks for Democratic Party organizations, to appoint blacks to judgeships and to membership on the University of North Carolina Board of Governors, as well as to positions in the State Bureau of Investigation, Paroles Office, Probation Office, and National Guard. They further urged him to direct the Department of Public Instruction to assist local school systems in formulating system-wide desegregation plans. Above all, civil rights activists wanted the Pupil Assignment Act and the Pearsall Plan repealed.[95]

Governor Sanford subsequently hired Jesse Jackson to work in the Governor's Office, preparing television programs that would enable black students to explain their concerns to the public.[96] By mid-summer 1963, public accommodations in Durham, Greensboro, Statesville, Winston-Salem, Raleigh, Charlotte, Asheville, Lumberton, Hickory, and Wilmington were desegregated as a result of continued demonstrations.[97] The Raleigh Merchants Association passed a resolution stating, "God-fearing people, as responsible citizens, and all people of good will, must face the fact that peace on human relations is essential. We are convinced that we should . . . remove all policies in both government and business which deny rights and services because of race."[98]

During that same period the Charlotte Chamber of Commerce Executive Committee unanimously called on all businesses catering to the general public to be opened to all patrons without regard to race.[99] C. A. McKnight, editor of the *Charlotte Observer*; Joe H. Robinson, vice-president of Wachovia Bank; and J. M. Wasson, general manager of Southern Bell, wrote the resolution. Chamber of Commerce president J. Edward Burnside spoke of negative economic consequences if segregation customs were not changed, but he emphasized moral obligations even more. From May 29 to 31, 1963, all of the chamber directors took black guests to lunch at prominent area restaurants. Mayor Stan Brookshire invited Fred Alexander, local civic leader and brother of Kelly Alexander. C. A. McKnight took Dr. Reginald Hawkins and attorney Thomas Wyche, who had been active in school desegregation. S&W Cafeterias owner Frank O. Sherrill soon announced the desegregation of his entire chain. Competitors followed suit.

During some demonstrations around the state, law enforcement authorities used limited force to disperse unruly crowds. In Oxford, an armed owner confronted a group of blacks who had been refused service at a local restaurant. A crowd of whites from a nearby poolroom began harassing them, resulting in several fights. The blacks went to the local police for help. Before the evening was over, firemen turned water hoses on the white mob to break it up. A state investigator reported that NAACP leaders had tried to quiet down the situation.[100] In Williamston, however, black demonstrators accused the police of attacking them without provocation.[101]

In July 1963, Governor Sanford issued a formal statement urging an end to all employment discrimination in North Carolina.[102] In addition to the Good Neighbor Council, Sanford organized conferences of local mayors.[103] Many of those attending developed what eventually became known as the North Carolina Mayors Cooperating Committee. Leaders included M. C. Benton of Winston-Salem, Wense Grabarek of Durham, David Schenck of Greensboro, Stan Brookshire of Charlotte, and Floyd Mehan of High Point. The Mayors Committee promoted local ordinances prohibiting segregation in public accommodations.[104] Governor Sanford appointed General Capus Waynick of High Point as special assistant to the governor and John Brooks as special legal advisor, both with specific responsibilities for racial matters.[105]

Sanford organized meetings with moderate black leaders, but he met with some of the more vocal leaders as well, in spite of criticism from conservative whites.[106] On one occasion he invited Golden Frinks, one of the state's most outspoken black leaders, to come inside from a march in front of the Governor's Mansion.[107]

The segregationist faction did not accept such changes quietly. When the Young Democrats changed their meeting site from the Sir Walter Hotel in Raleigh to another location that would admit blacks, Sam Worthington, who had been a prominent member of the prosegregationist faction in the legislature, bitterly denounced the organization's leaders. Worthington's letter to President David Reid reveals a great deal about the depth of opposition to civil rights among a segment of North Carolina's political elite. Worthington wrote:

> Dear Sir Galahad: It would have been travesty enough to have changed the place of the [Young Democrats] rally because of North Carolina niggers—to change it for the plants and emissaries of the Kennedys, NAACP and CORE constitutes you the prize stupid scapegoat and stool pigeon of all times. . . . Certainly, with the attendant publicity . . . that will spread throughout the sections from which you expect niggers you may well anticipate a rather large showing on their part, if for no other reason than to be able to rub shoulders with white girls who may at-

> tend. . . . My compliments to you and your nigger constituents. I hope NAACP and CORE send a raft of them and you get a complete belly full of niggers until they . . . spew out your ears.[108]

Civil rights demonstrations spawned even more severe reaction. The Ku Klux Klan began a resurgence in summer 1964. A June rally in Asheboro drew a crowd of two hundred.[109] Another Klan meeting near Salisbury in August drew a crowd of over two thousand, plus three hundred to four hundred robed Klansmen, who heard Grand Dragon Robert Jones denounce Governor Sanford for selling out the country "to the niggers."[110]

The year 1965 witnessed continued demonstrations along with corresponding violence. Dynamite damaged a black church in Craven County and a black elementary school near Smithfield.[111] Bombs exploded at the Charlotte homes of Frederick and Kelly Alexander, attorney Julius Chambers, and civil rights leader Reginald Hawkins.[112] Kelly Alexander commented that, if his house had been made of wood instead of brick, his son would have been killed.[113] The principal result of the Charlotte bombings, however, was an outpouring of sympathy and assistance from white and black citizens alike.[114] The cases were never solved, though.[115]

Litigation, 1963

In spite of opposition and efforts at intimidation, individual families continued to press for desegregation. All the desegregation cases filed prior to 1963 had involved black children. Segregation, however, was more broadly based. Nine North Carolina counties operated separate schools for Native American children.[116] In 1963 a group of Native Americans residing in Harnett County sought transfer for their children from an Indian school to a white school. The Board of Education denied their application.[117] U.S. Eastern District Court Judge Wilson Warlick's opinion in *Chance v. Board of Education of Harnett County* said as much about racial attitudes of the period as it did about the disposition of the case: "Until the hearing of this matter I had never had any personal contact with the Indians of Eastern North Carolina, and was obviously unaware of their habits, customs, and behavior. During the trial . . . I closely observed those present . . . , and came to the conclusion that they were not only very intelligent, but particularly well behaved, and well dressed. From their testimony I was impressed with the fact that they not only were well informed but that they had made of themselves first-class citizens."[118]

Judge Warlick no doubt considered these remarks complimentary, though in retrospect they seem elitist, condescending, and patronizing. That such remarks came from a respected judge, and no adverse reaction ensued in the press or from the public, constitutes yet another measure of the extent to which attitudes reflecting assumptions of racial inferiority and superiority were considered normal during this period. Warlick found for the plaintiffs and ordered admission to the schools of their choice. A restraining order prohibited the Harnett Board from using race as a consideration in administering applications for reassignment.

The pace of desegregation was accelerating. In response, significant political reaction and realignments were underway.

1964: A Watershed Year

Lyndon Baines Johnson, the vice-president, ascended to the presidency following the assassination of President John F. Kennedy on November 22, 1963. The following year, Johnson ran for his own term as president against Barry Goldwater, a strong conservative senator from Arizona. Support for a new civil rights act, previously initiated by President Kennedy, was a centerpiece of Johnson's campaign. According to Taylor Branch, eminent historian of the civil rights era, Goldwater adopted the strategy of opposing the proposed act as an outcome of discussions with two key advisors, William Rehnquist and Robert Bork, who advised Goldwater to base his opposition on states' rights, while vowing no motivation related to race or segregation. This verbal gymnastic would become a key element in discussions related to race in the future. The Republican Party, previously the party of Lincoln, thus shifted to become the party opposing desegregation initiatives, while the Democratic Party, formerly the bedrock of the "Solid South" and segregation, became the party that supported civil rights.[119]

After Johnson's resounding victory, Congress passed the Civil Rights Act of 1964. Title IV required the U.S. Office of Education (USOE) in the Department of Health, Education, and Welfare (HEW) to provide technical assistance to school systems in the development of desegregation plans. When satisfactory progress toward desegregation did not occur, the U.S. Attorney General's Office was authorized to file civil suits to compel desegregation.[120] Such authorization had the effect of lifting the burden of desegregation initiatives from individuals and organizations such as the NAACP while shifting the executive branch of the federal government into a proactive role.

Individual complaints were still part of the law, however. Before filing suit, the attorney general had to have a signed complaint from a pupil or parent and had to determine that the complainant was unable to bring action on his or her own. The attorney general was also required to give school boards a reasonable period of time to correct an alleged condition before filing suit.

Another restriction involved what was to become known as busing. By the 1960s, widespread reaction to desegregation initiatives among moderate and liberal whites did not oppose desegregation outright and often acknowledged that ending discrimination was a worthy goal. But whites did not take kindly to the idea of transporting their children to new locations, especially if the new location involved a formerly black school that was situated some distance from the white neighborhood. Title IV thus limited courts' authority to order district reorganization: "[N]othing herein shall empower any official or court of the United States to issue any order seeking to achieve a racial balance in any school by requiring the transportation of students from one school to another."[121]

Title VI of the Civil Rights Act of 1964 required every federal agency that provided funds to eliminate discrimination on the grounds of race, color, or national origin in all programs supported.[122] Agencies were empowered to terminate support for programs where discrimination was found. This provision would bear significant impact on education. The Office of Civil Rights (OCR) began collecting pupil population data by race, enabling accurate monitoring of desegregation progress.

Equal employment opportunity, to be enforced by the Equal Employment Opportunity Commission (EEOC), became an additional requirement.[123] Employers, labor unions, and employment agencies were required to treat all persons equally, without regard to race, color, religion, gender, or national origin. Equal opportunity in all phases of employment, including hiring, promotion, firing, training, and job assignments were required as well.

A key issue of concern during the development of the Civil Rights Bill involved state sovereignty. Senator Sam Ervin of North Carolina became one of the principal voices of opposition as the legislation worked its way through Congress. Education had heretofore been regarded as a function of state governments, with only a limited federal role. But Congress had periodically appropriated federal funds to support supplemental programs for economically disadvantaged children. Southern school systems had been particular beneficiaries, although black children had been systematically denied equal access to such programs.

The question of state sovereignty was resolved on the basis of litigation originating in Greensboro. Dr. George Simkins and a group of other black health-care professionals challenged provisions in the federal Hill-Burton Hospital Construction Act that allowed local budgeting, and hence racial discrimination, in funding distribution. In a decision issued in 1963, the Fourth Circuit Court of Appeals concluded that states had engaged in voluntary participation in the receipt of federal funds, so federal guidelines did not constitute a violation of state sovereignty. Denial of equal protection on the basis of race was, therefore, illegal. The U.S. Supreme Court declined to hear an appeal.[124] From that point forward, when states elected to receive federal funds, they also accepted responsibility to follow federal rules, especially regarding racial discrimination. Although not as significant as *Brown* and its progeny, what came to be known as the Moses Cone Hospital case rests among a second tier of cases in terms of long-range impact.

Governor Sanford publicly opposed the Civil Rights Bill.[125] He argued that the states were handling the civil rights issue, and federal intervention was neither necessary nor warranted.[126] Once the law was passed, however, Sanford vowed to obey and urged all North Carolinians to do the same. He advised the public that the Civil Rights Act was the law of the land, and he knew the people of North Carolina would obey the law. Sanford pointed out that, before enactment of the law, many towns and cities in the State had been making voluntary efforts to provide the greater opportunities which black citizens had been seeking. At the state level, the Good Neighbor Council had been conducting programs to increase job opportunities. Governor Sanford closed with an appeal to people of both races: "[H]onor the law, . . . deal justly, love mercy and walk humbly with God."[127]

In 1965, the Johnson administration convinced Congress to expand federal funding for education dramatically. The Elementary and Secondary Education Act (ESEA) would reward desegregation with significant funds, whereas previous legislation had been oriented to compelling desegregation.[128] HEW began requiring school systems to prepare full-scale desegregation plans as a condition for receipt of federal funds. The State Board of Education filed forms promising to assist in the acquisition of desegregation compliance statements from local boards.[129]

In 1961, over bitter protests and blocking efforts from southern senators, President Kennedy had appointed Thurgood Marshall, formerly chief legal counsel for the NAACP Legal Defense Fund, to the U.S. Court of Appeals for the Second Circuit. President Johnson appointed him to the post of solicitor general in 1965. Marshall would be elevated to the Supreme Court two years later, the first black to hold the latter two seats. Clearly, the pace of desegregation was about to grow less deliberate.[130]

The Moore Administration

In the Democratic primaries of 1964, race was less overt than in 1960. L. Richardson Preyer of Greensboro was closely identified with the progressive policies of the Sanford administration.[131] Dan K. Moore of Jackson County positioned himself as a middle-of-the-road candidate. I. Beverly Lake, whose political and social philosophy lay well to the political right of the other Democratic candidates, ran again, this time emphasizing conservative economic policies.[132]

Race, and racially oriented code words, however, played an underlying role. Moore, for example, charged that the NAACP was backing Preyer.[133] Moore also denounced the Sanford administration, and Preyer by association, for appointing civil rights leaders to positions of responsibility, charging that their actions had been disruptive.[134] Although Lake tried to smooth over his image as an overt segregationist, he was still referred to as the "white man's candidate."[135] Media commentator Jesse Helms explicitly sought to publicize the high level of black support for Preyer.[136] North Carolina Senator Sam Ervin joined the voices denouncing Preyer's association with civil rights.[137] All three candidates opposed the Civil Rights Act of 1964.[138] But Preyer and Moore both said they would enforce the act if it passed. Lake vowed that he would not.[139] Lake also backed a new law, known as the Speaker Ban, that would prohibit alleged communists from speaking on state university campuses, while Preyer and Moore opposed it.

In the first primary, on May 30, 1964, Preyer ran strong in the Piedmont, while Moore took the West.[140] Lake won a majority of votes in an area from east of the Piedmont to the coastal plain but did not carry the tidewater, which split between Moore and Preyer. The actual vote tallied 281,430 for Preyer; 257,872 for Moore; and 217,172 for Lake.[141] None of the candidates won a majority. Moore called for a runoff. In the campaign leading up to the second primary, Lake endorsed Moore.[142] In the June 27, 1964, primary, Moore garnered 480,431 votes to Preyer's 293,863. In the fall, Moore defeated repeat Republican candidate Robert Gavin, 790,343 to 606,165. Upon receiving the Lake endorsement, Moore assured the public that Lake requested no favors or rewards.[143] In August 1965, however, Governor Moore appointed Lake to a seat on the State Supreme Court.[144]

The Tone of the Moore Administration

As the campaign rhetoric and alliances foretold, Governor Moore did not emerge as a promoter of civil rights or of school desegregation, although he did devote considerable attention to maintaining order. Early in the Moore administration, State Board of Education Chair Dallas Herring and State Superintendent Charles F. Carroll visited Governor Moore to seek counsel regarding adaptation to the Civil Rights Act. Moore listened to their questions and responded, "That's your problem,"[145] and ended the conversation. Moore supported some educational improvements, though. During the Moore administration, educator salaries rose by 30 percent, and special appropriations went to state institutions of higher education for blacks.[146]

Governor Moore attempted to make inroads into the black community. As a native of the mountains, the region containing the smallest black population, he brought few, if any, such contacts with him. Early in his administration, Governor Moore reappointed Dr. Harold L. Trigg, a black educator, to the State Board of Education.[147] That appointment, though, may not represent as much of a progressive initiative on the governor's part as it might appear. Dr. Trigg was regarded in the black press as an appeaser of whites, and he had resigned as president of St. Augustine's College, allegedly under pressure from the trustees due to financial irregularities and nepotism.[148]

Governor Moore spoke on August 10, 1965, to the Christian Education Convocation of the African Methodist Episcopal Church, meeting in Winston-Salem, advising the convention that the real problem between races was lack of communication.[149] Later in the fall, he warned that the people of North Carolina could no longer afford to deny equal opportunities to anyone who was qualified for a job.[150] Governor Moore ordered state personnel departments to recruit on traditionally black college campuses.[151]

Governor Moore and state education leaders tended to rally around the concept of freedom of choice, opposing district reorganization and busing. Governor Moore condemned what he termed HEW's "far-reaching and dangerous . . . intervention in State matters."[152] When school systems faced hearings that could have resulted in the cutoff of federal funds, Moore utilized the Attorney General's Office as well as state funds to retain a large Washington law firm in their defense.[153]

The U.S. Office of Education (USOE) in HEW issued school desegregation guidelines in April 1965, tacitly indicating approval of freedom of choice plans. The guidelines were revised the following year, however, recognizing both freedom of choice and geographic zones of attendance, but adding cautions that approval of plans would depend on actual levels of desegregation.[154] The new guidelines further mandated integration of faculties and warned that qualified teachers could not be dismissed because of race.[155]

State Superintendent Charles F. Carroll advised local superintendents to "hold in abeyance further action on the development of desegregation plans and other compliance documents."[156] Superintendent Carroll held fast to the idea that school systems merely had to cease requiring segregation, not integrate.[157] Governor Moore urged North Carolina's congressional delegation to seek legislation countermanding the HEW guidelines.[158] Delegations from North Carolina and the other southern states mounted a vigorous effort in Congress,[159] but the effort came to no avail.[160]

Support for segregation remained widespread in the early 1960s. In the decade following the *Brown* decisions, no gubernatorial candidate openly supported desegregation. But the people of North Carolina never elected a strong segregationist governor, either, although they certainly had the opportunity in I. Beverly Lake. A moderate, Terry Sanford, set a more liberal tone after he was elected than he had during the campaign, promoting the elimination of racial discrimination in the state. No school board in North Carolina vowed to fight desegregation as a matter of policy. The state, through local board control, continued to provide education to black and white students with no new restrictions.

North Carolina, the South, and indeed the nation underwent a period of trauma. The civil rights movement made clear that blacks would no longer accept second-class citizenship. Gradually, political and business leaders in North Carolina began to support desegregation, in harmony with the tone set by the Sanford administration. Moral values played an influential role, although economic motivations were important as well. Some unsettling incidents took place, but for the most part, a significant degree of change was accomplished peacefully.

In the 1960s, judges began to focus on whether actual desegregation had occurred, rather than how individual transfer applications had been processed. The federal Civil Rights Act shifted the burden of desegregation from individual families to the federal government, now empowered to institute proceedings against entire school systems and cut off funding when desegregation had not occurred. Whereas no school system had achieved any significant measure of desegregation in 1960, from 1964 to 1966 all systems began to develop comprehensive desegregation plans.

6

Early, Limited Desegregation

THE MID- TO LATE 1960S

The Chapel Hill–Carrboro Board of Education pioneered rezoning to achieve system-wide desegregation on a voluntary basis in the early 1960s. But voluntary desegregation did not produce results elsewhere in the state. The Civil Rights Act of 1964 imparted dramatic impetus to school desegregation. As in the 1950s and 1960s, black families filing on behalf of individual students continued to seek redress through the courts, usually with backing from the NAACP. Comprehensive desegregation commenced, however, because all school systems were required to prepare desegregation plans as a part of the federal funding process.

Before 1965, federal court decisions had upheld school systems as long as courts perceived the valid operation of appeals procedures when school administrators processed individual transfer requests. From the mid-1960s forward, however, courts also focused on actual levels of desegregation. Freedom-of-choice plans that had been approved previously were rejected later, when little desegregation actually occurred. Consequently, entire school systems all over the South entered periods of supervision either by federal courts or by the Office of Civil Rights in the Department of Health, Education, and Welfare (OCR/HEW).

What degree and pace of desegregation would the OCR and federal courts require? How would local school systems and the state comply? How would student reassignments affect black educators? And what political outcomes would be associated with changes in education and the pattern of practices related to race?

Litigation in North Carolina, 1965–1966

Two cases reported from North Carolina shortly after passage of the Civil Rights Act involved court approval of system-wide desegregation plans. In *Jones v. Pamlico County Board of Education,*[1] black parents and the local board agreed that all students would be assigned to the same schools they had attended the previous year, but any students could transfer to schools of their choice. Students entering school for the first time in the fall of 1965 would have free choice regarding school assignment. In the event of overcrowding, pupils would be reassigned only to schools containing members of another race.

Bryant v. Carteret County Board of Education[2] constituted consent to a desegregation plan that had already been approved by the OCR. The Carteret County Board adopted a freedom-of-choice policy, effective fall 1965. Teacher transfers for the purpose of integrating staff would begin, and all future staff meetings and workshops would be held on an integrated basis. The board agreed not to dismiss teachers, principals, or other staff members because of actual or expected loss of enrollment resulting from desegregation.

Bowditch v. Buncombe County Board of Education[3] was the first case decided at the appellate level in North Carolina after the passage of the Civil Rights Act. The public schools of Buncombe County remained segregated at the elementary and junior high levels in 1963. Buncombe County had never operated a high school for blacks, assigning black students who wanted to attend upper grades to Lee High School in the Asheville city system. This was a common arrangement for county school systems in North Carolina. The number of rural black students who attended high schools was small, since no transportation was provided.

Conrad Pearson, Robert L. Harrell of Asheville, and Julius Chambers[4] of Charlotte, as well as Derrick A. Bell Jr., Jack Greenberg, and James Nabrit III of New York, represented the NAACP-backed plaintiffs in *Bowditch.* Plaintiffs objected to the requirement of individual transfer requests, to the continued assignment of black students to a city high school, and to the lack of a reassignment plan to integrate teachers and other staff. The U.S. Fourth Circuit Court of Appeals pointed out that high-school students, against whom the board had most seriously discriminated, would be victims of continued delay under the proposed plan.[5] The Court of Appeals thus ordered acceleration but held that no cause of action existed regarding employees.

The same NAACP team argued *Nesbit v. Statesville City Board of Education.*[6] R. A. Collier of Statesville represented the board. U.S. Western District Court had approved a plan which prescribed an approximate three-year progression for desegregation. Transfers would be allowed in grades one through six in 1964–65, in grades ten through twelve in 1965–66, and in grades seven through nine in 1966–67. The plan still provided for dual attendance zones, however. Furthermore, the plan had not actually been written; it existed only in discussions between district court judge J. Braxton Craven Jr. and the board's representatives.[7] The Fourth Circuit Court of Appeals decided that it was unable to determine the validity of the system's desegregation plan and remanded the case.[8]

I. Beverly Lake and Robert Morgan defended the Harnett County Board of Education against the NAACP team in *Felder v. Harnett County Board of Education.*[9] The Harnett County schools remained segregated in 1965, but the board claimed that such segregation was the result of voluntary acts of parents, not action by the board. The Fourth Circuit Court of Appeals found that the Harnett Board had never intended to allow freedom of choice. In a tersely worded repudiation of the arguments Lake and Morgan presented, the court held, "The appeal presents no issue which has not long since been settled beyond all question."[10]

Several other cases extended consent orders recorded in 1965. *Clayton v. Person County Board of Education*[11] established a freedom-of-choice plan. In 1966 another consent order had provided for faculty and staff integration.[12] Vacant teaching positions were to be filled with qualified black applicants, if they were available; and if a decrease in the number of teaching positions occurred, the board promised not to use race as a factor in determining which teachers would not be reemployed. *Gill v. Concord City Board of Education*[13] also consented to a freedom-of-choice plan for student assignments, as well as faculty and staff desegregation.

In *Barrow v. Washington City Board of Education,* however, the U.S. Eastern District Court found that the board had failed to implement a desegregation plan to which it had consented. The court ordered several faculty transfers in addition to those already made, and five student reassignments which had been denied. The court included provisions similar to those in *Clayton* regarding teacher retention resulting from decreased positions.[14] In *Dilday v. Beaufort County Board of Education,*[15] the North Carolina Supreme Court left desegregation matters unresolved until the board and county commissioners could agree on funding for a new school.

Protracted litigation involving the Durham City Schools continued through the mid- to late 1960s. *Wheeler*[16] resurfaced in 1966, when the

U.S. Middle District Court found that only white teachers taught white students in Durham schools and that only one white teacher had been assigned to teach black students. Except for the six hundred black students who had been granted transfers, black students attended all-black schools. The court ordered the integration of faculty and staff through the employment of black teachers to fill vacancies, while expressing reluctance to order involuntary transfers.[17]

Another case appeared to be similar in nature to other ongoing litigation, but over the next decade it would become another of the most significant school desegregation cases in history. In *Swann v. Charlotte-Mecklenburg Board of Education,*[18] NAACP attorney Julius Chambers complained that certain districts in the school system had been gerrymandered to prevent desegregation. The suit further contended that the pace of desegregation ought to be increased, specifically in the matter of ten schools serving black students that had not been included in the system's desegregation plan. The board had delayed desegregation of those schools because of ongoing construction projects. Finally, Chambers argued that faculty and staff desegregation ought to begin immediately.

At the time, Dr. Craig Phillips was superintendent of the Charlotte-Mecklenburg system. Brock Barkley represented the board. U.S. Middle District Court judge J. Braxton Craven Jr. found the system's desegregation plan reasonable, voicing the opinion that courts were ill equipped to deal with such matters. Craven found no evidence of gerrymandering, but he ordered the board to integrate faculty and staff.[19] Chambers appealed the pupil desegregation portion of Craven's decision, but the Fourth Circuit Court of Appeals upheld the lower court.[20] Chambers did not appeal, because he thought precedents indicated that the Supreme Court would affirm.[21]

Invalidation of the Pearsall Plan

Although local boards had processed requests for pupil transfers under the Pupil Assignment Act from the latter 1950s through the mid-1960s, the other aspects of the Pearsall Plan had lain dormant. No one applied for a tuition grant to attend a private school until 1961. That year, Mr. and Mrs. Reece Birmingham of Carrboro asked the Chapel Hill–Carrboro Board of Education to assign their daughters to an all-white school instead of Carrboro Elementary School, where two black students had been admitted.[22] The board found no "reasonable or practical" alternative to the original assignment and denied the family's request.

The Birminghams then sought a grant to support tuition at the private Twaddle School in Durham, where their children were already enrolled,[23] and the Chapel Hill–Carrboro Board approved the application.[24] The North Carolina Department of Public Instruction, however, found that the Twaddle School did not meet state requirements.[25] The State Board of Education thus rejected the application.

The state board received no other tuition grant applications until 1965, when the parents of Terrence McClain, a resident of Mecklenburg County, sought a grant to pay tuition to Carolina Military Academy in Maxton.[26] The board had admitted black students to West Mecklenburg High School, where McClain had previously been assigned. William E. Poe, an attorney who served on the board, warned that he thought education expense grants were neither proper nor legal. Board attorney Brock Barkley, however, advised the board that approval was required, since McClain's application met all requirements of the education expense grant law. The board thus approved the application. Ironically, Carolina Military Academy had previously committed itself to admitting black cadets.

At the same time the State Board of Education received the Mecklenburg application, Mr. and Mrs. William F. Tyson of Pitt County sought tuition at Hargrave Military Academy in Chatham, Virginia. The state board denied the Pitt County request because Hargrave was located out of state.[27] The board approved the Mecklenburg application, however.[28] Deputy Attorney General Ralph Moody held that state grants could be used to support tuition in an integrated, private school, since the law had made no such prohibition. In spite of the state board's approval, Dallas Herring, along with State Treasurer Edwin Gill, criticized the grant because it appeared to be a mechanism enabling parents to transfer their children to private schools at state expense. State board members also wondered aloud about the implications of the new federal Civil Rights Act regarding such grants.

Within a week, Rev. Darius Swann, Rev. E. J. Moore, and Dr. Reginald Hawkins, civil rights activists who lived in Charlotte, sought an injunction to restrain payment of the grant and a permanent injunction to ban all such payments.[29] Moreover, the suit asked the U.S. Western District Court to void the remainder of the Pearsall Plan, making illegal any local school closings in order to avoid integration. The Department of Justice intervened for the plaintiffs.[30]

Ironically, by this time the U.S. attorney for the Western District was William Medford, a former member of the second Pearsall Committee who had managed the Pearsall Plan legislation through the North Carolina Senate. He now argued that, although the Pearsall Plan had avoided the massive resistance characteristic of some southern states, it no longer served a useful purpose and was now unconstitutional. Julius Chambers, representing the plaintiffs, told the court the tuition grants were designed to circumvent the *Brown* rulings.[31]

Andrew Vanore Jr., who had recently joined the Attorney General's Office after graduating from law school, was assigned to defend the tuition grant law. Inside the Attorney General's Office, opinion held that the Pearsall Plan was indeed unconstitutional. Nevertheless, the attorney general was obligated to defend the state. Vanore argued that the plan did not discriminate or deny benefits because of race, and that it did not require segregation. No schools had been closed in North Carolina because of integration, and no student had been excused from compulsory attendance.[32] As expected, however, U.S. Western District Court ruled that the laws establishing the Pearsall Plan were unconstitutional and enjoined their enforcement.[33] The state elected not to appeal.[34]

Educator Dismissals Related to Race

Throughout the 1950s and 1960s, attorneys in North Carolina had used the state's extensive employment of black educators as evidence of a positive climate regarding racial matters and of the state's efforts to educate black students. Yet one of the first acts passed by the General Assembly following the *Brown* decisions had subjected teachers and principals to annual renewal of their employment, making terminations relatively easy.[35]

E. B. Palmer, executive secretary of the North Carolina Teachers Association, the organization of black educators,[36] reported that, after the onset of system-wide desegregation, black educators "swamped" the NCTA with complaints. The NCTA, in cooperation with the National Education Association, provided legal assistance to a number of black professionals whose continued employment was in jeopardy.[37]

In a Halifax County case, *Johnson v. Branch,*[38] prominent civil rights attorney William Kunstler represented teacher Willa Johnson.[39] Johnson alleged that her contract had not been renewed because of her involvement in the civil rights movement. The U.S. Eastern District Court expressed reluctance to interfere with state procedures that included "no conditions or vested rights . . . to employment or re-employment." The court warned, however, that the authority the state had conveyed to local school officials to exercise discretion in employment matters could not "extend to an arbitrary denial of . . . protected rights."

The court found that board members were probably not aware of Johnson's civil rights activities. Johnson's complaint "tended to minimize her professional transgressions while maximizing her notoriety as a known participant in the civil rights movement." Her actual involvement was not extensive and not well known. She had, however, failed on a number of occasions to report to work on time, the charges alleged, and her principal had written her a letter about such matters. The court thus dismissed the case.[40]

The Fourth Circuit Court of Appeals disagreed, holding that the school system had acted in an arbitrary and capricious manner by allowing trivial incidents to overshadow twelve years of excellent service. Moreover, a member of the school board had warned that teachers participating in civil rights activities would be fired. Those voting against Johnson's renewed employment had "conceded frankly that they were opposed to integration of the schools."[41] In the absence of her civil rights activities, therefore, nonrenewal of her teaching contract would not have been considered. The Court of Appeals thus instructed the District Court to order the renewal of Johnson's teaching contract. The school board subsequently paid her a cash settlement.[42]

The NAACP team of attorneys, with NCTA support, handled *Chambers v. Hendersonville City Board of Education*. Conrad Pearson, Jack Greenberg, and Julius Chambers argued that Grace Chambers, Doris Yvonne Greene, and Mary Ann White had been denied reemployment because of race. Arthur B. Shepherd, L. B. Prince, and Jonathan W. Jackson of Hendersonville represented the board. The Hendersonville Board had denied reemployment to sixteen of the system's twenty-four black teachers. A reduction of five positions in the teaching force had occurred as a result of the system's abandoning a freedom-of-choice plan and redistricting the attendance zones of its four schools so as to desegregate them. As a part of the redistricting plan, the Hendersonville schools had lost 217 black students living outside the Hendersonville district.

The U.S. Western District Court divided the teachers into three groups. Six situations did not seem to be related to race. Five others did not appear to be qualified for employment in the reorganized system. Black teachers in the segregated system had been employed with lower qualifications than those required for whites, and lower than the system was requiring as it desegregated. Of the five remaining teachers, the court found that four held credentials inferior to those hired, including lower recommendations and evaluations from their principal, who was also black. The District Court thus found for the board.[43]

Once again, however, the Fourth Circuit Court of Appeals overturned the ruling. The superintendent, in determining which teachers to retain, had subjected black and white teachers to different evaluation criteria. A loss of black pupils did not in any way justify a corresponding elimination of black teachers, the court found. Meanwhile, all of the teachers seeking reemployment had found other teaching positions by the time the decision was issued. The Court of Appeals thus remanded the case to federal District Court with instructions to order the Hendersonville system to employ teachers without discrimination, and to offer reemployment to the affected teachers the next year.[44]

A similar sequence of events characterized *Wall v. Stanly County Board of Education*. The transfer of approximately three hundred black pupils under a freedom-of-choice plan caused the school system to reduce teaching positions for black teachers. The U.S. Middle District Court found the nonrenewal justified.[45] Again, the Fourth Circuit Court of Appeals reversed. Julius Chambers represented the teacher, Audrey Gillis Wall, and the NCTA; Henry C. Doby Jr. of Albemarle represented the board. The Court of Appeals noted that during and prior to the 1965–66 school year, black teachers taught only black students and white teachers taught only white students in Stanly County. When enrollment in the black schools declined, no plan for reassignment of black teachers was developed, and white principals were not told they could hire black teachers. The Court of Appeals concluded, "Mrs. Wall was not employed as a teacher in the Stanly County school system but . . . *as a Negro teacher in a Negro school* [original emphasis]. Such a premise is unlawful." On remand, the District Court awarded Wall damages and attorney's fees. In addition, the court enjoined the board from considering race in employment matters.[46]

In a case originating in Asheboro, the U.S. Middle District Court initially found for the Asheboro Board under circumstances similar to previous teacher-dismissal cases. On appeal, the Fourth Circuit Court of Appeals cited the *Wall* precedent. Some of the teachers involved were entitled to damages, and all the teachers involved were entitled to reemployment.[47]

With regard to black administrators, E. B. Palmer of the North Carolina Teachers Association tallied North Carolina's employment of 525 black principals, including 252 in schools containing high-school grades, in 1963–64, as opposed to 250, with 25 in schools containing high-school grades, in 1970.[48] Another tally compiled by A. C. Davis, State Board of Education controller, for State Board member Dr. Harold Trigg, showed that in 1972 North Carolina employed 359 black principals, along with 15 Native American, Oriental, or Hispanic surnamed, in addition to 1,435 white and 235 of unidentified race or ethnicity.[49]

During the period of system-wide desegregation, therefore, the number of black principals in North Carolina was reduced by at least 50 percent, with the number of black principals in schools containing high-school grades reduced by approximately 90 percent. Such a figure is significant enough in itself, but the fact that black principals constituted a core element of leadership within the black community amplifies its importance.

Black children bore the burden of reassignment in school desegregation through the mid- to late 1960s. Black professionals paid the price in loss of status and in some cases loss of livelihood. School desegregation, in retrospect, produced the unintended consequence of decimating a leadership class within the black community. This pattern of dismissals, as well as reassignments to lower levels of responsibility, strongly implies that superintendents and school boards had either accepted a lower level of performance from black principals than they expected in the administration of white schools, or they did not consider black principals qualified to administer the emerging new, desegregated, but still predominantly white schools, or they believed white parents would not accept black administrators exercising discipline over white students and/or teachers. This constitutes yet another powerful indicator of the level of racial prejudice prevalent in North Carolina through the 1960s.

White superintendents also experienced significant turnover during desegregation. Precise numbers are difficult to ascertain, and the relationship to issues surrounding race and desegregation is inferred, not proven. Superintendents were torn between the demands of local citizens, boards of education, and requirements of the courts. Facts revealed in litigation as well as judgments issued by the courts show a pattern of resistance to desegregation among the local populace, and at least a widespread determination among boards of education members to obey the law, but to go no further than the courts required. A significant number of North Carolina superintendents thus lost their jobs in the 1960s and 1970s, not because they resisted desegregation or failed to comply with legal mandates, but because they obeyed the law and did comply with desegregation requirements in spite of resistance in the community and from local boards who controlled superintendents' employment.[50]

Racial Unrest in the Latter 1960s

This early phase of system-wide school desegregation occurred in an atmosphere of widespread racial unrest. In January 1965 three cross burnings in Craven County foreshadowed the bombing of civil rights attorney Julius Chambers's car while he was working in New Bern.[51] Chambers was not injured, although his car was destroyed. During the summer of 1965, rumors regarding the possibility of school bombings spread, and threats circulated involving black parents whose children attended newly desegregated schools.[52] Governor Moore assisted school officials by utilizing the Highway Patrol and the State Bureau of Investigation.

Between 1965 and 1968, Ku Klux Klan activity expanded throughout the state.[53] Klan rallies occurred in numerous localities, with attendance usually in the hundreds.[54] On one occasion in Dunn, in Harnett County, approximately 1,300 Klansmen participated.[55] Rallies in Rowan County drew the largest crowds, up to 2,000. But only 75 showed up in Mecklenburg County.[56] Governor Moore subsequently explored various legal alternatives aimed at shutting down Klan activities.[57] The Klan remained a shadowy, malevolent presence throughout the mid-1960s, however. Law enforcement officials infiltrated the Klan and received reports from informers, including some of the Klan's leaders, but they were never able to assess with confidence the extent of the Klan's power, and much of what they learned produced valid concern.

Some of the most serious racial incidents grew out of tragic developments at the national level. In April 1968, Dr. Martin Luther King Jr. was scheduled to visit North Carolina to support the gubernatorial candidacy of Dr. Reginald Hawkins. But Dr. King canceled his appearance in order to continue assisting sanitation workers in Memphis,

Tennessee.[58] There, he was assassinated. Riots broke out in a number of North Carolina towns, and serious disruptions lasted nearly a week.[59] Peaceful memorial services were held in a number of North Carolina communities as well. One of the few whites seen in Wilson County's candlelight parade was a young man named Jim Hunt, a member of the county's Good Neighbor Council.[60]

Governor Moore ordered the Highway Patrol and the National Guard to assist local law enforcement agencies and urged local Good Neighbor Councils to help quiet things down.[61] He also dispatched a telegram to a broad range of clergy, black and white, appealing for peace and order. "Let us resolve to associate ourselves in a close communion with each other and with the benevolent teachings of our God, so that strife may be dispelled from every neighborhood . . . , and . . . the violence of these past days may be ended," he urged.[62] State NAACP President Kelly Alexander added his voice to the call for peace. He urged black citizens to "use restraint and work with law abiding citizens of both races to act promptly and sternly to bring an end to the riotous destruction of property. . . . Insurrection is not the instrument for the attainment of the goal of absolute and complete equality,"[63] he advised.

The most serious events of the latter 1960s occurred in Greensboro, on and near the campus of the North Carolina Agricultural and Technical (A&T) State University. A National Guard force of six hundred, in an effort to quell three days of disorder, used tear gas and gunfire to drive out dozens of students occupying campus buildings. One student was killed, and a police officer was seriously injured.[64] A series of related walkouts and class boycotts disrupted the formerly all-black Dudley High School during the same period.[65] President Lewis C. Dowdy closed A&T before the end of the semester and sent all students home for an early summer vacation.

More than seven hundred black students in Hyde County boycotted the schools for a full year, beginning in fall 1968.[66] The protest grew out of the failure of the Hyde County system to desegregate to any significant extent prior to 1968, in combination with a new desegregation plan that included the closing of the two formerly black schools in the system. A team of investigators from the National Education Association denounced the board's actions.[67]

These disorders occurred in the context of a continued, stronger civil rights movement combined with general unrest related to the war in Vietnam; another assassination, of Robert F. Kennedy; and violent confrontations involving Chicago police during the Democratic National Convention, all resulting in a period of turmoil for the United States. The fabric of the nation had been torn.

Whereas the NAACP had seemed militant and radical during the 1950s, in comparison to some of the organizations that developed in the 1960s, the NAACP began to appear relatively conservative, certainly moderate, as it continued to operate within the legal system.[68] The Student Nonviolent Coordinating Committee, the Congress of Racial Equality (Floyd McKissick of Durham became one of CORE's chief officers), and the Southern Christian Leadership Conference shared the NAACP's goal of full equality for black people, but these organizations utilized methods of direct confrontation, such as sit-ins, large scale marches, boycotts, and other approaches designed to bring society and the economy to a standstill if prompt change were not forthcoming. Other organizations, such as the Black Panthers, advocated even more extreme tactics, approaching revolution. Controversy developed among black leaders regarding which methods to use. The NAACP, however, continued its efforts through the courts. Public accommodations were desegregated largely as a result of direct action from the civil rights movement. School desegregation came about because of lawsuits.

The Coleman Report

One of the largest and most important research studies ever undertaken was published in 1966. Written by James S. Coleman, then of Johns Hopkins University, and colleagues, *Equality of Educational Opportunity* was commissioned by HEW as required by the Civil Rights Act. Coleman found that, although wide variations existed based on location, black students, in comparison to white students, had less access to language, physics, or chemistry laboratories, fewer books per pupil in libraries, lower supplies of textbooks, and less access to curricular and extracurricular programs related to academics. Black students were much more likely to attend unaccredited schools staffed by teachers whose qualifications were generally lower than those found in schools attended by whites.

Families of black children tended to have lower educational levels than those of whites. Scores on achievement tests for black children were lower, on average, than scores for whites. Coleman cautioned, however, that these tests were "culture bound," warning that they did not measure intelligence. Minority students tended to enter school at an academic disadvantage, due to poverty, community attitudes, and lower levels of parent education. Academic deficiencies tended to increase over time, indicating that the schools they attended usually failed to overcome initial deficiencies.

Coleman reported that the achievement of black students was more a function of the schools they attended than white students. "The inference might . . . be made that improving the school of a minority pupil may increase . . . achievement more than would improving the school of a white child. . . . [I]t is for the most disadvantaged children that improvements in school quality will make the most differences in achievement."

Teacher quality, as indicated by educational background and test scores on verbal assessments, showed a strong relationship to improved academic achievement for black students, with cumulative effects appearing in higher grades when students were exposed to a series of better-qualified teachers. White students from families that support education, when placed in a school with similar student characteristics, tended to achieve much like their peers. Black students, however, when placed in a school where most families valued education and where most families were better educated, improved their achievement significantly. Therefore, "[I]ntegration should be expected to have a positive effect on Negro achievement." Black students who had spent most of their education in integrated schools showed consistently higher levels of academic achievement.[69] That finding became a crucial empirical foundation for court decisions requiring the transportation of students to other schools.

Litigation in North Carolina, 1967–1969

Litigation in the latter 1960s revealed that little actual desegregation had taken place under freedom-of-choice plans. Courts, therefore, began to produce edicts insisting on the achievement of full-scale desegregation.

In *Teel v. Pitt County Board of Education,* the U.S. Eastern District Court declared Pitt County's previously accepted freedom-of-choice plan invalid because intimidation had interfered with the free exercise of choice by black students. Moreover, board members and others charged with implementing the plan had failed to support the plan effectively. The court ordered the expansion of faculty and staff integration.[70]

U.S. Eastern District Court held in *Coppedge v. Franklin County Board of Education* that, even though the board had a freedom of choice plan in effect, at the conclusion of the 1965–66 school year, only six black students attended school with white students. In 1967–68 the figure stood at a mere forty-five. Marked hostility to desegregation existed in Franklin County, according to the court, and blacks had been subjected to threats and intimidation. The court thus ordered the board to prepare a redistricting plan that would produce a fully desegregated system, with free transportation to be provided to all students. Faculty integration was ordered as well.[71]

Federal district courts in North Carolina decided two far-reaching cases in 1968. In *Boomer v. Beaufort County Board of Education,* the U.S. Eastern District Court found that the Beaufort County Board continued to operate a dual school system. Moreover, the board had taken no steps toward faculty desegregation. The court's order required district reorganization, as well as teacher reassignment, integration of extracurricular activities, transportation, and the location of new schools without regard to race.[72]

United States v. Bertie County Board of Education was the first case to reach the federal district courts in which the U.S. Department of Justice proceeded directly against a North Carolina school system. In 1968 less than 10 percent of the county's black students were attending desegregated schools. In 1966–67 only 1 black teacher out of 160 had been assigned to a white school, with that number increasing to 8 white and 8 black teachers assigned across racial lines the following year. The Eastern District Court's orders required integration of all students in grades ten through twelve into a single high school, effective in the fall of 1968, with reassignment in grades eight and nine to follow a similar pattern, space allowing. Faculty and staff assignments, promotions, and retentions were to be made on a nondiscriminatory basis.[73]

By 1968, therefore, the position of the courts had hardened: full desegregation must proceed apace, and further delays would not be allowed. No discrimination with regard to faculty or staff hiring or transfer would be permitted, and faculties must be integrated. These findings were in concert with desegregation guidelines from the OCR.

A case decided in summer 1969 finally gained for NAACP attorneys the statewide leverage they had been seeking. Pointing out that the Civil Rights Act of 1964 defined the term "school board" to mean any agency or agencies which administer a system of one or more public schools, the U.S. Eastern District Court held in *Godwin v. Johnston County Board of Education* that the duty to effect transition from a dual system of schools to a unitary nonracial school system "falls not only upon the local school boards, but also upon the State Board of Education and the State Superintendent of Public Instruction."[74] From this time forward, therefore, the state could be made the defendant in a class-action suit. Local boards no longer bore sole responsibility for desegregation.

Legislation and Constitutional Amendments, 1967–1970

The 1967 legislative session restored a measure of the job security that teachers had lost in 1955. The North Carolina General Assembly passed a law providing that teacher and principal contracts in effect at the end of the 1966–67 school year would continue unless terminated by the board by certified mail prior to the end of the school year. Although the new law eliminated the requirement for annual renewals, terminating a teacher or principal's employment remained relatively simple, with no specific grounds required.[75]

Federal court decisions in the latter 1960s had rendered some sections of the North Carolina Constitution clearly unconstitutional, among them certain education clauses that still included the Pearsall Plan's provisions for educational expense grants and local option school closing in order to avoid desegregation. Governor Moore appointed a commission, chaired by former State Supreme Court chief justice Emery B. Denny, to study improvements to the public school system and revisions to the State Constitution.[76] The commission developed amendment proposals for submission to the legislature and to the voters, deleting the Pearsall Plan,[77] extending the mandatory school term to nine months, making school attendance compulsory, and eliminating the poll tax and literacy test as requirements for voting.[78] The requisite three-fifths majority of both House and Senate approved the package,[79] and the electorate approved all the constitutional amendments except abolition of the literacy test.[80] The literacy test was unenforceable, anyway, due to federal legislation that prohibited the use of literacy tests to prevent blacks from voting.

The Election of 1968

The election of 1968 once again revealed deep feelings in North Carolina regarding race. In the Democratic Primary, Lieutenant Governor Robert W. Scott, son of former governor Kerr Scott and a member of the progressive Sanford wing of the Democratic Party, ran against Dr. Reginald Hawkins of Charlotte, a prominent black civil rights activist, and J. Melville Broughton, also the son of a former governor. In spite of Scott's standing in the relatively liberal wing of the party, he kicked off his campaign with a strong law-and-order speech in Harnett County.[81] The vote tally in May was 337,368 for Scott, 233,924 for Broughton, and 129,808 for Hawkins.[82]

In the general election, Scott faced Republican James C. Gardner. Hawkins endorsed Scott. Scott responded that he had not sought the endorsement but did not believe it would have an adverse effect on his campaign.[83] This virtual repudiation of Hawkins's endorsement grew out of Scott's belief that North Carolina voters would not support a candidate strongly identified with civil rights.[84] Scott defeated Gardner, 821,232 to 737,075.[85] Robert Morgan of Harnett County, former ally of I. Beverly Lake, was elected attorney general.[86]

In the presidential election, Republican Richard M. Nixon carried North Carolina with 627,192 votes. Nixon based his campaign to a significant extent on a strategy designed to appeal to southern whites who were angry over the threat of busing and alienated by affirmative action and other employment practices growing out of the civil rights movement.[87] Nixon couched strong, race-related sentiments in respectable language in public, while ranting in private. Nixon's media adviser, Roger Ailes, would later found the Fox News Network, dedicated to presenting news from a conservative point of view.[88]

Liberal Democratic candidate Hubert H. Humphrey received 464,113 votes in North Carolina. Humphrey placed third among the state's voters, however. The runner-up was Alabama governor George C. Wallace, an avowed segregationist, who received 496,188 votes.[89] The votes for Wallace thus imply that popular sentiment toward strong racial conservatism, even in support of segregation, was growing, as people perceived desegregation as moving apace. The totals for Nixon suggest at least opposition to liberalism in racial matters, certainly opposition to large-scale school district reorganization to support desegregation, as well as opposition to busing. The election also brought into office a new state superintendent, A. Craig Phillips, former superintendent of the Charlotte schools.[90] Phillips was committed to desegregation. Under Phillips, the State Department of Public Instruction would no longer play a passive role.

New National Precedents

Two U.S. Supreme Court decisions in 1968 and 1969 established new, stronger mandates for school desegregation. The national NAACP team argued *Green v. County School Board of New Kent County* in Virginia. The local board had adopted a freedom-of-choice plan in 1965 under pressure of litigation. In three years, however, no white student had chosen to attend a black school, and 85 percent of the black students in the system still attended all-black schools. This clear pattern of separate white and black schools, originally established under compulsion of law, represented "precisely the pattern of segregation . . . which [*Brown*] declared unconstitutionally denied Negro children equal protection of the laws," the court concluded.

Green further admonished district courts to assess the effectiveness of proposed desegregation plans with regard to actual results. A freedom-of-choice plan no longer bore any standing as an end in itself. The court concluded, "The burden on a school board today is to come forward with a plan that promises realistically to work, and promises realistically to work *now* [original emphasis]."[91] *Green* thus established the actual level of integration as the only relevant test of whether a school system was practicing racial discrimination.[92] In impact, *Green* became the decision that ranked second only to *Brown* in desegregation litigation.

Alexander v. Holmes County Board of Education, another NAACP-backed case originating in Mississippi, further warned that the "all deliberate speed" standard for desegregation was no longer applicable. "Under explicit holdings of this Court the obligation of every school district is to terminate dual school systems *at once* [emphasis added, but used by the court in subsequent decisions] and to operate now and hereafter only unitary schools."[93] President Nixon publicly supported Mississippi's side of the argument, generating praise from South Carolina Senator Strom Thurmond. Governor George Wallace of Alabama denounced the court's decision.[94]

Green and *Alexander* clearly mandated that schools had to be desegregated without further delay. The only remaining question involved remedies that would be utilized. By the late 1960s the issue of busing had become volatile. President Nixon issued a lengthy statement, stating his opposition to busing and urging that children be permitted to attend neighborhood schools.[95] The North Carolina General Assembly of 1969 passed legislation outlawing assignment of pupils based on race, creed, color, or national origin, but also prohibiting busing pupils for the purpose of racial balance.[96]

The tuition grant phase of the Pearsall Plan had been in existence for five years before anyone tried to use it. That application was rejected. After almost five more years, following another application, a federal district court voided the plan altogether. No one ever made formal application to implement the school-closing feature of the plan. The only effect the Pearsall Plan ever had was placating strong segregationists who wanted the power to close schools rather than desegregate. That "safety valve" was precisely what Governor Luther H. Hodges had claimed he intended, and it worked. Neither Hodges nor any of his associates sought to manipulate racial issues for personal or political gain. They saved the public school system while staving off precipitous efforts from strong segregationists to shift to a system of public funding for private schools.

Litigation in North Carolina showed that freedom-of-choice plans and measures that depended on individual initiatives produced little actual desegregation, as well as revealing the depth of discrimination practiced throughout the state. Freedom-of-choice plans, the hallmark of white response to desegregation, became invalid because they produced almost no results. Desegregation required more than the reassignment of pupils. Teachers and administrators had to be reorganized as well. The period of desegregation witnessed negative consequences for some black teachers. For black administrators, the impact was devastating, virtually wiping out a leadership class in the black community.

Desegregation was carried out during a time of racial unrest in the state and the nation. Southern whites grew angry over busing and felt alienated by affirmative action and other employment practices growing out of the civil rights movement. White anger manifested itself in politics, resulting in the success of conservative candidates at the national level, most notably Richard Nixon, who was elected president in large measure on the basis of a strategy designed to appeal to alienated whites while maintaining no positions overtly related to race.

North Carolina followed suit, supporting Nixon while also providing a substantial number of votes for extreme conservative George Wallace, whose campaign was clearly based on racism. In response to demonstrations and public unrest, Governor Moore tended to focus on maintaining order, not advancing civil rights. In 1968, the state elected Bob Scott, who positioned himself as a conservative. As desegregation moved forward, reaction was beginning to grow, a trend that would become dominant a couple of decades later.

At the same time the population was beginning to grow more conservative, courts were pressing forward with ever stronger desegregation orders. Litigation in Virginia produced another pivotal case. *Green v. County School Board of New Kent County* warned school systems that they must desegregate forthwith. Plans and procedures would no longer be the focus of court review. By the end of the 1960s, only actual results mattered. A pattern of practices created by government action that resulted in racial subordination would have to be dismantled by government action.

7

System-wide Desegregation

LATE 1960S TO LATE 1970S

By the late 1960s, token desegregation had been carried out in school districts all over North Carolina. Boards of education in the state had not resisted desegregation. Their common response, however, utilized freedom-of-choice plans, which had become standard throughout the South. These plans placed the burden of desegregation on individual families, applying for transfers one child at a time. As an outgrowth of the Civil Rights Act of 1964, desegregation guidelines were developed requiring boards to prepare comprehensive desegregation plans. The federal government, through the Office of Civil Rights in the Department of Health, Education, and Welfare (OCR/HEW), therefore, became the primary driving force behind desegregation. School boards also continued to face litigation.

Public opposition to busing had become widespread, however, and the growing conservative movement had developed a strong political base. In North Carolina, that base did not go as far as the strong race-related conservatism of George Wallace of Alabama, but it did solidify allegiance to Richard Nixon and the veiled racial conservatism embodied by the new orientation of the Republican Party.

How far would boards of education have to go in order to desegregate schools? How would the public react? Further litigation in North Carolina would provide the answer.

Federal Courts in North Carolina in the 1970s

When school systems were sued, in most cases by black parents with support from the NAACP, desegregation was ordered and monitored by federal courts. The jurisdictions of three federal courts covered North Carolina. The number of judges on each court expanded to two during the 1960s.[1] Six judges, therefore, heard most of the North Carolina cases from the late 1960s through the late 1970s that resulted in system-wide desegregation orders. Appeals from U.S. District Courts led to the Fourth Circuit Court of Appeals.

Judges Algernon Butler and John Larkins presided over the Eastern District of North Carolina. Judge Butler had studied law at the University of North Carolina and served in the legislature in 1931. A Republican, he had been nominated by President Eisenhower in 1959.[2] He served as chief judge from 1961 to 1975, assuming senior status in 1975. At the time of his death three years later, the Wilmington *Star-News* described him as "the man considered most responsible for the desegregation of schools in eastern North Carolina."[3] Judge Larkins attended Wake Forest Law School.[4] He did not have enough money to complete the required coursework, but the dean arranged for him to take the bar exam early. He passed the bar exam at age twenty, a year before the age required for a law license.[5] A 1961 Kennedy appointee, he succeeded Butler as chief judge, serving in that status from 1975 to 1979, when he assumed senior status. Prior to appointment to the bench, he had served several terms in the North Carolina Senate; he was president pro tem 1941–43, and he chaired the Democratic Party from 1954 to 1958. He served as counsel for Governor Hodges in 1955, when the Pearsall Plan was being developed and passed. In an unsuccessful campaign for governor against Terry Sanford in 1960, Larkins had not supported desegregation.

Judge Edwin Stanley presided over one seat on the U.S. Middle District Court from the 1960s through the early 1970s. A Wake Forest law graduate, Stanley was appointed by President Eisenhower in 1957; he served as chief judge from 1961 until his death in 1971. Hiram Ward succeeded him, on an appointment by President Nixon. Ward served as chief judge from 1982 to 1988, assuming senior status in 1988; he continued in that role until his death in 2002. President Johnson nominated Eugene Gordon in 1964 to the other Middle District seat. A graduate of Duke Law School, he served as chief judge from 1971 to 1982, assuming senior status in 1982.

For the Western District, Woodrow Wilson Jones, a Wake Forest law graduate, was appointed by President Johnson in 1967. He served as chief judge from 1968 to 1984, assuming senior status in 1985, continuing until his death in 2002. He had served in the legislature from 1947 to 1949, and in the U.S. Congress from 1950 to 1957. He was a member of the commission appointed by Governor Hodges to consider constitutional revisions.[6] Judge James B. McMillan was a Robeson County native who had graduated from the University of North

Carolina and then received his law degree from Harvard. McMillan's appointment by President Johnson in 1968 had followed a recommendation from Senator Sam Ervin, based to some extent, McMillan believed, on the perception that he had not been vocal in support of desegregation.[7] He assumed senior status in 1989; his service terminated in 1995, upon his death.

Nothing in their personal histories would suggest that any of these judges would be zealots for desegregation. But although their personal, political, and professional backgrounds were different, and some had been appointed by Democratic administrations, others by Republicans, the patterns of their decisions would be quite similar. They would follow the course compelling desegregation, as guided by the U.S. Supreme Court.

Swann II

After the *Green* decision, Julius Chambers refiled *Swann,* based on his perception that *Green* signaled a Supreme Court shift in favor of more rapid desegregation.[8] Judge James B. McMillan heard *Swann II,* his first important case after appointment to the federal bench.[9] Judge McMillan complimented the board for achieving a higher level of desegregation than any of the other school systems reviewed in appellate court decisions.[10] But the policies the board had implemented, no matter how well they compared to other districts, were no longer adequate. Approximately fourteen thousand of the Charlotte-Mecklenburg school system's twenty-four thousand black students still attended all-black schools taught by black teachers. Pointing to *Green,* McMillan directed the board to submit a new desegregation plan.

The Supreme Court issued *Alexander* after McMillan's initial, April 1969 ruling. In December, Judge McMillan reviewed the board's revised plan. This time McMillan found that more than sixteen thousand black students would still attend virtually all-black schools. Approximately 90 percent of the faculties in the system remained obviously black or white. Moreover, student achievement varied considerably according to attendance in racially identifiable schools.[11] McMillan therefore ordered the system to prepare another plan. A key element, and a source of much controversy, was the inclusion of racial ratios as target goals.[12] In February 1970, McMillan found that the board had still failed to submit a plan that would effectively desegregate all the schools.

Consequently, he issued new orders based on suggestions from a consultant, Dr. John Finger of Rhode Island College.[13] The board appealed, and the Fourth Circuit Court of Appeals vacated the orders with regard to busing elementary students.[14] The U.S. Supreme Court reinstated McMillan's judgment,[15] however, and remanded the case.[16] In August 1970, Judge McMillan found that more than nine thousand black students still attended all-black schools; fifty-seven schools remained clearly white, twenty-five clearly black.[17]

Many people in the community ostracized McMillan, and he and his family received threats. During the appeals process, Governor Scott and the State Board of Education denounced McMillan's busing orders. An organized opposition group of white parents conveyed petitions bearing more than sixty-seven thousand signatures to a sympathetic Nixon administration.[18] President Nixon issued a statement reinforcing his opposition to busing, again urging that students be permitted to attend neighborhood schools.[19]

The Supreme Court agreed to review the remanded order.[20] Chief Justice Warren Burger, a recent Nixon appointee, broke with court tradition by electing to write the opinion himself, even though initial discussions indicated that only Burger and Hugo Black favored overturning McMillan's orders. Burger wanted to narrow the decision.[21] His initial draft fell in line with the Nixon administration's anti-busing, neighborhood-school positions. As finally issued, however, *Swann* placed the court firmly on the side of eliminating segregation, using whatever means necessary. *Swann* cautioned that a district court could not require quotas at specific schools. McMillan's order, however, had only mentioned ratios as a general guide. Racially identifiable schools created a burden of proof for the school system that assignments had not grown out of discrimination. Where discrimination was found, courts possessed broad powers to order school redistricting and busing.[22]

The white public reacted bitterly. A bomb exploded at Julius Chambers's office in 1971.[23] During the 1970–71 and 1971–72 school years, nine of Charlotte-Mecklenburg's ten high schools had to be closed for several days during tense periods. Charlotte-Mecklenburg lost approximately ten thousand white students as white parents moved their families to rural districts over the next few years.

Moderate leadership prevailed, though, and a constructive response emerged. Editorials in the *Charlotte Observer* helped set the stage. In February 1972, C.D. Spangler Jr., a prominent real estate developer, announced his candidacy for the Board of Education, advising citizens that the court had spoken and the law had to be obeyed. Board chair William Poe, who had been opposed to busing, told school patrons that the question was no longer whether students would be bused but what kind of schools they would find when they arrived. W. T. Harris, who chaired the Mecklenburg County commissioners, joined in promotion of the moderate tone. Within schools, students staged "love-ins" in concert with the mood of the 1960s and early 1970s, pledging mutual respect and cooperation.[24]

Draft plans developed by the board had protected wealthy neighborhoods and placed the burden of bus rides on black children, along with middle- and lower-income whites. New plans were prepared in cooperation with parent groups during 1972–73, spreading the impact of busing.[25] These developments occurred under the leadership of Superintendent William Self, whose term ended in 1973. Dr. Rolland Jones succeeded him. In 1974, Judge McMillan entered an order approving the revised plan and expressing gratitude to the board, to citizens who had assisted in development of the plan, and to the school system staff. In 1975 McMillan closed the case.[26] Implementation and maintenance of widespread busing would fall to another superintendent, Dr. Jay Robinson, who served from 1977 to 1987.[27]

Patterns of Compliance

Why was reopening *Swann* necessary? The meaning of the *Brown* decisions was clear, the Civil Rights Act had outlawed segregation in 1964 and authorized enforcement by the federal government, and federal courts had ordered school systems to desegregate forthwith. School systems in the South had not been desegregated, though, and doubt remained as to how far the courts would go to ensure the elimination of dual school systems.

HEW had cut off federal funds to school systems in Alabama, Arkansas, Georgia, Mississippi, Tennessee, and South Carolina.[28] But in North Carolina, by summer 1965, desegregation plans in 31 North Carolina school systems had been approved. Of the remaining 138 systems, 72 had submitted plans that were still being reviewed.[29] But only 5 percent of the State's black students were attending school with whites.[30] The Caswell, Lenoir, Granville, Hyde, Chowan, Richmond, Elm City, Kinston, Fremont, Franklinton, and Morven systems received notice in the mid-1960s that federal funds for new programs would be held in abeyance until further desegregation was achieved. But no North Carolina system experienced outright termination of funds in the manner of other southern states.

All school systems were submitting desegregation plans to the OCR. But school administrators felt that lack of clarity plagued negotiations with the office. OCR officials avoided using the word "quota," but school systems found themselves trying to hit a moving target. Salisbury, for example, received a series of letters congratulating them on achieving unitary status, but later threatening them with funds elimination as punishment for inadequate progress.[31]

Developments in the Guilford County system illustrate the quandary school administrators and boards faced. Board attorney John Hardy advised in 1965 that board members could submit a signed form to HEW certifying full compliance with desegregation guidelines. But since such certification was patently not true, that was not an appropriate course of action. Or the board could do nothing, in which case they could expect to be sued. Or they could submit a voluntary plan for further desegregation to HEW.[32] Board members and Superintendent E. P. Pearce, following an outline supplied by State Superintendent Charles F. Carroll and Assistant Attorney General Ralph Moody, approved a freedom-of-choice plan for early grades, combined with reassignments of sixteen students in ninth grade to formerly white schools.

Guilford County had never provided a comprehensive high school for black students. Such deficits were typical among county school systems in the state. If county systems provided any high school education at all for black students, and most did not, those grades were housed in union schools that also contained elementary grades. The sort of coursework and laboratory facilities associated with comprehensive high schools were seldom, if ever, available to rural black students, and sometimes not to rural white students.

So another 62 students in high-school grades were assigned to black city high schools, a measure often used by county school systems. HEW rejected Guilford County's proposal, without specifying why or providing suggestions for revision. An appointment with HEW officials was arranged. But when Pearce, Hardy, and board chair Howard Carr arrived, the HEW officer failed to show up, and the individual who met with them was obviously not familiar with the plan the board had submitted. The delegation returned to Greensboro in a state of severe frustration.

A new plan provided for freedom of choice in all grades in 1967. In the interim, 119 black students were reassigned to formerly white schools. Several dozen more were reassigned before fall 1966. HEW subsequently demanded freedom of choice for all grades by 1966, a year earlier than requested in previous communications with HEW officials. All transfer requests had to be approved for 1965–66. The board acquiesced. Francis Keppel, the U.S. commissioner of education, notified the board of approval in October 1965.

Faculties throughout the district were reassigned on a desegregated basis by 1967. By 1967–68, only two schools remained all-white, although the black schools remained all-black. In 1970, OCR director Leon Panetta notified Guilford County that the schools were out of compliance, previous approvals notwithstanding. Multiple meetings with different HEW officials eventually produced district reorganization based on pairing formerly all-white with formerly all-black schools, splitting grade levels kindergarten through second and third through sixth between paired schools. Consolidated junior and senior high schools, most new or under construction, would enroll all students, black and white. District administrators and board members expressed dissatisfaction with the plan, but considered it preferable to further negotiations with HEW or a court order that would probably be even more unpalatable. By 1970–71, all of Guilford County's black students were attending desegregated schools. HEW declared Guilford County in full compliance (again) in October 1970.

Desegregation in Guilford County thus benefited all students, white as well as black, in the form of new, consolidated, comprehensive high schools that replaced white union schools that had contained all grades from primary through high school, and providing black students with their first opportunity in history to attend a comprehensive high school within their own neighborhoods within the same school district.

Similar experiences along with comparable progress took place among other districts in North Carolina. In 1966–67, 12.8 percent of the state's black students were attending desegregated schools.[33] HEW commended North Carolina, Florida, Tennessee, Virginia, Texas, and Arkansas for progress. South Carolina, Alabama, Georgia, Mississippi, and Louisiana had attained levels of desegregation less than half the North Carolina level. By 1968–69, 27.8 percent of North Carolina's black students were attending desegregated schools.[34] Among the southern states, only Texas had achieved more. In 1970–71, approximately 50 percent of North Carolina's black students attended desegregated schools.[35]

Most of this progress was initiated and sustained under the Scott administration. Once in office, Governor Scott moved the state's position regarding school desegregation from neutrality to assistance. The policy shift came about as a result of the *Godwin* case and growing pressure from the courts and the federal government, as well as initiatives from the new state superintendent, Craig Phillips.

In the latter days of the Moore administration, the state had established a Technical Assistance Center for desegregation, funded by a federal grant. Phillips initiated the application prior to taking office. He met with a warm response at the federal level. No other southern state had sought to establish a desegregation assistance office.[36] Bob Strother,[37] former superintendent of the Greene County Schools, headed the new agency. Gene Causby, a white principal from Goldsboro, and Dudley Flood, a black principal from Pitt County, were the team's field representatives.[38] The Department of Public Instruction (DPI) team provided most of the direct support for local school systems, with the Governor's Office marshaling additional resources as needed. Whenever a difficult situation appeared to be developing, Flood and Causby contacted David Murray in Governor Scott's office, who had direct access to the State Highway Patrol and the State Bureau of Investigation, under Director Charles Dunn. The State Human Relations Council and local Good Neighbor Councils were involved as well.

Governor Scott took personal action, too. Early in his administration, when his daughter's school in eastern Alamance County opened following implementation of a desegregated pupil-assignment plan, he paid a personal visit. His symbolic action generated extensive television news coverage. One other key member of the Scott administration was Attorney General Robert Morgan, who had earned a reputation as a staunch conservative. But he also believed deeply in obeying the law. Morgan could go into a resistant community and tell people they had to obey the law, and they would accept his counsel out of respect for him, when they were not willing to follow admonitions from anybody else.[39]

At first, the DPI desegregation assistance team operated under two basic tenets: they had to be invited by the local school superintendent, and the school system had to have been declared out of compliance with desegregation orders, either by a court or by HEW. Soon, however, the team began working with any schools that asked for help.[40] Virtually all assistance was carried out verbally, through personal mediation; hardly anything was documented.[41]

Flood and Causby eventually consulted with every school district in the state, either as intermediaries with OCR, helping school systems develop desegregation plans, or by eliciting public cooperation with plans that had been developed. They held meetings in churches, community centers, even tobacco barns, but they tried not to meet in schools, carefully avoiding symbols of authority. Their strategy centered on establishing at the outset that no one intended to do wrong to any child. But if a plan could lead to more children being better taught, that would become the goal. Three guidelines had to be followed. Whatever the group decided had to be educationally sound. It had to be legal. And a consensus had to be formed that was approved by school administrators and that would generate broad support in the community.

As in Guilford County, one of the most common solutions to pupil assignments involved pairing formerly black and white schools that were located within some proximity of each other. In rural areas, where black residences were scattered, desegregation usually proceeded fairly smoothly. Where large, multifamily housing resulted in high concentrations of poverty and large numbers of black families, desegregation and everything else related to improving schooling proved much more difficult. Commonalities appeared among successful situations: strong, positive leadership on the part of the superintendent and board, as well as teachers and administrators; supportive involvement from prominent business leaders; the maintenance of a moral tone, often voiced by local ministers; and widespread community participation in the development and promulgation of desegregation plans.

Potentially volatile issues often centered on participation in athletics and other extracurricular activities. Symbols were important. The pupil populations of formerly black and white schools had to be merged. But what school colors would become the symbols for a newly desegregated school? Many schools settled on tricolors, where one color that had been common to both schools was added to two that were new. Another concern was the perception among black parents that the white schools were simply absorbing the black schools, retaining none of the traditions that had been valuable to the identity of the black community.

Flood and Causby found that, whenever they could get students together, help them talk to each other, and empower them, the students themselves invariably came up with good solutions. Flood recalls: "We never had any power, and we never talked to them in the context of power. They just thought we were some guys who liked them well enough to want to come by and talk to them. DPI didn't mean anything to them, and DPI did not mean much to community people. Gene and I were about as non-threatening as anybody you could find. Gene could laugh more freely than anybody I ever met. He could make others laugh, too. And whenever we could get people to see humor in a situation, we could start to teach through the use of that humor."[42]

Degrees of difficulty varied considerably, but every school district in the state experienced some level of disruption. The Piedmont, where blacks constituted a large minority, posed the most difficult problems. Organizing functions so that blacks received some degree of parity was difficult, because whites saw guaranteeing black participation as "tampering with a concept of color-blindness that had become almost religious,"[43] in Causby's words.

The Greensboro city system, located within Guilford County, provides a particularly positive illustration of the process. Greensboro was among the last of the state's largest cities to implement busing, but its plan featured unusually solid preparation.[44] In 1970, Dr. George Simkins, local NAACP branch president, and a group of black parents had filed suit. The Board of Education reached a settlement by the end of the year.

For Al Lineberry, who chaired the board, the decision to end segregation had been made long ago: "I was sitting in a little restaurant downtown, eating breakfast. It was rainy, icy. I remember to this day what I was eating—country ham, grits, and eggs. And I saw, behind the door, this black lady. I was brought up in Memphis, Tennessee, and I was taught the racial code just like any other white growing up in the South. She had two children with her. I could tell they were hungry. She looked in, but she waited. And waited. She wasn't asking for a handout, she had the money to pay. But then she had to go back out in the cold and give the food to her children to eat, outside, in the cold rain. Quietly, I began to cry."[45]

Early on, members of the business community, working through the Chamber of Commerce, created discussion groups so that blacks and whites could meet quietly and get acquainted. Lineberry and other business leaders concluded, "It was clear that we would be lagging [with regard to economic development] in this part of the country if we didn't do a better job of educating more of our children." Early on, the board initiated conversations with local ministers. Lineberry credits Rev. Otis Hairston, a black minister, for the positive influence he exerted on leaders of the white community.[46]

During the spring and summer of 1971, black and white community leaders attended retreats where they got to know each other and practiced techniques for cooperation. Three black administrators, Fred Cundiff, Julius Fulmore, and Mel Swann, prominent in the black community, played key roles. Meetings at schools enabled parents to visit with teachers and administrators and with each other. Mayor E. S. "Jim" Melvin proclaimed August 15 as "Public School Sunday," and on that day almost every minister in the city preached a sermon on the theme of racial harmony.[47] They spoke to their congregations about nurturing children and thinking about the changes that were underway. Sermons emphasized that the change was not about color, it was about doing the right thing by giving all children equal opportunities for education.[48]

The following Sunday, every school bus in the city carried approximately thirty thousand parents to the schools their children would be attending, where parents met their children's new teachers. In North Carolina, the state provides transportation to schools by allocating buses to local districts. Dudley Flood recalls discussing with Superintendent "Wink" House whether the use of state-owned buses to transport parents instead of students was legal. "We were pretty sure that if we asked the Department of Transportation for permission, they would say 'absolutely not.' So we volunteered that they go ahead and do it, and if Raleigh heard about it, we would swear that administrators in Greensboro could not possibly have been crazy enough to do anything like that."[49] Administrators in Raleigh probably found out about the use of the buses, but they never raised the issue.

During the early days of busing, Lineberry, his wife, and his children were threatened. He and his family had around-the-clock police protection. But gradually, students in a fully desegregated school system learned to experience normal school days. Regarding the progress of school desegregation, Dr. Simkins subsequently commented, "I feel so proud to say I'm from Greensboro."[50]

Other communities experienced similar successes, along with varying degrees of difficulty. But they all desegregated their schools.

North Carolina Politics and Education through the 1970s

North Carolina's political leaders competed to improve education during the mid- to late 1970s. In the election of 1972, the people chose Republican James Holshouser[51] over Democrat Hargrove "Skipper" Bowles, who had held a position in the Sanford administration.[52] Holshouser was the first Republican governor in the twentieth century. Bowles based his campaign on career education, a curriculum to serve a broader range of students. Some educators as well as voters in general perceived career education as a form of tracking students into lower academic courses, creating a stratified education system. Holshouser emphasized ways to improve traditional structures: expansion of kindergarten, class size reduction, and improved buildings, in addition to renovations to roads and bridges, as well as improving financial efficiency.[53] *Time* magazine termed Holshouser "notably liberal on racial matters."[54] In 1973, he gave the Founder's Day address for African Methodist Episcopal (AME) churches, one of the largest black denominations in the nation.

The Holshouser administration secured passage of a $300 million bond issue to supplement local efforts in school construction, added a tenth month to teacher employment, provided paid vacation for teachers, made principals year-round employees, and initiated state-funded kindergarten. Class sizes were reduced, and improved retirement benefits were funded for educators and other state employees.[55] An initiative begun in 1975, the Primary Reading Program, added an assistant in each classroom grades one through three and provided materials and professional development for reading teachers and assistants.[56] These initiatives were accomplished in spite of a serious recession and an energy crisis that plagued the economy.[57]

The 1972 election also brought in a Republican U.S. senator from North Carolina. One of the strongest voices in opposition to forced desegregation had emerged from Jesse Helms, the radio commentator whose political career had been forged during the Willis Smith–Frank Porter Graham campaign. Helms subsequently spent two years in Washington as a member of Smith's staff. He moved to WRAL television in Raleigh in 1960, where he broadcast editorials for twelve years. The voice track was rebroadcast over seventy rural radio stations, with the content reprinted in approximately two hundred newspapers.[58]

Helms ran for the Senate seat which had been held by B. Everett Jordan, who had been defeated in the Democratic Primary by Nick

Galifianakis. Helms won by 54 percent, the first time North Carolina had elected a Republican senator since 1903.[59] Helms's supporters organized the Congressional Club, first, to help raise funds to pay off campaign debts, but later, to serve the interests of other conservative candidates. Raleigh attorney Tom Ellis, former staff attorney for the second Pearsall Committee, was a key leader.[60] Helms won reelection over State Insurance Commissioner John Ingram in 1978, with 54.5 percent.[61]

Helms always maintained that he harbored no racist attitudes. "I thought it was wrong for people who did not know, and who did not care, about the relationships between neighbors and friends to force their ideas about how communities should work on the people who had built those communities in the first place." To Helms, the southern way of life was based on "customs and institutions people cared about. Black neighbors and white neighbors depended on each other, and the vast majority lived in harmony,"[62] Helms believed. But he and other conservatives used language that appeared neutral but carried racial undertones.[63] He and other Republicans were able to associate Democratic opponents with "black causes and cultural radicalism."[64] North Carolina's other seat in the U.S. Senate was held for twenty years (1954–74) by Sam Ervin, who, according to Senator Helms, was a consistent ally with Helms and the conservative cause.[65] When Ervin left office, Robert Morgan, an Ervin protégé, succeeded him. Although he had begun his political career as a strong conservative, Morgan by this time had earned significant respect across a broad political spectrum, due in part to his service as state attorney general. Morgan would serve only one term, however.

North Carolina also voted to reelect President Richard M. Nixon in 1972. The election occurred during a nationwide period of unrest.[66] The Nixon administration had already begun to unravel, however, first with the resignation of Vice-President Spiro Agnew in 1973, following revelations of financial irregularities while he was governor of Maryland,[67] then with the resignation of the president himself in 1974 due to the Watergate scandal.[68] During the Watergate hearings, one of the Senate's most memorable voices came from Senator Sam Ervin, whose deep reverence for the U.S. Constitution represented a variety of conservatism that appeared to have been lost in the Nixon administration's passion for power. Judicial appointments made during the Nixon administration would survive long after his administration, ultimately reversing the path of school desegregation.

The Federal Judiciary and National Litigation in the Mid-1970s

From 1968 to 1972, a combination of retirements and scandals enabled President Nixon to replace four justices on the U.S. Supreme Court. Earl Warren retired in 1968, and Warren Burger replaced him as chief justice in 1969. Abe Fortas resigned during the same period, after allegations that he had accepted, then returned, money from the family of an individual who had been indicted on charges of stock manipulation. Fortas denied any wrongdoing.[69] Harry Blackmun replaced Fortas. Justices Hugo Black and John Marshall Harlan retired in 1971. William Rehnquist and Lewis Powell took seats in 1972.[70] Those appointments created a court with a majority that tended toward conservatism.

The shift in membership produced two decisions in 1973 that began a pattern of retrenchment in pupil assignment requirements. In *San Antonio Independent School District v. Rodriguez,*[71] the court ruled that children had no *federal* right to education and that unequal funding in education did not violate the Constitution. This finding spawned a series of suits at the state level, producing rulings that *state* constitutions did create a right to education.[72]

The Supreme Court subsequently ruled in *Keyes v. Denver School District No. 1*[73] that, when school assignments produce segregated schools, the school system must bear the burden of proving that discriminatory intent was not present.[74] Justice Rehnquist dissented, arguing that *Green* had constituted a "drastic extension" of *Brown,* moving beyond the elimination of discrimination to requiring "racial mixing in schools" that should not be applied in situations where segregation did not grow out of state action. His opinion would have, in effect, made *de facto* segregation legal, as opposed to situations that had been mandated by law—*de jure* segregation.[75]

The year 1974 saw a case that would move the court toward Rehnquist's position. *Milliken v. Bradley*[76] looked at the overwhelmingly black school system of Detroit, situated among overwhelmingly white suburban school systems, and concluded that desegregation orders could not cross school-system boundaries. The decision effectively eliminated the prospect of judicial mandates to integrate big-city school systems in the North. All four of President Nixon's appointees joined Justice Stewart to create a five member majority.[77] This split opinion stood in contrast to previous school-desegregation cases, which usually had been unanimous.[78]

Although desegregation had been proceeding with general success, at least regarding compliance with legal mandates, a phenomenon termed "white flight" began to plague school officials in the state and nation. By 1970, more than 230 new private academies, most enrolling only white students, had opened in North Carolina.[79] More than thirty-five thousand white students had enrolled in private, all-white schools by 1971.[80] The private-academy movement was especially strong in the East, where the black population was largest. Even in the Piedmont area, Greensboro City, Winston-Salem City, Charlotte-Mecklenburg, and Wake County reported losing substantial numbers of white students. Most disconcerting was the loss of upper- and middle-class whites.[81] The fear that state leaders had expressed in the 1950s and early 1960s was becoming reality.

Desegregation in National Context: The Beginning of Retrenchment

Although some withdrew their children, a large majority of parents of all socioeconomic strata left their children in the public schools, and those schools were desegregated. By the 1970s, the utilization of busing to eliminate racial separation eliminated just about every all-black school in North Carolina.[82] At the end of the 1972–73 school year, 99.5 percent of the state's black students were attending desegregated schools. Over 90 percent of the state's school systems had been formally declared unitary, either by courts or by OCR/HEW. By the end of the 1973–74 school year, North Carolina was operating the most thoroughly desegregated school system in the South, and the South was the most thoroughly desegregated region in the nation.[83]

During this period, desegregation in the nation's large urban centers, primarily in the North and West, generated just as much resistance as early desegregation initiatives in the South had, a decade or more earlier. Violence erupted in connection with school desegregation in Denver, Colorado; Pontiac, Michigan; Trenton, New Jersey; as well as Lamar, South Carolina. In Boston, Judge Arthur Garrity ordered the transportation of some twenty-one thousand students across the city's racially identifiable neighborhoods. Riots broke out in the high schools of Hyde Park, Roxbury, and South Boston. Governor Francis Sargent mobilized the National Guard and sought federal assistance from the new president, Gerald Ford. Educators, students, and parents from Boston began visiting Charlotte to study how Charlotte had managed desegregation and busing peacefully and effectively.

Congress passed legislation in 1976 prohibiting HEW from withholding federal funds to force busing.[84] By the end of the 1970s, formal desegregation essentially ceased as a point of focus for federal enforcement in the legislative and executive branches, and thus also ceased for school systems, although efforts to avoid civil rights violations continued. OCR maintained monitoring of some school systems into the early 1980s, in the form of annual reports, but the level of intervention that had characterized the 1970s passed away.

Religion and a Moral Voice: A Third Impetus for Change

Awareness of discrimination and efforts to end discriminatory practices expanded under pressure from the civil rights movement that developed gradually, amplifying dissonance where white leaders had imagined harmony, eventually threatening to bring the economy of the state and nation to a standstill. White people realized that the demands of black citizens had to be accommodated if state and nation were to continue to move toward improved prosperity.

The civil rights movement utilized tactics that varied according to the temperaments of different organizations. Direct pressure produced admission to public accommodations and created a political and legal setting more favorable to desegregation in other walks of life. NAACP-sponsored litigation, however, constituted the primary impetus for the desegregation of public schools.

Until passage of the 1964 Civil Rights Act, the NAACP was the only organization in the nation using lawsuits as its primary strategy. In North Carolina, Kelly Alexander argued for years that courtrooms were the best venue to address racial injustice. Under his leadership, the state chapter sponsored more school desegregation litigation in the 1950s than any other chapter in the South. A decade later, the judicial system began to order what the political system had not been willing to provide.[85] Thus, the NAACP's legal strategy in pursuit of equal educational opportunity was validated.

The force of moral suasion created another impetus for social change. Michael B. Friedland, in his history of the clergy's role in the civil rights movement, relates how black ministers and other civil rights leaders couched the public struggle in the context of

> fellowship, justice, and love, of bringing people together in legal, moral and ethical terms. . . . Ministers, priests, and rabbis found it hard to

> ignore Martin Luther King Jr.'s skillful use of prophetic imagery from the Old Testament; even those moderates who were unwilling to support civil rights marches could condemn racial bigotry. Those who used the Bible to support segregation and racial inequality were generally looked upon as a fringe group, a minority. By appealing to Americans to live up to their creeds of equality and democracy, civil rights activists tried to invoke the most favorable images Americans had of themselves, even if the reality was found wanting.[86]

In North Carolina, leaders constantly appealed to the populace in the context of morality and religion. Jews, having shared a history of oppression, provided strong support for civil rights initiatives. A broad impetus in support of desegregation did not emerge from within southern Christian congregations, however. Formal, public, church-related initiatives supporting civil rights tended to flow from the upper reaches of denominations that had structured hierarchies. The North Carolina Council of Churches (NCC), one of the more liberal religious institutions, desegregated in the 1940s. With the onset of the civil rights movement, NCC initiated work in the improvement of race relations. The organization hired Rev. Jack Crum, a Methodist, to work on racial issues. Rev. Collins Kilburn, of the United Church of Christ, succeeded him. NCC was involved in many matters related to race, including desegregating public accommodations and with issues related to poverty, but seldom directly with school desegregation. Ministers often took the stance that some reasonable accommodation to civil rights was the right thing to do, but they addressed racial issues in a low-key manner. Few white ministers would dare participate in a civil rights demonstration or speak out strongly in specific support of integration.

A ministerial fellowship composed of mainline churches worked in conjunction with black churches, taking positions in support of civil rights, especially to the effect that churches should be open to membership without regard to race. Reverend Kilburn recalls a number of North Carolina ministers who took public positions in support of civil rights, including Eugene Owens of Myers Park Baptist in Charlotte; Randy Taylor, a Presbyterian minister in Charlotte; William C. Smith, a former campus minister at Duke University; Dan Sap of Christ Episcopal in Raleigh; Vernon Tyson of Edenton Street Methodist in Raleigh; Doug Aldrich, a Baptist minister in Raleigh and other parts of the state; Jack Bullard, a Baptist minister in Raleigh who moved to Charlotte to be head of the Charlotte Human Relations Council; and John Lewis of First Baptist in Raleigh, where Jesse Helms was a member.[87]

One of the strongest religious voices in the state came from W. W. Finlator, pastor of Pullen Memorial Baptist Church in Raleigh, which housed one of the more liberal congregations in North Carolina, including professors and theologians, as well as newspaper editors and reporters from the Raleigh *News and Observer* and the Associated Press. Finlator adds names to the list of North Carolina ministers who spoke out, albeit in soft tones, in favor of civil rights. The pioneer, he believes, was his predecessor at Pullen Memorial, Edwin McNeal Poteat. Robert Seymour of Binkley Memorial in Chapel Hill was also "out in the forefront."[88] A seminary professor, Jesse Weatherspoon, brother of the president of Carolina Power and Light, led early efforts to persuade the Southern Baptist Convention to adopt resolutions affirming the morality of desegregation. Others included Carlyle Marney, of Myers Park in Charlotte; and Dr. Carlyle Campbell, president of Meredith College, son of Archibald Campbell, founder of Campbell University.

Although he did not know it at the time, Finlator's sermons played an indirect role regarding developments in Charlotte's desegregation and adaptation to busing. William Friday, president of the University of North Carolina system, told Finlator that Jay Robinson, who had been superintendent of the Charlotte-Mecklenburg schools during the late 1970s through the 1980s, the period when busing was widespread, was very ill and probably was not going to live much longer. Finlator called Robinson in an effort to offer pastoral counsel and comfort. In their conversation, Robinson told Finlator, "When we were in the heart of all this, and none of us really knew what to do, silence descended among us. Then a voice was heard from Pullen Church, telling us that blacks had the right to be citizens. You'll never know how that one voice gave us room, let us move ahead. I cherish the memory of that conversation," Finlator recalls.[89] Robinson died in 2000.

Broad-based congregational change lagged, however.[90] Early in the civil rights period, leaders of the Southern Baptists, the largest white denomination in North Carolina, took a stand in support of ending discrimination on moral grounds.[91] The Southern Baptist Convention had a staff member, Corbin Cooper, whose job centered on racial issues, especially liaison with the black General Baptist Convention, which had been established after the Civil War.[92] But the body of the church, acting in the Baptist State Convention, would not formally respond positively to civil rights initiatives until 1989.[93]

Presbyterians tended to share the Baptists' ambivalence,[94] although in Charlotte, local Presbyterians helped push the city toward desegregation, utilizing the moral force of the church.[95] Other denominations—Quaker, Catholic, Episcopal, Lutheran, and Methodist—advanced a stronger moral imperative related to civil rights, albeit in varying degrees.[96] The United Church of Christ dissolved formal racial identification of churches in the 1960s, creating the most integrated religious body in the South, although individual churches tend to remain all or almost all of one race.[97]

Religion and appeals to morality thus exerted another important influence in support of civil rights in North Carolina, although quietly, in the background. Factors of a more worldly nature were certainly significant as well, especially recognition that the forces of the civil rights movement were capable of disrupting the state's economy. Davison M. Douglas has admirably analyzed the economic forces behind Charlotte's school desegregation. But Douglas also recognizes the existence of underlying moral forces.[98] The importance of the economic impetus should not be deemphasized, and this book has firmly established the legal impetus. Morality and religion, however, helped create and sustain momentum toward peaceful accommodation to civil rights, as well.

Swann v. Charlotte-Mecklenburg Board of Education became the third in a triumvirate of legal decisions that defined the parameters for school desegregation. *Brown* outlawed segregation but allowed an unspecified period of time for desegregation. *Green* warned that the time for adjustment had ended, that actual desegregation must be completed forthwith. *Swann* affirmed that courts could order virtually any means necessary, including busing, in order to achieve desegregation.

The 1970s also witnessed the beginnings of retrenchment in school desegregation, however, as a majority of conservative justices appointed after the Warren Court decided in *Milliken* that desegregation orders could not cross district boundaries, a decision that in essence validated *de facto* segregation and would become the guiding point of view in the future.

Three forces operated to shift North Carolina toward accommodation to desegregation and a more equitable pattern of practices related to race and education: legal, where lawsuits produced court-ordered redistricting in order to desegregate schools; economic, where business and community leaders realized that racial disruption threatened progress; and moral-religious, where leaders as well as the rank and file, especially mothers and fathers, began to consider equal educational opportunities for children in a framework of how they would want their own children to be treated.

North Carolina, in spite of its difficulties in adjusting to desegregation, continued to justify its moderate, relatively positive reputation regarding race. By the end of the 1970s, North Carolina had achieved more thorough school desegregation than any other state and had established a path toward more equitable practices that served as a model for other states.

Epilogue

REFORM AND RESEGREGATION

By the early 1980s, North Carolina and the other southern states had achieved the most thorough levels of desegregation in the nation. In the 1980s–90s, North Carolina, for the first time, sought to ensure that equal educational opportunities were provided to all children. The end of the twentieth century thus witnessed major reforms in education at the state and national levels, and those reforms benefited all students, regardless of race, gender, geography, or family socioeconomic level.

Key reform elements in North Carolina centered on a series of initiatives from the state:

- An emphasis on early childhood education, preventing failure before it became entrenched;
- Reduced class size, especially in primary grades;
- Professional advancement for teachers, in the form of higher pay for demonstrated levels of performance, based on criteria grounded in research associating teacher behaviors with improved student academic achievement;
- Professional development based on high-quality research associating pedagogy with improved outcomes;
- An articulated curriculum, effectively communicated to teachers in a way that enabled them to understand what students needed to know and be able to do;
- Assessments that were aligned with the curriculum and appropriately designed and field tested;
- Benchmark grades with demonstrated proficiency required for promotion, combined with opportunities for remediation and retesting;
- Accountability at the school rather than the district level, based

on a model that calculated academic growth of the same students from one year to the next; as well as
- Increased flexibility and local control regarding funding and pedagogy.

The impact of these reforms, mostly initiated under the administrations of Republican Governor James Holshouser (1973–77) and Democratic Governor James B. Hunt (1977–85, 1993–2001), but sustained and improved under Republican Governor James Martin (1985–93), moved North Carolina from one of the weakest educational systems in the nation to the strongest in the South, with achievement above the national average, measured on the basis of common assessments administered nationwide.

Academic achievement across the nation improved after desegregation, based on broad averages calculated for all students, a fact not widely recognized.[1] The strongest gains have appeared among black students, just as the Coleman Report predicted, with additional strong gains among white students from lower socioeconomic families. Achievement for students from middle and upper socioeconomic families has remained fairly constant at levels higher than the overall average. Addressing the racial achievement gap became a priority, within the context of improving achievement across the entire spectrum of pupils.[2]

Moreover, more students have stayed in school, so improved achievement has been occurring across a broader range of the pupil population. In 2012, North Carolina's four-year high-school graduation rate stood at 80.4 percent, the highest in history. (Students who did not graduate in four years did not necessarily drop out; some graduated after five or six years.) The annual dropout rate was 3.01 percent, the lowest in history. For students enrolled in the Career and Technical Education program, the graduation rate was 94 percent.[3]

In previous generations, low achievement for blacks had been considered normal and inevitable. Similar low expectations prevailed for females, especially in certain subjects such as math and science, as well as for children from lower socioeconomic families. Considering academic achievement to be a condition that can be improved through changes in the educational system represents significant progress in cultural norms.

During the same period that school reforms were producing improved results, however, federal courts, in decisions emanating primarily from conservative judges appointed by Republican administrations, especially the Reagan administration, shifted from a focus on desegregation to returning schools to local control. Pressure to reduce desegregation initiatives came primarily from middle- and upper-class whites, although blacks acquiesced. Large-scale court-ordered busing in the North and West as well as the South had spawned a backlash among whites, who relocated in large numbers from cities to suburbs, a phenomenon known as "white flight." The Republican Party capitalized on white resentments, becoming steadily more conservative, exploiting race as a political issue.[4] Opposition to busing was so widespread, however, that after the late 1970s no president of either party, not even Barack Obama, the nation's first black president, publicly supported busing or maintained efforts to sustain desegregation.

When boards of education were freed from judicial supervision, they tended to end busing and other policies supporting desegregation and reassign students to neighborhood schools. Although *de jure* segregation would never be reinstated in the form of state law, and no policy maker or government official would publicly advocate a return to schools where segregation by race was mandated by law, to a significant extent, widespread resegregation began to develop.

Neighborhoods are largely segregated by race and especially by socioeconomic status. So, although more students began attending schools closer to home, schools with high concentrations of low-income black and other racial and ethnic minority students resulted. Assignment patterns that would have been illegal in the 1980s–90s became widespread in the 2000s–2010s. To the historic issue of race, a new influx of Hispanic children into the pupil population introduced the additional circumstance of ethnicity, highly associated with poverty, as well as language barriers. Schools with high concentrations of black students, Hispanic ethnicity, non-English speakers, and poverty also tend to be staffed with teachers whose credentials are inferior to those found among teachers in more affluent schools.[5] These conditions are strongly associated with low academic achievement.

Within a school system, the board of education functions as a legislative body, and board policy has the force of law. When boards create school assignment patterns that highly concentrate pupils on the basis of race, ethnicity, and poverty, therefore, boards are not only reinstituting *de jure* segregation, albeit at the local level, they are creating schools that are, in their design, predisposed to fail.

In 2001, George W. Bush took office as president. Federal education policy during the Bush administration focused on accountability. No Child Left Behind, Bush's hallmark education legislation, could have ranked as one of the most positive initiatives in the history of education. But NCLB turned out to be deeply flawed and generated a backlash of its own. Ironically, Bush, one of the most conservative presidents in history, would join Lyndon B. Johnson as one of the two presidents who presided over this nation's largest expansion of the federal role in education.

Candidates for executive office at both the state and the national level began to support charter schools and vouchers to pay tuition in private schools as a core element of their vision of school reform, initiatives that originated in history as mechanisms to sustain racial segregation. Other initiatives seek to cure the problem of low achievement by reducing teacher job security and improve perceived financial inefficiency by reducing per-pupil appropriations to education. The political system has thus found a way to avoid the pain of systemic educational reform to support improved achievement of all students by isolating children whose circumstances of birth predispose them to lower achievement, while protecting political constituencies. New variations on an old pattern of practices have emerged.

In 2012, conservative Republicans took control of both the legislative and executive branches of North Carolina government, instituting sweeping changes in education policy and law. It is too soon to determine whether these practices will result in stalling or reversing the progress in academic achievement made during the reforms of the 1980s through the early 2000s. If achievement growth slows or is reversed, then conservative Republicans will have earned opprobrium for subordinating another generation of America's children to a lifetime of restricted freedom, access to employment that produces higher levels of income, and the better quality of life that has always represented the American dream. If achievement growth continues at the pace established from the 1980s through the early 2000s, then conservatives will earn a nation's praise for cutting costs in government without hurting educational outcomes. With regard to education, therefore, North Carolina and the nation have embarked on a period of great risk.

APPENDIX 1

Key Office Holders

U.S. PRESIDENTS, 1953–2012

1953–61	Dwight Eisenhower	Republican
1961–63	John F. Kennedy	Democrat
1963–69	Lyndon Johnson	Democrat
1969–74	Richard Nixon	Republican
1974–77	Gerald Ford	Republican
1977–81	Jimmy Carter	Democrat
1981–89	Ronald Reagan	Republican
1989–93	George H. W. Bush	Republican
1993–2001	William J. Clinton	Democrat
2001–9	George W. Bush	Republican
2009	Barack Obama	Democrat

Source: www.whitehouse.gov/history/presidents/.

NORTH CAROLINA'S U.S. SENATORS, 1946–2005

1946–48	William B. Umstead	Democrat
1948–49	J. Melville Broughton	Democrat
1949–50	Frank Porter Graham	Democrat
1950–53	Willis Smith	Democrat
1953–54	Alton A. Lennon	Democrat
1954–58	W. Kerr Scott	Democrat
1958–73	B. Everett Jordan	Democrat
1973–2003	Jesse Helms	Republican
1954–74	Samuel J. Ervin Jr.	Democrat
1975–81	Robert B. Morgan	Democrat

North Carolina's U.S. Senators, 1946–2005 (*continued*)

1981–86	John P. East	Republican
1986–86	James T. Broyhill	Republican
1986–93	Terry Sanford	Democrat
1993–99	Duncan McLauchlin (Lauch) Faircloth	Republican
1999–2005	John Edwards	Democrat

Source: www.senate.gov.

NORTH CAROLINA GOVERNORS (1953–2012)

1953–54	William B. Umstead	Democrat
1954–61	Luther H. Hodges	Democrat
1961–65	Terry Sanford	Democrat
1965–69	Dan K. Moore	Democrat
1969–73	Robert W. Scott	Democrat1
1973–77	James E. Holshouser Jr.	Republican
1977–85	James B. Hunt Jr. (first two terms)	Democrat
1985–93	James G. Martin	Republican
1993–2001	James B. Hunt Jr. (second two terms)	Democrat
2001–9	Michael F. Easley	Democrat
2009–12	Beverly Perdue	Democrat
2012	Pat McCrory	Republican

Sources: Lefler and Newsome, *North Carolina,* 711; statelibrary.dcr.state.nc.us/nc/stgovt/governor.htm; www.ncpublicschools.org/students/edhistory.html#NC%20State%20Superintendents%201852-Present.

STATE SUPERINTENDENTS OF PUBLIC INSTRUCTION, 1934–2004

1934–52	Clyde A. Erwin
1952–71	Charles F. Carroll
1971–88	A. Craig Phillips
1989–97	Bob Etheridge
1997–2004	Michael E. Ward

Source: History of the North Carolina State Board of Education (Raleigh: Department of Public Instruction, not dated), 7.

NORTH CAROLINA ATTORNEYS GENERAL, 1938–2001

1938–55	Harry McMullan
1955–56	William Rodman Jr.
1956–58	George B. Patton
1958–60	Malcolm Seawell
1960–69	Wade Bruton
1969–74	Robert Morgan
1974–75	James H. Carson Jr.
1975–85	Rufus L. Edmisten
1985–93	Lacy Thornburg
1993–2001	Michael F. Easley

Source: Linda Cox, North Carolina Attorney General's Office.

APPENDIX 2

Members of the First and Second Pearsall Committees

MEMBERS OF THE FIRST PEARSALL COMMITTEE (REPORT SUBMITTED DECEMBER 30, 1954)

Thomas J. Pearsall, Rocky Mount, attorney; chair, former member, Rocky Mount School Board; former Speaker of North Carolina House of Representatives

William T. Joyner, Raleigh, attorney; former chair, North Carolina Board of Elections

R. O. Huffman, Morganton, furniture executive; president, Drexel Furniture (the committee's only Republican)

Arthur D. Williams, Wilson, farmer; business owner; chair, Wilson County Board of Commissioners

I. E. Ready, Roanoke Rapids, educator; superintendent, Roanoke Rapids City Schools

James C. Manning, Williamston, educator; superintendent, Martin County Schools

Dr. F. D. Bluford, Greensboro, educator; president, A&T College (one of three black members)

Dr. J. W. Seabrook, Fayetteville, educator; president, Fayetteville State Teachers' College (one of three black members)

Hazel S. Parker, Tarboro, home economist, home demonstration agent (one of three black members)

Ruth Current, Raleigh, home economist, home demonstration agent

Helen S. Kafer, New Bern, hospital administrator, New Bern City School Board member

Dr. Paul A. Reid, Cullowhee, educator; president, Western Carolina College

Dallas Herring, Rose Hill, business owner; chair, Duplin County Board of Education

Fred B. Helms, Charlotte, attorney; former president, State Bar Association

Dr. Gordon Gray, Chapel Hill, educator; president, University of North Carolina

L. R. Varser, Lumberton, attorney; former associate justice, North Carolina Supreme Court

Clarence Poe, Raleigh, journalist; chair, Board of Editors, *The Progressive Farmer*

J. H. Clark, Elizabethtown, business owner; former member, North Carolina State Senate; chair, North Carolina Medical Care Commission

Holt McPherson, High Point, journalist; editor, *The High Point Enterprise*

Sources: Corbitt, ed. *Public Addresses, Letters, and Papers of William Bradley Umstead,* 211–13; Calaway, "The Pearsall Program—1954–1956," 64–69.

MEMBERS OF THE SECOND PEARSALL COMMITTEE (REPORT SUBMITTED APRIL 5, 1956)

Thomas J. Pearsall, Rocky Mount, attorney; chair, former member, Rocky Mount School Board; former Speaker of North Carolina House of Representatives (also member of first Pearsall Committee)

William T. Joyner, Raleigh, attorney; former chair, North Carolina Board of Elections (also member of first Pearsall Committee)

R. O. Huffman, Morganton, furniture executive; president, Drexel Furniture (the committee's only Republican; also member of first Pearsall Committee)

Lunsford Crew, Halifax County, attorney, member of State Senate

William Medford, Haywood County, attorney, member of State Senate

H. Cloyd Philpott, Lexington, furniture executive, member of State House of Representatives

Edward Yarborough, Franklin County, attorney, member of State House of Representatives

Source: Calaway, "The Pearsall Program—1954–1956," 96–97.

Notes

PREFACE

1. A. Leon Higginbotham Jr., *Shades of Freedom* (New York: Oxford University Press, 1996).

2. G. Edward White, "The Appellate Opinion as Historical Source Material," in *Patterns of American Legal Thought* (New York: Bobbs-Merrill, 1978), 149; see also 136–63.

3. White, "Appellate Opinion as Historical Source Material," 74.

CHAPTER ONE

1. Bernard Bailyn, *Education in the Forming of American Society* (Chapel Hill: University of North Carolina Press, 1960), xvi, 147.

2. Certain non-state entities in the Middle East, for example, function as governments, although they are not formally constituted as governments within boundaries defined by geography. Prohibiting or restricting access to education is part of their core mission.

3. David Tyack and Larry Cuban, *Tinkering Toward Utopia: A Century of Public School Reform* (Cambridge, MA: Harvard University Press, 1995), 17–18.

4. This insight was provided in a conversation with Larry R. Vaughn of Quality Leadership Resources, Inc., Edna, Texas (www.weimproveschools.com).

CHAPTER TWO

1. 163 U.S. 537 (1896). The *Slaughter-House Cases,* 16 Wallace 36 (1873) and *Civil Rights Cases,* 109 U.S. 3 (1883) were precedents for *Plessy.*

2. Ohio Historical Society, "The African-American Experience in Ohio, 1850–1920," dbs.ohiohistory.org/africanam/page.cfm?ID=17274.

3. *Plessy,* 163 U.S. at 538.

4. Albert P. Blaustein and Robert L. Zangrando, eds., *Civil Rights and the American Negro: A Documentary History* (New York: Trident Press, 1968), 294–96. McNeill Smith, "First Big Battles for Black Rights Were Lost," *Greensboro News and Record,* February 25, 1990.

5. 175 U.S. 528 (1899).

6. 211 U.S. 45 (1908).

7. Mark V. Tushnet, *The NAACP's Legal Strategy Against Segregated Education* (Chapel Hill: University of North Carolina Press, 1987), xi, 21–44.

8. Ibid., 111–12. Richard Kluger, *Simple Justice* (New York: Alfred A. Knopf, 1976), 14, 15, 187.

9. Elaine Jones, interview with National Public Radio, May 16, 1994.

10. Tushnet, *NAACP's Legal Strategy,* 35–36.

11. *State ex rel. Gaines v. Canada,* 113 S.W. 2d 783 (Mo. 1938). *Sipuel v. Board of Regents,* 332 U.S. 631 (1948). *McLaurin v. Oklahoma State Regents for Higher Education,* 87 F. Supp. 526 (W.D. Okla. 1948). *Sweatt v. Painter,* 339 U.S. 629 (1950), and *Bolling v. Sharpe,* 347 U.S. 497 (1954) were precedents in higher education for *Brown.*

12. 347 U.S. 483 (1954).

13. *Brown,* 347 U.S. at 495.

14. *Brown v. Board of Education of Topeka,* 349 U.S. 294 (1955).

15. *Brown,* 349 U.S. at 301. See also Albert P. Blaustein and Clarence Clyde Ferguson, *Desegregation and the Law* (New York: Vintage Books, 1962), 219.

16. Samuel Lubell, *The Future of American Politics* (New York: Harper and Brothers, 1952), 124.

17. Charles L. Coon, *The Beginnings of Public Education in North Carolina: A Documentary History, 1790–1840* (Raleigh: Edwards and Broughton, 1908), xxii.

18. Quoted in Coon, *Beginnings of Public Education in North Carolina,* 478–79.

19. Marion Nolan O'Quinn, "Carpetbagger Samuel S. Ashley and His Role in North Carolina Education, 1865–1871," MA thesis, North Carolina State University, 1975, 61–63, 98–99.

20. Hugh T. Lefler and Albert Ray Newsome, *North Carolina: The History of a Southern State* (Chapel Hill: University of North Carolina Press, 1973), 531–37. Raymond Gavins, "The Meaning of Freedom: Black North Carolina in the Nadir, 1880–1900," in Jeffrey J. Crow, Paul D. Escott, and Charles L. Flynn Jr., eds., *Race, Class, and Politics in Southern History* (Baton Rouge: Louisiana State University Press, 1989), 188.

21. Dennis Hargrove Cooke, *The White Superintendent and the Negro Schools in North Carolina* (Nashville: George Peabody College, 1930), 132. Charles L. Coon, The Beginnings of North Carolina City Schools, 1867–1887." *South Atlantic Quarterly* 12 (1913): 237–38.

22. A. W. Bolenius, Sub-Assistant Commissioner's (or Agent's) Monthly Report, June 12–September 28, 1867, RG 105, National Archives, qtd. in John E. Batchelor, *The Guilford County Schools: A History* (Winston-Salem, N.C.: John F. Blair, 1991), 21.

23. Hugo Hillebrandt, Sub-Assistant Commissioner's (or Agent's) Monthly Report, October 1868, RG 105, National Archives, qtd. in Batchelor, *Guilford County Schools,* 21.

24. Coon, "Beginnings of the North Carolina City Schools," 237.

25. Quotation from Bruce Beezer, "North Carolina's Rationale for Mandating Separate Schools: A Legal History," *Journal of Negro Education* 52 (1983): 215–16. See also Edwin M. Speas Jr., "The Legal Principles of Desegregation," in Robert E. Phay, and Janine M. Murphy, eds., *Education Law in North Carolina* (Chapel Hill, N.C.: Institute of Government, 1991), 17-1. and "An Ordinance to Amend Section Two, Article Nine, of the Constitution," in John L. Cheney Jr., ed., *North Carolina Government, 1585–1974: A Narrative and Statistical History* (Raleigh: Secretary of State, 1975), 883.

26. Cooke, *White Superintendent and the Negro Schools,* 133. Lefler and Newsome, *North Carolina,* 534–37. Henry Allen Bullock, *A History of Negro Education in the South* (Cambridge, Mass.: Harvard University Press, 1967), 86–87. Robert F. Durden, "North Carolina in the New South," in Lindley S. Butler and Alan D. Watson, eds., *The North Carolina Experience* (Chapel Hill: University of North Carolina Press, 1984), 315, 318.

27. Batchelor, *Guilford County Schools,* 47.

28. Charles L. Coon, "School Support and Our North Carolina Courts, 1868–1926," *North Carolina Historical Review* 3 (1926): 399–438; rpt. Raleigh: Edwards and Broughton, 1926), 3–4. Page numbers in citations refer to the reprint, in the North Carolina Col-

lection, Louis Round Wilson Library, University of North Carolina, Chapel Hill. See also Bullock, *History of Negro Education,* 56.

29. 65 N.C. 153 (1871) at 153, 157. The court further held that education was the responsibility of the state, not of local government.

30. 93 N.C. 473 (1885). A series of North Carolina Supreme Court cases from the mid-1880s have been repaginated. This citation uses the original page number, although the case actually appears on page 444 of currently printed volumes.

31. Coon, "Beginnings of North Carolina City Schools," 239.

32. Coon, "School Support and Our North Carolina Courts," 4, 6–15.

33. See James L. Leloudis, *Schooling the New South* (Chapel Hill: University of North Carolina Press, 1996), 177–81.

34. Qtd. in Coon, "Beginnings of North Carolina City Schools," 245.

35. Beezer, "North Carolina's Rationale for Separate Schools," 217. Coon, "Beginnings of North Carolina City Schools," 244.

36. Coon, "School Support and Our North Carolina Courts," 20–21.

37. Coon, "Beginnings of North Carolina City Schools," 245.

38. 94 N.C. 709 (1886); the case actually appears on page 514 of currently printed editions. *Puitt,* 94 N.C. at 514, 519.

39. 94 N.C. 800 (1886); the case actually appears on page 577 of currently printed editions.

40. Coon, "Beginnings of North Carolina City Schools," 246.

41. 96 N.C. 127 (1887).

42. See also Coon, "School Support and Our North Carolina Courts," 4, 6–15.

43. *Puitt,* 94 N.C. at 514.

44. Beezer, "North Carolina's Rationale for Separate Schools," 219.

45. Women did not have the right to vote during this period. Enfranchisement for women was an issue that would not arise for decades. Black males received the right to vote much earlier than white females, or females of any other race.

46. Richard L. Watson Jr., "Furnifold M. Simmons and the Politics of White Supremacy," in Crow, Escott, and Flynn, eds., *Race, Class, and Politics in Southern History,* 129–31.

47. Watson, "Furnifold M. Simmons and the Politics of White Supremacy," 134–36.

48. Jeffrey J. Crow, "Cracking the Solid South: Populism and the Fusionist Interlude," in Butler and Watson, eds., *North Carolina Experience,* 341.

49. Jack M. Balkin and Cristina M. Rodriguez, *Civil Rights Chronology* (www.yale.edu/lawweb/jbalkin/brown/1903.html).

50. 189 U.S. 475 (1903). Balkin and Rodriguez, *Civil Rights Chronology,* 1903.

51. Watson, "Furnifold M. Simmons and the Politics of White Supremacy," 137.

52. The impact of Populism, Fusion, and the Democratic backlash is admirably described in Leloudis, *Schooling the New South,* 107–76.

53. Jeffrey J. Crow, "An Apartheid for the South: Clarence Poe's Crusade for Rural Segregation," in Crow, Escott, and Flynn, eds., *Race, Class, and Politics in Southern History,* 216–20.

54. Watson, "Furnifold M. Simmons and the Politics of White Supremacy," 142–48. See also Leloudis, *Schooling the New South,* 136–41.

55. Watson, "Furnifold M. Simmons and the Politics of White Supremacy," 139, 165.

56. William S. Powell, *North Carolina: A Bicentennial History* (New York: W. W. Norton, 1977), 182–84. Watson, "Furnifold M. Simmons and the Politics of White Supremacy," 155.

57. Cooke, *White Superintendent and the Negro Schools,* 133. *Hooker v. Town of Green-*

ville, 130 N.C. 472 (1902). *Lowery v. School Trustees of Kernersville,* 140 N.C. 33 (1905). Davison M. Douglas, *Reading, Writing, and Race: The Desegregation of the Charlotte Schools* (Chapel Hill: University of North Carolina Press, 1995), 15.

58. 145 N.C. 170 (1907). The case actually appears on page 123 of currently printed volumes.

59. 93 N.C. 473 (1885).

60. Coon, "School Support and Our North Carolina Courts," 19–20.

61. The discussion of classification by race is based on Beezer, "North Carolina's Rationale for Separate Schools," 220–24.

62. *Laws and Resolutions of North Carolina,* 1889, C. 199, Section 42.

63. 113 N.C. 10 (1893).

64. *Laws and Resolutions of North Carolina,* 1903, C. 435, Section 22, qtd. in Beezer, "North Carolina's Rationale for Separate Schools," 220.

65. Beezer, "North Carolina's Rationale for Separate Schools," 221.

66. 141 N.C. 482 (1906).

67. 166 N.C. 468 (1914).

68. *Johnson,* 166 N.C. at 471.

69. 167 N.C. 239 (1914).

70. *Medlin,* 167 N.C. at 242. Precedent for observing a child had been established in *Warlick v. White,* 76 N.C. 166 (1877).

71. Beezer, "North Carolina's Rationale for Separate Schools," 224.

72. *Biennial Report of the Superintendent of Public Instruction* (Raleigh: Edwards and Broughton, 1902), vi. Later editions of these reports were published by the Department of Public Instruction.

73. *Biennial Report of the Superintendent of Public Instruction* (1904–6), 28; (1906–8), 8; (1908–10), 15.

74. Leloudis, *Schooling the New South,* 183–228, 195, 213–22.

75. Joyner, *Biennial Report* (1905–6), 259.

76. Tyack and Cuban, *Tinkering Toward Utopia,* 22–24, 43.

77. *Biennial Report* (1905–6), 251.

78. Ibid. (1942–44), 102–4.

79. Brooks, *Biennial Report* (1920–22), 35.

80. Allen, *Biennial Report* (1930–32), 5.

81. Erwin, *Biennial Report* (1940–42), 98.

82. "Governor Broughton Hits Race Issue in Campaign," *The Carolinian,* May 22, 1948.

83. Tushnet, *NAACP's Legal Strategy,* 159.

84. State Education Commission, *Education in North Carolina Today and Tomorrow* (Raleigh: United Forces for Education, 1948), 32.

85. 95 F. Supp. 441 (M.D.N.C. 1951). The decision applied only to Durham city schools, however, not to the state as a whole (Jeffrey J. Crow, Paul D. Escott, and Flora J. Hatley, *A History of African Americans in North Carolina* [Raleigh: Division of Archives and History, 1992], 165).

86. Higginbotham, *Shades of Freedom,* xxx.

87. Discussion of the *Hocutt* case is based on Augustus M. Burns III, "Graduate Education for Blacks in North Carolina, 1930–1951," *Journal of Southern History* 66 (1980): 195–218, and Gilbert Ware, "*Hocutt:* Genesis of *Brown,*" *Journal of Negro Education* 52 (1983): 227–33.

88. Burns, "Graduate Education for Blacks in North Carolina," 196.

89. Ware, "*Hocutt:* Genesis of *Brown,*" 228.

90. Hastie eventually became the first black federal judge in the United States; he was later elevated to the U.S. Court of Appeals. See Ware, "*Hocutt:* Genesis of *Brown,*" 229, and Kluger, *Simple Justice,* 271, 158.

91. Ware, "*Hocutt:* Genesis of *Brown,*" 229.

92. Qtd. in Burns, "Graduate Education for Blacks in North Carolina," 204.

93. Burns, "Graduate Education for Blacks in North Carolina," 204. The law school at North Carolina College was established in 1939 following *Missouri ex rel. Gaines v. Canada,* although the school was not compelled to do so by any direct litigation. See also *McKissick v. Carmichael,* 187 F. 2d 949, 951 (4th Cir. 1951).

94. Burns, "Graduate Education for Blacks in North Carolina," 204.

95. Qtd. in Burns, "Graduate Education for Blacks in North Carolina," 207. Burns cites *News and Observer,* March 6, 1941, 4.

96. Burns, "Graduate Education for Blacks in North Carolina," 209–12.

97. *Epps v. Carmichael,* 93 F. Supp. 327 (M.D.N.C. 1950).

98. Ibid., at 328. Umstead was elected governor soon thereafter.

99. Burns, "Graduate Education for Blacks in North Carolina," 211–12. By the time the case reached Middle District Court, accreditation had been granted. The court also pointed out that black lawyers in North Carolina represented only black clients (*Epps v. Carmichael,* 93 F. Supp. at 329).

100. *Epps,* 93 F. Supp. at 327.

101. Qtd. in Burns, "Graduate Education for Blacks in North Carolina," 215.

102. Burns, "Graduate Education for Blacks in North Carolina," 216.

103. 187 F. 2d 949 (4th Cir. 1951).

104. *McKissick,* 187 F. 2d at 954.

105. *Carmichael v. McKissick, cert. denied,* 341 U.S. 951, 952 (1950). Royall served as secretary of war in the Truman administration.

106. McMullan to Kenneth Royall, June 8, 1961, University of North Carolina Archives, qtd. in Burns, "Graduate Education for Blacks in North Carolina," 217.

107. Balkin and Rodriguez, *Civil Rights Chronology,* 1919, 1920, 1921.

108. Paul Luebke, *Tar Heel Politics 2000* (Chapel Hill: University of North Carolina Press, 1998), 129.

109. V. O. Key Jr., *Southern Politics in State and Nation* (New York: Alfred A. Knopf, 1950), 206.

110. John Hope Franklin, *From Slavery to Freedom* (New York: Alfred A. Knopf, 1967), 547–52. With regard to its response to the civil rights movement, Franklin has commented, "North Carolina was not much better than any other state." Fannie Flono, "After Freedom," *Charlotte Observer,* July 7, 1996. Bullock, *History of Negro Education,* 176, lists North Carolina, Texas, Virginia, and Kentucky as the least discriminatory southern states.

111. "The Inevitable," *The Carolinian,* April 17, 1948.

112. See, for example, Arthur F. Raper, *The Tragedy of Lynching* (Chapel Hill: University of North Carolina Press, 1933); James Harmon Chadbourn, *Lynching and the Law* (Chapel Hill: University of North Carolina Press, 1933); James Elbert Cutler, *Lynch-Law* (London: Longmans, Green, 1905); Jesse Daniel Ames, *The Changing Character of Lynching.* (Atlanta: Commission on Interracial Cooperation, 1942), *Lynchings and What They Mean* (Atlanta: Southern Commission on the Study of Lynching, [n.d.]). All works are in the North Carolina Collection.

113. Walter White, *Rope and Faggot* (1929; rpt. New York: Arno Press and New York Times, 1969), 21–23.

114. Chadbourn, *Lynching and the Law,* 190–92. See also *N.C. Code Annotated* (Charlottesville, Va.: Michie, 1931), Section 1266, Section 3945, Section 4377, Section 4600, Section 4636, Sections 4570–4573; and White, *Rope and Faggot,* 201–2.

115. Jerry Bledsoe, "Dousing the Fires of Bigotry," *Greensboro News and Record,* November 26, 1991, A11. The article deals with W. Horace Carter, *Virus of Fear* (Tabor City, N.C.: Atlantic, 1991).

116. *The Tabor City Tribune* was the smallest and the first weekly newspaper to win a Pulitzer Prize for meritorious public service. Carter, *Virus of Fear,* v–vi, xiv. www.nytimes.com/2009/09/21/us/21carter.html?_r=0

117. Dargan Frierson, interview with author, February 3, 1983.

118. Donald R. Matthews and James W. Prothro, *Negroes and the New Southern Politics* (New York: Harcourt, Brace & World, 1966), 148, 154.

119. Harry S. Ashmore, *The Negro and the Schools* (Chapel Hill: University of North Carolina Press, 1954), 48–49.

120. William C. Havard, ed., *The Changing Politics of the South* (Baton Rouge: Louisiana State University Press, 1972), 710. Lefler and Newsome, *North Carolina,* 592. Thomas D. Clark and Albert D. Kirwan, *The South Since Appomattox* (New York: Oxford University Press, 1967), 292–95. Irwin Ross, *The Loneliest Campaign* (New York: Signet, 1968), 232.

121. The Kerr Scott material is based on Robert W. Redwine, "The Kerr Scott Administration," in David Leroy Corbitt, ed., *Public Addresses, Letters, and Papers of William Kerr Scott* (Raleigh: Council of State, 1957), xii-xxvi; Lefler and Newsome, *North Carolina,* 592–94; and Powell, *North Carolina,* 190.

122. "The Better Man," *The Carolinian,* May 29, 1948. "Overwhelming Vote Cast for Broughton in Negro Precincts," *The Carolinian,* June 5, 1948.

123. "Umstead Learns a Lesson," *The Carolinian,* June 12, 1948.

124. Lefler and Newsome, *North Carolina,* 593.

125. Lubell, *Future of American Politics,* 101.

126. Julian M. Pleasants and Augustus M. Burns III, *Frank Porter Graham and the 1950 Senate Race in North Carolina* (Chapel Hill: University of North Carolina Press, 1990), 19. "Dr. Frank Graham—International Repute," *The Carolinian,* May 20, 1950.

127. Redwine, "The Kerr Scott Administration," 123.

128. "Health, Family Life Problems Aired at Confab," *The Carolinian,* November 20, 1948.

129. "Teachers Repudiate Trigg," *The Carolinian,* April 8, 1950.

130. Corbitt, ed., *Public Addresses, Letters, and Papers of William Kerr Scott,* 123.

131. Qtd. in Lefler and Newsome, *North Carolina,* 575.

132. "Phony Post-Cards Used To Lessen Graham's Chance," *The Carolinian,* May 27, 1950.

133. Pleasants and Burns, *Frank Porter Graham,* 186, 198–99. A third candidate won 58,752 votes (9.3 percent), and a fourth candidate won 5,900 votes (1.3 percent).

134. The decisions were *McLaurin v. Oklahoma State Regents for Higher Education,* 87 F. Supp. 526 (W.D. Okla. 1948), and *Sweatt v. Painter,* 339 U.S. 629 (1950), two of the higher education cases, plus *Henderson v. United States,* 339 U.S. 816 (1950), which outlawed segregation on Pullman railroad cars.

135. Pleasants and Burns, *Frank Porter Graham,* 91, 98, 198–99. The role of the Supreme Court decisions is reinforced by John B. Wilson Jr. and Martin Clark, *Dr. Frank: The Life and Times of Frank Porter Graham* (Chapel Hill: UNC Arts and Sciences Foundation and UNC Center for Public Television, 1994).

136. Lubell, *Future of American Politics,* 101–2.

137. Lubell uses the word "Negro," although it seems likely that a whispering campaign would have used more base terminology.

138. Pleasants and Burns, *Frank Porter Graham,* 214, 221.

139. John Egerton, *Speak Now Against the Day* (New York: Alfred A. Knopf, 1994), 531.

140. Pleasants and Burns, *Frank Porter Graham,* 203–46, 84.

141. Lubell, *Future of American Politics,* 101–2, 107–16. Lefler and Newsome, *North Carolina,* 593.

142. See Pleasants and Burns, *Frank Porter Graham,* 247, 253–54; "Whose Defeat?," *The Carolinian,* July 8, 1950; "Negro Vote May Be Deciding Issue in the May 27 United States Senatorial Election," *The Carolinian,* May 20, 1950.

143. Lubell, *Future of American Politics,* 107–16. In retrospect, Lubell forecast the political impact of the emerging black vote in the 1960s, followed by Republican ascendancy and the so-called Reagan revolution. Paul Luebke, in *Tar Heel Politics: Myths and Realities* (Chapel Hill: University of North Carolina Press, 1990), 17, 103, refers to the survey conducted in North Carolina by Melvin Tumin (*Desegregation: Resistance and Readiness* [Princeton, N.J.: Princeton University Press, 1958]), but no citation for the Tumin study appears in Luebke's notes or bibliography. He evidently did not review Tumin, relying only on Chafe. The new edition, *Tar Heel Politics 2000* (Chapel Hill: University of North Carolina Press, 1998), 134, does not change the entry, although Luebke remarks later (141) that no advocate of desegregation could have won a statewide election.

144. Pleasants and Burns, *Frank Porter Graham,* 197, 269. This point also appears in Earl Black, *Southern Governors and Civil Rights* (Cambridge, Mass.: Harvard University Press, 1976), 333.

145. Egerton, *Speak Now Against the Day,* 532.

146. William H. Chafe, *Civilities and Civil Rights* (New York: Oxford University Press, 1980).

147. Ibid., 7–8, 50–55, 57–58, 65–82, 78.

148. Ibid., 78.

149. Tumin, *Desegregation.*

150. For population data, see Carolina Population Center, *County Population Trends, North Carolina, 1790–1960, State / Region / County* (Chapel Hill: Carolina Population Center, University of North Carolina, and Dept. of Administration, 1969). See also Thomas E. Steahr, *North Carolina's Changing Population* (Chapel Hill: Carolina Population Center, 1973), 49; and Paul E. Zopf Jr., *North Carolina: a Demographic Profile* (Chapel Hill: Carolina Population Center, [n.d.]), 123–26.

151. Tumin, *Desegregation,* 81–82, 87, 90, 103–4.

152. Chafe, *Civilities and Civil Rights,* 80.

153. Tumin, *Desegregation,* 46.

154. McKnight, *Charlotte News,* June 7, 1950, qtd. in Douglas, *Reading, Writing, and Race,* 59.

155. Egerton, *Speak Now Against the Day,* 422–26, 556–57.

CHAPTER THREE

1. Edward L. Rankin Jr., "William Bradley Umstead," in David Leroy Corbitt, ed., *Public Addresses, Letters, and Papers of William Bradley Umstead* (Raleigh: Council of State, 1957), xvii, 36. Beth G. Crabtree, *North Carolina Governors* (Raleigh: Division of Archives and History, 1974), 132.

2. Corbitt, ed., *Public Papers of William Bradley Umstead,* 4.

3. Julian M. Pleasants, "'Call Your Next Case': H. F. 'Chub' Seawell Jr., the Gubernatorial Election of 1952, and the Rise of the Republican Party in North Carolina," *North Carolina Historical Review* 76 (1999): 74.

4. Rankin, "William Bradley Umstead," xix.

5. Virginius Dabney, *Virginia: The New Dominion* (Charlottesville: University Press of Virginia, 1971), 528–47. Kilpatrick later became a popular network television commentator.

6. Balkin and Rodriguez, *Civil Rights Chronology,* 1954.

7. Henry S. Stroupe, "Irving Edward Carlyle," in William S. Powell, ed., *Dictionary of North Carolina Biography* (Chapel Hill: University of North Carolina Press, 1979), vol. 1: 324–25.

8. Mary Belo Carlyle, qtd. in Calaway, "The Pearsall Program—1954–1956 in North Carolina," MA thesis, Wake Forest University, 1972, 40.

9. Stroupe, "Irving Carlyle," 325, reinforced by Albert Coates, *Talks on the Rule of Law and the Role of State Government in the Cities, the Counties, and the State of North Carolina* (Chapel Hill, N.C.: Professor Emeritus Fund, [n.d]), 86–87.

10. Calaway, "Pearsall Program," 42.

11. Carlyle, interview with Calaway, 45.

12. Rankin, "William Bradley Umstead," xix.

13. Stroupe, "Irving Carlyle," 325. Chafe considers the Democratic Convention's applause evidence that North Carolina was receptive to desegregation in the 1950s (*Civilities and Civil Rights,* 65–66).

14. Sam J. Ervin Jr., "Alexander Hamilton's Phantom," address before Harvard Club, New York, April 28, 1955, 114.3/F18, William Dallas Herring Papers, State Archives, Raleigh.

15. Corbitt, ed., *Public Papers of William Bradley Umstead,* 201.

16. Black, *Southern Governors and Civil Rights,* 13–15, 309–41.

17. James C. N. Paul, in Albert Coates, ed., *A Report to the Governor of North Carolina* (Chapel Hill: Institute of Government, 1954), 105, 120, 167–74, 180–81, 185.

18. Coates, ed., *Report to the Governor,* ii–iii.

19. Chafe, *Civilities and Civil Rights,* 65–69.

20. Ibid., 65–68. William B. Umstead to the following: John L. Marshburn Jr., Wilmington, September 15, 1953; John B. Lewis Jr., Farmville, November 23, 1953; E. E. Barringer, Salisbury, December 15, 1953; Mrs. David Burns, Asheboro, December 17, 1953; R. N. White, Winston-Salem, December 18, 1953; W. N. Jefferies, Burlington, January 14, 1954; Reverend H. F. Beaty, Peachland, January 14, 1954; Helen Bain, Winston-Salem, February 12, 1954; Box 47, Umstead Papers, State Archives, Raleigh.

21. Holt McPherson to William B. Umstead, July 20, 1954;.Charles F. Carroll to William B. Umstead, July 7, 1954, Box 47, Umstead Papers.

22. J. Martin Umstead to William B. Umstead, July 30, 1954, Box 47, Umstead Papers.

23. Press Release, August 4, 1954, Box 47, Umstead Papers.

24. Umstead announced Gray's appointment without conferring with him first. Gray subsequently expressed doubts about helping make a policy that he would have to administer. Gordon Gray to William B. Umstead, August 26, September 8, 1954, Box 58, Umstead Papers.

25. Rev. G. A. Fisher to William B. Umstead, August 10, 1954, Box 47, Umstead Papers. "43 Proposed for Governor Umstead's Advisory Group," *The Carolina Times,* July 31, 1954.

26. Fisher to Umstead, August 10, 1954. Kelly M. Alexander, "Implementation of the United States Supreme Court Decision of May 17, 1954 in North Carolina, Report Made In Atlanta Georgia at the Meeting of NAACP Leaders on Ending Racial Segregation in Public Schools in Southern and Border States. June 4, 1955," Folio 37-15, Kelly Alexander Papers, J. Murrey Atkins Library, University of North Carolina at Charlotte. "Governors Need Broader Acquaintance," *The Carolinian,* August 14, 1954. "The Governor's Advisory Committee," *The Carolina Times,* August 14, 1954.

27. Pleasants and Burns, *Frank Porter Graham,* 52, 74, 88, 93, 250.

28. Crow, "Apartheid for the South," 216–59.

29. Gordon Gray to William B. Rodman, December 3, 1953, Box 47, Umstead Papers.

30. Almost the entire contents of Box 1, Thomas Jenkins Pearsall Papers #4300, Southern Historical Collection, Wilson Library, University of North Carolina at Chapel Hill.

31. Boxes 58.1, 58.2, 58.3, Umstead Papers, are devoted to segregation petitions. Roy L. Deal to Thomas J. Pearsall, August 11, 1954, 114.2/E18, Herring Papers.

32. Raleigh *News and Observer,* August 12, 1954, 114.2/E18, Herring Papers.

33. Holt McPherson, interview with Calaway, "Pearsall Program," 70–71.

34. William B. Umstead to Attorney General Harry McMullan, December 23, 1953, Box 47, Umstead Papers.

35. Attorney General Harry McMullan to William B. Umstead, November 25, 1953; R. Gregg Cherry to William B. Umstead, December 18, 1953, Box 47, Umstead Papers.

36. Luther H. Hodges, *Businessman in the Statehouse* (Chapel Hill: University of North Carolina Press, 1962), 79–80.

37. Kelly M. Alexander to William B. Umstead, June 14, 1954, Box 47, Umstead Papers. The Kelly M. Alexander referred to throughout this study is Kelly M. Alexander Sr. His son, Kelly M. Alexander Jr., became president of the North Carolina NAACP in the mid-1980s. Pleasants and Burns consistently refer to Kelly M. Alexander Jr. in *Frank Porter Graham,* but Kelly M. Alexander Jr., was only two years old at the time Graham was running for Senate.

38. William B. Umstead to Kelly Alexander, June 24, 1954, Box 47, Umstead Papers.

39. Thurgood Marshall to C. O. Pearson, September 2, 1954, Folio 37-18, Kelly Alexander Papers.

40. Kelly M. Alexander, "Implementation of the United States Supreme Court Decision of May 17, 1954 in North Carolina," report to NAACP leaders, Atlanta, June 4, 1955; "A Discussion of the Function of a Community Desegregation Process," July 30, 1954; Folio 37-15; Herbert Wright, president, Davidson County Branch, NAACP, to Kelly M. Alexander, July 22, 1954; Folio 37-17; blank petition form, Folio 37-17, Kelly Alexander Papers.

41. Kelly M. Alexander, "Implementation of the United States Supreme Court Decision of May 17, 1954.

42. Wyche, Bell, and Pearson, contract with blank spaces, Folio 37-15, Kelly Alexander Papers.

43. Thurgood Marshall to Charles A. McLean, August 16, 1954; G. H. Bostic to Kelly Alexander, October 27, 1954; C. C. Lipscomb to Rev. A. D. Owens, December 1, 1954; Donald E. Ramseur to Kelly M. Alexander, February 3, 1955; C. O. Pearson to J. Kenneth Lee, August 26, 1954; Thurgood Marshall to Herbert Wright, August 16, 1954; C. W. Stanford to Edgar Collins, September 9, 1954; Rev. L. R. McKnight to Kelly Alexander, September 14, 1954; W. M. Turner to Kelly M. Alexander, October 7, 1954; W. O. Thomas to Kelly Alexander, October 12, 1954; Kelly M. Alexander to Troy Lassiter, February 7, 1955, Folio 37-18, Kelly Alexander Papers.

44. "Resolution of Educators Backs Integration in North Carolina's Public School," *The Carolina Times,* August 21, 1954. See also "Principals and Supervisors Support Court Decision In Durham Confab," *The Carolinian,* August 21, 1954.

45. Raleigh *News and Observer,* August 14, 1954, 114.2/E18, Herring Papers.

46. Thomas J. Pearsall to Committee, September 11, 1954, Box 47, Umstead Papers.

47. Thomas J. Pearsall to the Governor's Special Advisory Committee on Education, September 11, 1954, Box 47; October 6, 1954, Box 58, Umstead Papers. "Two Churches March Forward," *The Carolinian,* June 26, 1954. Harry Golden, *Mr. Kennedy and the Negro* (Greenwich, Conn.: Fawcett, 1964), 143–48, 154, 163.

48. Alice Owens, "YWCA Honors a Pioneer in Desegregation in Triad," *The News and Record,* January 31, 2014, B3.

49. "City Council Meeting To Consider Plan," *The Carolinian,* July 10, 1954. "Local Groups Plan To Study Integration," *The Carolinian,* July 24, 1954.

50. "White and Negro Ministers Vote to Unite in Greensboro," *The Carolina Times,* February 12, 1955.

51. "Supt. L. Stacy Weaver, Dr. Chas. Stewart Speakers for Berean S.S. Class Annual Homecoming," *The Carolina Times,* October 9, 1954.

52. Quoted in Michael B. Friedland, *Lift Up Your Voice Like a Trumpet: White Clergy and the Civil Rights and Antiwar Movements, 1954–1973* (Chapel Hill: University of North Carolina Press, 1998), 21.

53. Friedland, *Lift Up Your Voice Like a Trumpet,* 22.

54. J. P. Strother to William B. Umstead, September 6, 1954, Box 47, Umstead Papers.

55. "Progress and Reaction, 1955," NAACP *Annual Report,* 1955, Box 114A, Folio 4, Frederick Alexander Papers, J. Murrey Atkins Library, University of North Carolina at Charlotte. North Carolina Council on Human Relations, "Human Relations Bulletin," July 1955, Box 121, Folio 86, Frederick Alexander Papers.

56. Ben L. Smith to Attorney General Harry McMullan, September 23, 1954, Box 47, Umstead Papers.

57. North Carolina Council on Human Relations, "Human Relations Bulletin," July 1955, Box 121, Folio 86, Frederick Alexander Papers. See also Calaway, "Pearsall Program," 45.

58. Petitions, Boxes 58.1, 58.2, and 58.3; Thomas J. Pearsall to the Governor's Special Advisory Committee, September 22, 1954, Box 47, Umstead Papers.

59. Golden, *Mr. Kennedy and the Negro,* 143–48.

60. Allison James, Executive Secretary, Patriots of North Carolina, to Members of the North Carolina Legislature and Other State Officials, [n.d.], Box 131, Series 4, Folio 22, Frederick Alexander Papers. See also Calaway, "Pearsall Program," 45–50.

61. W. C. George, *The Race Problem from the Standpoint of One Who Is Concerned about the Evils of Miscegenation* (Birmingham, Ala.: American States Rights Association, February 1955), 10, 13.

62. Fred C. Owen to William B. Umstead, June 4, 1954; Basil M. Watkins to William B. Umstead, May 24, 1954; John H. Kerr Jr., to William B. Umstead, May 25, 1954, Box 47, Umstead Papers.

63. W. T. Joyner to Attorney General Harry McMullan, September 13, 1954, Box 47, Umstead Papers.

64. W. B. Rodman Jr. to William B. Umstead, November 28, 1953; William B. Rodman Jr., to William B. Umstead, December 8, 1953, Box 47, Umstead Papers.

65. Qtd. in *North Carolina Education* (September 1955): 40–41.

66. Thomas J. Pearsall to the Governor's Special Advisory Committee, September 22, 1954, Box 47, Umstead Papers.

67. Dallas Herring to Henry M. Marrow, December 27, 1954, 114.2/E18, Herring Papers.

68. Weaver to Calaway, May 5, 1972, cited in Calaway, "The Pearsall Program," 71–75.

69. Thomas J. Pearsall to the Governor's Special Advisory Committee, November 19, 1954, Box 41; L. S. Weaver to Luther Hodges, January 1, 1955, Box 76, Hodges Papers.

70. Chafe believes that Hodges changed to a policy supporting segregation (*Civilities and Civil Rights,* 65–69).

71. James W. Patton, ed., *Messages, Addresses, and Public Papers of Luther Hartwell Hodges, Governor of North Carolina, 1954–1961* (Raleigh: Council of State, 1960), xxi–xxv; quotation, xxv.

72. Edwin L. Rankin Jr., telephone conversation with author, Concord, N.C., July 13, 1983.

73. Hodges, *Businessman in the State House,* 3, 17–18.

74. "The New Governor an Unknown Quantity," *The Carolina Times,* December 4, 1954.

75. Robert E. Giles, interview with author, April 20, 1992.

76. John Ellsworth Batchelor, "Rule of Law: North Carolina School Desegregation from *Brown* to *Swann,* 1954–1974," EdD diss., North Carolina State University, 1992, 127–31.

77. Herring, "Save Our Schools," unpublished essay, in MS speeches, "Essays on Education." 2 vols., photocopies, loaned to author by William Dallas Herring.

78. Dallas Herring to Thomas Pearsall, October 11, 1954, 114.2/E18; Notes, on *North Carolina Teachers Record,* October, 1954, 114.2/E18, Herring Papers. Herring, "Save Our Schools."

79. Dallas Herring to Charles F. Carroll, November 11, 1954, 114.2/E18, Herring Papers.

80. Thomas Pearsall, interview with Calaway, "Pearsall Program," 75–79.

81. For more detail on Herring's deliberations and other discussions within the Pearsall Committee, see Batchelor, "Rule of Law," 127–34.

82. I. Beverly Lake to Thomas J. Pearsall, November 23, 1954, Box 1, in Thomas Jenkins Pearsall Papers #4300.

83. Thomas J. Pearsall to the Governor's Special Advisory Committee, November 16, 1954, 114.2/E18, Herring Papers. Thomas J. Pearsall to Luther Hodges, November 20, 1954, Box 41, Hodges Papers.

84. Luther Hodges, handwritten notes attached to Thomas J. Pearsall to Luther Hodges, November 20, 1954, Box 41, Hodges Papers.

85. Dr. J. W. Seabrook to Calaway, April 3, 1972, cited in Calaway, "Pearsall Program," 78–79.

86. Thomas J. Pearsall to the Governor's Special Advisory Committee, December 21, 1954, 114.2/E18, Herring Papers.

87. Herring, "Supplement" to "Save Our Schools."

88. Thomas J. Pearsall to the Governor's Special Advisory Committee, December 21, 1954, 114.2/E18, Herring Papers.

89. Dallas Herring to Guy B. Phillips, January 7, 1955, 114.2/E18, Herring Papers.

90. "Report of the Governor's Special Advisory Committee," December 30, 1954, 114.3/F18, Herring Papers.

91. Dr. J. W. Seabrook to Calaway, April 3, 1972, cited in Calaway, "Pearsall Program," 83–84.

92. Holt McPherson, interview with Calaway, "Pearsall Program," 84.

93. "Report of the Governor's Special Advisory Committee."

94. Dallas Herring, interview with author, March 8, 1983.

95. Thomas Pearsall to Dallas Herring, December 30, 1954, 114.2/E18, Herring Papers.

96. Thomas Pearsall, interview with Calaway, "Pearsall Program," 85.

97. Thomas J. Pearsall to Members of the Governor's Special Advisory Committee, January 10, 1955, 114.3/F18, Herring Papers.

98. "A Bill to Be Entitled to [*sic*] Act Amending G.S. 115-132 by Repealing a Part Thereof and Authorizing County and City Boards of Education to Assign Pupils to Schools or Attendance Centers; To Provide that No Child Shall Attend Any School or Attendance Center Except that to Which He Has Been So Assigned; To Provide for a Review of the Decisions of the City and County Boards of Education by the Courts," Box 58, Umstead Papers.

99. Attorney General Harry McMullan to William B. Umstead, July 29, 1954, Box 58, Umstead Papers.

100. W. Lunsford Crew to William B. Umstead, July 8, 1954, Box 58, Umstead Papers.

101. Attorney General Harry McMullan to William B. Umstead, July 29, 1954, Box 58, Umstead Papers. "An Act to authorize the boards of trustees of school districts to assign pupils to schools or attendance centers; to provide that no child shall attend any school or attendance center except that to which he has been so assigned; to provide for appeals from the decision of the board of trustees; and for other related purposes," Legislature of the State of Mississippi [n.d.], Box 58, Umstead Papers.

102. Thomas J. Pearsall to Members of the Governor's Special Advisory Committee, January 10, 1955, 114.3/F18, Herring Papers.

103. J. C. Manning to Dallas Herring, January 8, 1955; Thomas J. Pearsall to the Governor's Special Advisory Committee, January 10, 1955, 114.3/F18, Herring Papers.

104. Thomas J. Pearsall to the Governor's Special Advisory Committee, January 10, 1955, 114.3/F18, Herring Papers.

105. Dallas Herring to Luther Hodges, November 29, 1954, Box 41 Hodges Papers. Luther H. Hodges to Dallas Herring, December 1, 1954, 114.2/E18, Herring Papers.

106. Thomas Pearsall to Members of the Governor's Special Advisory Committee, January 10, 1955, 114.3/F18, Herring Papers.

107. Institute of Government, "Analysis," January 8, 1955, 114.3/F18, Herring Papers.

108. Hodges, *Businessman in the Statehouse,* 12.

109. Robert Carr to Dallas Herring, February 17, 1955, 114.3/F18; "A Bill to Be Entitled an Act to Amend the Constitution of North Carolina So as to Authorize the General Assembly to Provide for Grants of State, County, or Municipal Funds for Educational Purposes," 114.3/F18, Herring Papers.

110. Dallas Herring to L. C. Kerr, Sr., March 9, 1955, 114.3/F18; Dallas Herring to Guy B. Phillips, January 7, 1955, 114.2/E18, Herring Papers.

111. Herring to Kerr, March 9, 1955. Chafe contends that legislators withdrew bills to close the public schools and to provide tuition grants for private schools because they were resigned to the inevitability of integration (*Civilities and Civil Rights,* 79).

112. Crow, Escott, and Hatley, *History of African Americans in North Carolina,* 168–69.

113. "The 1955 General Assembly and Segregation in the Public Schools," *The Carolina Times,* January 8, 1955.

114. "An Act to Provide for the Enrollment of Pupils in Public Schools," 1955 Session Laws, Chapter 366, S.B. 9, H.B. 12.

115. Patton, ed., *Public Papers of Luther Hartwell Hodges,* xxx.

116. *Journal of the House of Representatives of the General Assembly of the State of North Carolina, Session 1955,* 644.

117. General Statute, 115-142.

118. Thomas J. Pearsall, interview with Calaway, "Pearsall Program," 89.

119. Brief of Harry McMullan, Attorney General of North Carolina, Amicus Curiae, *Brown v. Board of Education of Topeka,* 349 U.S. 294 (1955), U.S. Supreme Court Records and Briefs (Microform, Inc.), 3.

120. Ibid., 18, 19.

121. I. Beverly Lake, Argument on Behalf of the State of North Carolina as the Friend of the Court of the United States: The Warren Court, 1953 Term—1968 Term, *Brown v. Board of Education,* 349 U.S. 294 (1955), Fiche 1, Case 1 (University Publications of America), 264.

122. Fred B. Helms to Luther Hodges, April 18, 1955, Box 39, Hodges Papers.

123. Balkin and Rodriguez, *Civil Rights Chronology,* 1955.

124. "Extract from Letter from William F. Womble," June 2, 1955, Box 120, Hodges Papers.

125. Dallas Herring to Luther Hodges, June 9, 1955, Box 39, Hodges Papers.

126. Handwritten notes, Charles Carroll, [n.d.], Box 39, Hodges Papers.

127. Ben L. Smith to Luther Hodges, June 13, 1955, Box 117, Hodges Papers.

128. "Address by Gov. Luther H. Hodges before the Forty-seventh Annual Farm and Home Week," June 22, 1955, Box 39, Hodges Papers.

129. "Hodges' Vision and Sense," *Greensboro Daily News,* June 8, 1955.

130. "Desegregation Policies in North Carolina Public Schools," *Southern School News,* July 1955, rpt., Box 39, Hodges Papers.

131. Patton, ed., *Public Papers of Governor Luther Hartwell Hodges,* 624.

132. Victor S. Bryant to Luther Hodges, June 9, 1955, Box 39, Hodges Papers.

133. Holt McPherson to Luther Hodges, June 17, 1955, Box 117, Hodges Papers.

134. John Kerr Jr., N.C. Senate, Warrenton, Personal and Confidential, to Luther Hodges, June 17, 1955, Box 117, Hodges Papers.

135. Hodges, *Businessman in the State House,* 82–83.

136. Patton, ed., *Public Papers Governor Luther Hartwell Hodges,* 624.

137. Carolina Population Center, *County Population Trends, North Carolina, 1790–1960,* 17, 34, 40, 38, 47, 49, 69, 97.

138. Thomas J. Pearsall to Luther Hodges, July 6, 1955, Box 42, Hodges Papers.

139. "North Carolina's Wake County Takes Far-Reaching Step," *Southern School News,* August 1955, 3, 114.3/F18, Herring Papers.

140. Patton, ed., *Public Papers of Governor Luther Hartwell Hodges,* 608. Edward N. Rodman, son of William B. Rodman Jr., telephone conversation with author, March 17, 1992.

141. Thomas J. Pearsall to Members of the Advisory Committee, July 5, 1955, Box 39, Hodges Papers.

142. Hodges, *Businessman in the State House,* 83.

143. Handwritten note from Thomas Pearsall, July 7, 1955, Box 42, Hodges Papers. Thomas Pearsall, interview with Calaway, "Pearsall Program," 111.

144. Thomas J. Pearsall to W. W. Taylor Jr., July 22, 1955, Box 39, Hodges Papers.

145. Carolina Population Center, *County Population Trends, North Carolina, 1790–1960,* 98.

146. From the Governor's Office, Raleigh, For Immediate Release, July 21, 1955, Box 39, Hodges Papers. W. W. Taylor, telephone conversation with author, July 14, 1992. "N.C. Governor Asks Voluntary Segregation: NAACP Balks," *Southern School News,* September 1955. Taylor advised that such a relationship did not necessarily imply that he agreed

with Lake on segregation, or other issues. W. W. Taylor Jr., interview with author, July 14, 1992.

147. Thomas J. Pearsall to W. W. Taylor Jr., July 22, 1955, Box 39, Hodges Papers.

148. From the Governor's Office, Raleigh, For Immediate Release, July 21, 1955, Box 39, Hodges Papers.

149. Pleasants and Burns, *Frank Porter Graham,* 88, 98.

150. Thomas J. Pearsall to W. W. Taylor, July 22, 1955, Box 39, Hodges Papers.

151. Dallas Herring to Mr. Kerr, July 25, 1955, 114.3/F18; Dallas Herring to Mr. Kerr (handwritten notation on typed letter, "About Aug 1 55"), 114.3/F18; Chevis Kerr Sr., Clinton, to Dallas Herring, July 19, 1955, 114.3/F18, Herring Papers.

152. "North Carolina's Wake County Takes Far-Reaching Step," *Southern School News,* August 1955, 3, 114.3/F18, Herring Papers. It is not clear whether Fisher had NAACP backing.

153. "Resolution of Wake County Board of Education Affecting Operation of the Wake County Schools, 1955–56," 114.3/F18; "NAACP Says Wake Plan Unacceptable," *Charlotte Observer,* August 2, 1955, 114.3/F18, Herring Papers.

154. "North Carolina's Wake County Takes Far-Reaching Step." "Desegregation Policies in North Carolina Public Schools."

155. "The Supreme Court Order on School Desegregation, May 31, 1955: What It Means and How to Use It," NAACP Bulletin, June 1955, 7, Box 114A, Folio 4, Frederick Alexander Papers.

156. "The Supreme Court Order on School Desegregation," 9–10.

157. "NAACP Says Wake Plan Unacceptable."

158. 227 F. 2d 789 (4th Cir. 1955), commonly referred to as the Old Fort case.

159. *Carson v. Board of Education of McDowell County,* 227 F. 2d (4th Cir. 1955) at 790.

160. 242 N.C. 500 (1955).

161. 132 F. Supp. 776 (E.D.S.C. 1955). Civ. A. No. 2657, July 15, 1955 in 114.4/G18, Herring Papers.

162. Kluger, *Simple Justice,* 141–44. According to Kluger, Parker's nomination was not confirmed due in large part to opposition from the NAACP. For additional information on Parker, the decision, and reaction in North Carolina, see "Judge Parker's Analysis," Raleigh *News and Observer,* n.d., clipping, 114.3/F18, Herring Papers.

163. 132 F. Supp. 776 (E.D.S.C. 1955). Copy of Civ. A. No. 2657 (E.D.S.C. July 15, 1955) in 114.4/G18, Herring Papers.

164. Bascom N. Timmons, "Judge Parker's Analysis," Raleigh *News and Observer,* n.d., clipping, 114.3/F18, Herring Papers. "In a Confused, Inflamed Debate, an Intelligent Voice Is Welcome," *Charlotte Observer,* July 13, 1955, 2-B.

165. "N.C. Governor Asks Voluntary Segregation: NAACP Balks." Hodges, *Businessman in the State House,* 84. "Lake Advises Substitute Plan for Public Schools," n.d., clipping, handwritten note, "*Observer,*" Box 39; "Private Schools Planned," *Charlotte Observer,* August 2, 1955, 114.3/F18, Herring Papers. *Senate Journal, Session 1955,* 2.

166. Patton, ed., *Public Papers of Governor Luther Hartwell Hodges,* 561.

167. "Remarks by Gov. Luther H. Hodges before Lincoln County Kiwanis and Farmers Club," Lincolnton, July 19, 1955, Box 39, Hodges Papers.

168. "Dr. Beverly Lake Amplifies Upon Position Taken in Asheboro Speech," Raleigh *News and Observer,* July 20, 1955, in *Negroes in North Carolina,* 423, clipping file, North Carolina Collection.

169. "Private Schools Planned," *Charlotte Observer,* August 2, 1955, 114.3/F18, Herring Papers.

170. Hodges, *Businessman in the Statehouse,* 85. Patton, ed., *Addresses and Papers of Governor Luther Hartwell Hodges,* 561.

171. Patton, ed., *Public Papers of Governor Luther Hartwell Hodges,* 561. Hodges, *Businessman in the State House,* 86.

172. Luther Hodges to Thomas Pearsall, July 21, 1955, Box 39, Hodges Papers. Letters to Hodges: Mrs. J. M. Atkisson Jr., June 27, 1955; Robert W. Austin Jr., June 30, 1955; Elmore L. Addison and approximately 110 others, July 8, 1955; Emma Adams, July 18, 1955; J. H. Apple, July 18, 1955; R. G. Angel, July 19, 1955; Mrs. Spurgeon Ayscue, July 19, 1955; W. L. Allen, July 19, 1955; Frank L. Austin (a principal in Concord), July 20, 1955; G. E. Andrews, July 20, 1955; J. E. Anderson, July 22, 1955; E. S. Askew, July 22, 1955; John O. Askew, July 22, 1955; A. J. Ashley and 18 others, July 26, 1955; J. M. Atkisson Jr., June 27, 1955 Roy J. Atkinson, July 27, 1955; Mr. and Mrs. Roy Allen, July 29, 1955; W. B. Aldridge, August 2, 1955; Blount Arthur, August 29, 1955; Vernon G. Avery, September 23, 1955; E. S. Anderson, December 8, 1955; Box 39, Hodges Papers.

173. Sam O. Worthington, State Utilities Commission, to Luther Hodges, July 19, 1955, Box 39, Hodges Papers.

174. Edwin Rankin Jr., telephone conversation with author, July 13, 1983.

175. "If Public School System Is Abolished: Dr. I. Beverly Lake," Raleigh *News and Observer,* November 11, 1955; in *Negroes in North Carolina,* 479.

176. Rankin, telephone conversation with author.

177. "Suggestions as to the pros and cons of calling a special session," n.d., Box 39, Hodges Papers. The context of the memorandum strongly suggests it was written in summer 1955. Chafe believes that reference to public apathy on the issue indicates that Hodges and his advisors believed that the people were not concerned about desegregation and were receptive to change in racial matters (*Civilities and Civil Rights,* 79).

178. "Suggestions as to the pros and cons of calling a special session." Calaway, "Pearsall Program," 133–34.

179. Patton, ed., *Public Papers of Governor Luther Hartwell Hodges,* 205.

180. "Address on State-Wide Radio-Television Network," August 8, 1955, in Patton, ed., *Addresses and Papers of Governor Luther Hartwell Hodges,* 199–214. See also "Voluntary Separate Schools Seen as Best Hope by Hodges," Raleigh *News and Observer,* August 9, 1955, for a media account of the address. Patton, ed., *Public Papers of Governor Luther Hartwell Hodges,* 206.

181. Statement by Governor Luther H. Hodges, n.d., Box 39, Hodges Papers. See also D. L. Alford Jr., Chairman, Nash County Board of Education, to Luther Hodges, August 16, 1955, Box 39; C. H. Hamlin, Department of Social Science, Atlantic Christian College, to Luther Hodges, August 16, 1955, Box 39, Hodges Papers.

182. North Carolina Education Association, Division of Superintendents, "Resolution," August 12, 1955, Box 39, Hodges Papers.

183. "Sam Ervin Sees Hope in 'Voluntary Segregation,'" *Charlotte Observer,* November 15, 1955, 114.3/F18, Herring Papers.

184. "Resolution of Young Democrats," date stamped, "Received Governor's Office Sept 23, 1955," Box 39, Hodges Papers.

185. "Hodge-Podge," *The Carolinian,* August 13, 1955.

186. See, for example, Luther Hodges to Messrs. Pearsall, Taylor, and Johnston, August 22, 1955, Box 39, Hodges Papers. Thomas J. Pearsall to W. D. Herring, September 16, 114.3/F18, Herring Papers. Nat S. Crews, Forsyth County Attorney, to Thomas J. Pearsall, April 20, 1956, Box 120, Hodges Papers.

187. "Address Before the North Carolina Teachers' Association," Shaw University, Ra-

leigh, August 26, 1955, in Patton, ed., *Public Papers of Governor Luther Hartwell Hodges,* 214–21.

188. Patton, ed., *Public Papers of Governor Luther Hartwell Hodges,* 214–15.

189. "Teachers Nix Gov.'s Proposal," *The Carolinian,* September 3, 1955. Clipping, "Teachers Hit 'Voluntary' Segregation," Associated Press, August 27, [1955], Box 120, Hodges Papers.

190. W. I. Morris, NEA-NCTA Field Representative, to Luther Hodges, August 30, 1955, Box 120, Hodges Papers.

191. "Address at the Founders' Day Program of the Agricultural and Technical College of North Carolina," Greensboro, November 4, 1955, in Patton, ed., *Public Papers of Governor Luther Hartwell Hodges,* 249–57.

192. Patton, ed., *Public Papers of Governor Luther Hartwell Hodges,* 250.

193. Hodges, *Businessman in the State House,* 90.

194. Patton, ed., *Public Papers of Governor Luther Hartwell Hodges,* 250.

195. "The A. and T. Affair," *Carolina Times,* November 12, 1955.

196. Hodges, *Businessman in the State House,* 91.

197. Patton, ed., *Public Papers of Governor Luther Hartwell Hodges,* 250.

198. Hodges, *Businessman in the State House,* 90–91.

199. Handwritten note in Luther Hodges handwriting, n.d., Box 39, Hodges Papers.

200. "'Patriots of North Carolina' to Promote Segregation Plan," Raleigh *News and Observer,* August 23, 1955, 114.3/F18, Herring Papers.

201. Allison James, Executive Secretary, Patriots of North Carolina, to Luther Hodges, November 3, 1955, Box 39, Hodges Papers.

202. "'Patriots of North Carolina' To Promote Segregation Plan."

203. Allison James, Executive Secretary, Patriots of North Carolina, Inc., Greensboro, to All Superintendents of Schools in North Carolina, n.d., Box 117, Hodges Papers.

204. Allison James to All North Carolina Newspapers, Radio and Television Stations, n.d., ca. November 11, 1955, on Patriots of North Carolina, Inc., letterhead, which includes the names of the officers and directors; Box 39, Hodges Papers. *House Journal, Session 1955,* 3–5; *Senate Journal, Session 1955,* 3.

205. Allison James to All North Carolina Newspapers, Radio and Television Stations, n.d., ca. November 11, 1955, on Patriots of North Carolina, Inc., letterhead. "'Patriots of North Carolina' To Promote Segregation Plan," Raleigh *News and Observer,* August 23, 1955, 114.3/F18, Herring Papers.

206. The terminology refers to Chafe, *Civilities and Civil Rights,* 57.

207. Luther Hodges to E. L. Gavin, Attorney, Sanford, March 19, 1956, Box 117; "Statement from the Governor's Office," August 24, 1955, Box 39, Hodges Papers.

208. Paul A. Johnston, Administrative Assistant, to Octavious Lovin, Patriots of Richmond County, January 13, 1956, Box 117, Hodges Papers.

209. Dr. W. C. George to Luther Hodges, Dec. 10, 1955, Box 120, Hodges Papers.

210. Luther Hodges to Dr. W. C. George, UNC School of Medicine, December 19, 1955, Box 120, Hodges Papers.

211. Luther Hodges to Dr. Lee F. Tuttle, First Methodist Church, Charlotte, December 21, 1955, Box 117, Hodges Papers.

212. Thomas J. Pearsall to Members of the Advisory Committee, July 22, 1955, Box 39, Hodges Papers.

213. W. W. Taylor Jr. to the Members of the North Carolina Advisory Committee, October 26, 1955, Box 39; W. W. Taylor Jr., to the Members of the North Carolina Advisory Committee, October 18, 1955, Box 120; North Carolina Advisory Committee to Super-

intendents of Public Schools of North Carolina, December 20, 1955, Box 120, Hodges Papers.

214. Attorney General William B. Rodman to Luther H. Hodges, September 26, 1955, Box 39; Luther Hodges to Attorney General William B. Rodman, August 30, 1955, Box 39, Hodges Papers.

215. "Analysis of Legislation Adopted by Other States Affecting Public School Systems," Box 39; William W. Taylor Jr., to Members of the North Carolina Advisory Committee, November 23, 1955, Box 117, Hodges Papers.

216. "Analysis of Legislation Adopted by Other States Affecting Public School Systems," Box 39, Hodges Papers.

217. "The Segregation Problem in the Public Schools of North Carolina: Summary of Statements and Actions by Governor Luther H. Hodges," October 3, 1957, Box 227, Hodges Papers.

218. "Confusion and the Schools," October 20, 1955; "Ignorance as a Policy for the South," October 10, 1955; "Would Turn Back the Clock a Century," October 14, 1955, Raleigh *News and Observer.*

219. Luther Hodges to the following: Hon. Larry I. Moore Jr., Wilson; Luther E. Barnhardt, Concord; Carl T. Hicks, Walstonburg; C. Gordon Maddrey, Ahoskie; W. W. Taylor Jr., Raleigh; J. K. Doughton, Stratford; Carl B. Venters, Jacksonville; George R. Uzzell, Salisbury; Calvin Graves, Winston-Salem; J. C. Eagles, Wilson; Nelson Woodson, Salisbury; A. Pilston Godwin Jr., Gatesville; Paul E. Jones, Farmville; all dated October 11, 1955, Hodges Papers. Luther Hodges to John Larkins Jr., Trenton; Luther Hodges to Thomas Pearsall, Rocky Mount, both dated October 21, 1955, Box 120, Hodges Papers.

220. 165 F. Supp. 957 (M.D.N.C. 1958). W. W. Taylor, Jr., Confidential, to the Members of the North Carolina Advisory Committee, October 12, 1955, Box 117, Hodges Papers.

221. W. W. Taylor Jr., Confidential, to the Members of the North Carolina Advisory Committee, October 12, 1955, Box 117, Hodges Papers; quotations from this memo.

222. W. W. Taylor Jr. to Luther Hodges, Oct 18, 1955, Box 120, Hodges Papers.

223. "Memorandum on Possible Legislation Which Might Be Recommended to, or Considered by, the General Assembly at Its Next Session," October 18, 1955, Box 120; W. W. Taylor Jr. to the Members of the North Carolina Advisory Committee, November 23, 1955, Box 117, Hodges Papers.

224. W. W. Taylor Jr. to All Members of the North Carolina Advisory Committee, December 14, 1955, Box 120, Hodges Papers.

225. Ibid., 7–9.

226. "Interim Report of the North Carolina Advisory Committee on Education," attached to Thomas J. Pearsall to Luther Hodges, January 16, 1956, Box 120, Hodges Papers.

227. Balkin and Rodriguez, *Civil Rights Chronology,* 1955.

228. "Dixie Lawmakers Vow to Reverse High Court," *Charlotte Observer,* March 12, 1956. "N.C. Congressmen Who Signed Rebel Manifesto Listed," *Durham Morning Herald,* March 12, 1956, in *Negroes in North Carolina,* 508; "Four Tar Heel Names Missing in Signatures," Raleigh *News and Observer,* March 12, 1956, in *Negroes in North Carolina,* 509.

229. "From the Governor's Office," For Immediate Release, March 2, 1956, Box 312, Hodges Papers.

230. W. W. Taylor Jr., to Luther Hodges, March 16, 1956, Box 120, Hodges Papers.

231. "The Pearsall Plan to Save Our Schools" (Raleigh: North Carolina Advisory Committee, [1956]), Box 120, Hodges Papers.

232. Calaway, "Pearsall Program," 143–44.

233. Patton, ed., *Addresses and Papers of Governor Luther Hartwell Hodges,* 56.

234. "The April 5th Report of the North Carolina Advisory Committee on Education to the Governor, the General Assembly, the State Board of Education, and the County and Local School Boards of North Carolina," 9, Box 227, Hodges Papers.

235. North Carolina Advisory Committee on Education, For Release: 7:30 p.m. EST, Thursday, April 5, 1956, Box 120, Hodges Papers.

236. Thomas J. Pearsall to Luther Hodges, June 4, 1956, Box 120, Hodges Papers.

237. Thos. J. Pearsall to Luther H. Hodges, Luther Barnhardt, Larry Moore, and William Friday, July 7, 1956, Box 120, Hodges Papers.

238. Thomas J. Pearsall to Members of Governor's Advisory Committee, July 9, 1956, Box 120, Hodges Papers.

239. Thomas J. Pearsall to Members of the Special Advisory Committee, Mar 20, 1956, Box 120; Thomas J. Pearsall to the Governor's Special Advisory Committee, July 16, 1956, Box 120, Hodges Papers.

240. H.B. 1, "An Act to Amend Article IX of the Constitution of North Carolina So As to Authorize Education Expense Grants and to Authorize Local Option to Suspend Operation of Public Schools," in *Proposed Constitutional Amendment and Implementing Acts Relating to Public Education* (Raleigh: Secretary of State, 1956), 3.

241. H.B. 4, "An Act to Provide for a Local Option to Suspend Operation of Public Schools," in *Proposed Constitutional Amendment and Implementing Acts Relating to Public Education,* 12.

242. H.B. 5, "An Act to Amend G.S. 115-166 Relating to Compulsory School Attendance," in *Proposed Constitutional Amendment and Implementing Acts Relating to Public Education,* 17.

243. S.R. 11, *Senate Journal, Extra Session 1956,* 19. H.R. 8, *House Journal, Extra Session 1956,* 17.

244. Hodges, *Businessman in the State House,* 98.

245. S.B. 12, *Senate Journal, Extra Session 1956,* 20. H.B. 9, *House Journal, Extra Session 1956,* 17.

246. "Daily Bulletin," Institute of Government, July 25, 1956, Box 66, Hodges Papers. Woodrow Price, "Adjournment of Special Session Today Regarded as Likely," Raleigh *News and Observer,* July 27, 1956, in *Negroes in North Carolina,* 563.

247. Hodges, *Businessman in the State House,* 98. Price, "Adjournment of Special Session Today Regarded as Likely."

248. H.B. 12, *House Journal, Extra Session 1956,* 20.

249. H.B. 13, *House Journal, Extra Session 1956,* 20.

250. "Daily Bulletin," Institute of Government, July 27, 1956, Box 66, Hodges Papers.

251. "Statements by Members," *House Journal, Extra Session 1956,* 24, 25.

252. H.B. 2, "An Act to Provide for a General Election on September 8, 1956," in *Proposed Constitutional Amendment and Implementing Acts Relating to Public Education,* 4.

253. Hodges, *Businessman in the State House,* 102.

254. "Resolution," Pitt County Branch of the Patriots of North Carolina, Inc., July 12, 1956, Box 117, Hodges Papers. Hodges, *Businessman in the State House,* 99.

255. "N.C. Editors State Pearsall Plan Views," *Durham Morning Herald,* September 6, 1956, in *Negroes in North Carolina,* 574.

256. "Special Release," N.C. Schools Boards Association, August 7, 1956, Box 66; Guy B. Phillips, Executive Secretary, NCSBA, to Luther Hodges, August 7, 1956, Box 21.4; Luther Hodges to Jack Mitchell, President, Junior Chamber of Commerce, Asheville, August 22, 1956, Box 21.4; Luther Hodges to Members of General Assembly, August 24, 1956, Box 66, Hodges Papers.

257. Letters to Luther Hodges from Harold D. Cooley (4th Cong. Dist. N.C.), August 28, 1956; Woodrow W. Jones (11th Cong. Dist. N.C.), August 28, 1956; George A. Shuford (12th Cong. Dist. N.C.), August 28, 1956; Box 120, Hodges Papers.

258. Luther Hodges to Sam J. Ervin Jr., September 4, 1956, Box 120, Hodges Papers.

259. "This is a list of people supporting Governor Hodges in his stand on segregation, compiled from correspondence file in Governor's office," July 27, 1956, Box 130, Hodges Papers.

260. Hodges, *Businessman in the State House,* 99. "Lawyers Differ on Pearsall Plan," Raleigh *News and Observer,* July 17, 1957, in *Negroes in North Carolina,* 549–50; "Greensboro Superintendent Against School Amendment," Raleigh *News and Observer,* August 25, 1956, in *Negroes in North Carolina,* 581.

261. "Address by Governor Luther H. Hodges in Behalf of Special Session School Amendment," September 7, 1956, Box 120, Hodges Papers.

262. "Mixing the Races—from Top of 'Powder Keg,'" Raleigh *News and Observer,* July 1985 (400th Anniversary Special Edition), 9.

263. Hodges, *Businessman in the Statehouse,* 104. *North Carolina Manual* (Raleigh: Secretary of State, 1957), 253, 255–56.

264. Votes Cast For and Against Special Session School Amendment, September 8, 1956, Box 21.4, Hodges Papers.

CHAPTER FOUR

1. Luther Hodges, handwritten notes, n.d., context suggests fall 1956, Box 39, Hodges Papers. "On the Desegregation Front," *The Carolinian,* June 25, 1955.

2. "School Segregation Policy," *Winston-Salem Journal,* November 14, 1956, Box 227, Hodges Papers. "Integration's Spread in N.C. Schools Is Seen," Asheville *Citizen,* July 25, 1957, in *Negroes in North Carolina,* 599.

3. "Human Relations Bulletin" (Charlotte: North Carolina Council on Human Relations, October 1957).

4. Luther Hodges, Personal, to Reed Sarratt, Executive Editor, Piedmont Publishing Company, December 4, 1956, Box 227, Hodges Papers.

5. Robert E. Giles, interview with author, April 22, 1992. Dallas Herring, telephone conversation with author, April 28, 1992.

6. Robert E. Giles, interview with author, April 20, 1992. A. Craig Phillips, telephone conversation with author, April 28, 1992. Lunsford Crew, telephone conversation with author, July 15, 1992.

7. Frye Gaillard, *The Dream Long Deferred* (Chapel Hill: University of North Carolina Press, 1988), 20.

8. Ibid., 3.

9. Craig Phillips, telephone conversation with author, April 28, 1992.

10. Dallas Herring, telephone conversation with author, April 28, 1992. Craig Phillips, telephone conversation with author, April 28, 1992.

11. "Three Tar Heel Cities 'Mix,'" *The Carolinian,* September 7, 1957. "Officials Credited With Smooth Change," *The Carolina Times,* September 14, 1957. See also Ralph Lee Smith, "The South's Pupil Placement Laws," *Commentary* 30 (October 1960), 326.

12. Gaillard, *Dream Long Deferred,* xvii, 12.

13. *In Re: Applications for Reassignment,* 247 N.C. 413 (1958).

14. "Integration's Spread in N.C. Schools Is Seen." "Three Cities Settling Down After Integrating Schools," Raleigh *News and Observer,* September 7, 1957.

15. The exact number of requests denied varies slightly according to the source. A speech by Governor Hodges, in "Excerpt from an Address by Governor Luther H. Hodges at Greensboro, North Carolina," September 13, 1957, Box 227, Hodges Papers, indicates thirty-nine. A newspaper account, "Integration's Spread in N.C. Schools Seen," cited above, says forty-one. This figure is repeated in "Admissions May Help State's Legal Position," Raleigh *News and Observer,* July 24, 1957, in *Negroes in North Carolina,* 600. The applications cited in that article add up to thirty-nine, however.

16. "Admissions May Help State's Legal Position," Raleigh *News and Observer,* July 24, 1957, in *Negroes in North Carolina,* 600. The city of Charlotte and the county of Mecklenburg maintained separate school systems at the time.

17. Statement by Gov. Luther H. Hodges, August 29, 1957, Box 227, Hodges Papers.

18. John L. Sanders, Assistant Director, Institute of Government, to Robert E. Giles, Administrative Assistant to the Governor, August 30, 1957, Box 227, Hodges Papers.

19. Robert E. Giles, interview with author, April 20, 1992.

20. North Carolina Highway Patrol reports, Box 227, Hodges Papers.

21. Major David T. Lambert, State Highway Patrol, to Colonel James R. Smith, Commanding, September 4, 1957.

22. Lambert to Smith, September 4, 1957, Box 227, Hodges Papers.

23. "Kasper, the Klan and Public Opinion," Southern Pines *Pilot,* September 5, 1957, in *Negroes in North Carolina,* 606.

24. Lambert to Smith, September 4, 1957, Box 227, Hodges Papers. This document does not contain the principal's name. The Public Information Office of the Charlotte-Mecklenburg Schools provided his identity.

25. Sgt. O. R. Roberts to Col. James R. Smith, September 4, 1957, Box 227, Hodges Papers.

26. Gaillard, *Dream Long Deferred,* 6, 7, 10–11.

27. Report #7, #8—Maj. Lambeth, September 5, 1957, Box 227, Hodges Papers.

28. "Southern Newsletter," October 1957, Box 114A, Folio 4, Frederick Alexander Papers.

29. Report #4, #10—Maj. Lambert, September 5, 1957, Box 227, Hodges Papers.

30. Meredith Barkley, "Court Mixed Races in School 30 Years Ago," *Greensboro News and Record,* May 17, 1984.

31. Report #5—Maj. Lambert, September 6, 1957; Report #1—Maj. Lambert, September 10, 1957; Report #2—Maj. Lambert, September 10, 1957, Box 227, Hodges Papers.

32. Walter F. Anderson to Robert E. Giles, September 17, 1957, Box 227, Hodges Papers. "Greensboro Superintendent's Yard Scene of Cross Burning," *The Carolinian,* September 14, 1957.

33. The author lived one block from Superintendent Smith's home. I was one of several neighborhood boys who visited after school and took coffee and cake at night to the undercover officers in an unmarked car parked on Cypress Street. The car remained across the street from Aycock School, twenty-four hours a day, for several months. One of the officers was Conrad Wade, who later became chief of police. He was a strong, positive influence on a boy who had no father in the home.

34. Louise C. Smith, former teacher at Greensboro Senior High, telephone conversation with author, July 18, 1983.

35. "Integration, Forced Busing Ignited Strong Opposition," Raleigh *News and Observer,* July 1985, 10. "Human Relations Bulletin" (Charlotte: North Carolina Council on Human Relations, July 1958), Box 121, Folio 87, Frederick Alexander Papers.

36. "Public Schools and the Racial Problem," Address by Luther Hodges in Greensboro, September 13, 1957, Box 227, Hodges Papers.

37. Typed notes, n.d., Box 227, Hodges Papers.

38. Loye Miller, "NAACP Will 'Wait' for N.C. Progress," *Charlotte Observer,* October 12, 1957, Box 227, Hodges Papers.

39. "The NAACP and the South," Asheville *Citizen-Times,* January 12, 1958, in *Negroes in North Carolina,* 973.

40. "Negro Teachers Resign Rather Than Sign Pledge," Raleigh *News and Observer,* May 17, 1956, in *Negroes in North Carolina,* 968.

41. Bernard Schwartz, *Swann's Way* (New York: Oxford University Press, 1986), 6–8.

42. "Failed to Register, Eure Is Informed," Durham *Morning Herald,* November 15, 1955, in *Negroes in North Carolina,* 965.

43. "Rodman Informs NAACP Law Applies to Its Activities," Raleigh *News and Observer,* February 3, 1956, in *Negroes in North Carolina,* 500.

44. "N.C. Wins Round Against NAACP," Asheville *Citizen,* March 13, 1956, in *Negroes in North Carolina,* 965–66. "$500 Check Paid State By NAACP," Raleigh *News and Observer,* April 2, 1957, in *Negroes in North Carolina,* 965. "NAACP Files With State as Foreign Corporation," Raleigh *News and Observer,* February 18, 1957, in *Negroes in North Carolina,* 968.

45. H.B. 984, *House Journal, 1957,* 688, 50–52. Other cosponsors included R. Frank Everett of Martin County, Dr. J. M. Phelps of Washington County, C. Blake Thomas of Johnston County, Joe A. Watkins of Granville County, Ashley M. Murphy of Pender County, and P. R. Vann of Sampson County.

46. Roy Parker Jr., "9 Representatives Would Tell NAACP to Bare Member List," Raleigh *News and Observer,* May 7, 1957, in *Negroes in North Carolina,* 966.

47. H.B. 1137, *House Journal, 1957,* 804. S. B. 433, 434, *Senate Journal, 1957,* 499.

48. Roy Parker Jr., "Administration Measures Are Directed at NAACP," Raleigh *News and Observer,* May 17, 1957, in *Negroes in North Carolina,* 971.

49. Robert E. Giles, interview with author, April 20, 1992.

50. 139 F. Supp. 161 (M.D.N.C. 1956).

51. *Covington,* 139 F. Supp. at 162 (no author indicated), Analysis of *Covington,* 114.4/G18, Herring Papers. The context of this document and its placement in the Herring Papers suggests that it was written either by a member of the attorney general's staff or by one of the attorneys on the first or second Pearsall Committee.

52. *Covington,* 139 F. Supp. at 163.

53. 244 N.C. 164 (1956).

54. *Joyner,* 244 N.C. 169.

55. 238 F. 2d 724 (4th Cir. 1956).

56. *Carson,* 238 F. 2d at 729.

57. *Carson v. Warlick, cert. denied,* 353 U.S. 910 (1957).

58. 244 N.C. 221 (1956).

59. Additional commentary in Beezer, "North Carolina's Rationale for Mandating Separate Schools," 225.

60. *In Re: Applications for Reassignment,* 2 Race Relations Law Reporter 967 (Superior Court, Guilford County, September 4, 1957).

61. Ibid., 969.

62. *In Re: Applications for Reassignment,* 247 N.C. 413 (1958).

63. Ibid., at 421.

64. Daniel J. Meador, "The Constitution and the Assignment of Pupils to Public Schools," *Virginia Law Review* 45 (1959): 539, 540.

65. *Adkins v. School Board of Newport News,* 148 F. Supp. at 442. Meador, "The Constitution and the Assignment of Pupils to Public Schools," 540.

66. Robert G. Webb, "Constitutional Law—Little Rock School Litigation—Reexamination of North Carolina Laws," *North Carolina Law Review* 37 (1959): 181, n. 31. *Adkins v. School Board of Newport News,* 148 F. Supp. 430 (E.D. Va. 1957), *aff'd* 246 F. 2d 325 (4th Cir. 1957).

67. N.C. Council on Human Relations, "Special Report, Little Rock: A Look at the Record," September 16, 1958, Box 312, Hodges Papers. The report is based on information supplied by the Southern Regional Council.

68. *Faubus v. United States,* 254 F. 2d 797 (8th Cir. 1957).

69. "From the Governor's Office," September 27, 1957, Box 522, Hodges Papers.

70. "Opening Statement to the President by Governor Luther H. Hodges, Chairman of Special Committee to See the President," n.d., Box 522, Hodges Papers.

71. "Text of Joint Statement Issued by President and Governors' Committee After Conference on Tuesday, October 1, 1957," Box 523, Hodges Papers.

72. N.C. Council on Human Relations, "Special Report, Little Rock: A Look at the Record," 4.

73. *Cooper v. Aaron,* 358 U.S. 1 (1958), at 16, at 7.

74. Statement by Governor Luther H. Hodges, September 30, 1958, Box 312, Hodges Papers.

75. Douglas, *Reading, Writing, and Race,* 74.

76. Luther H. Hodges to Malcolm B. Seawell, Attorney General, November 24, 1958, Box 312, Hodges Papers.

77. Malcolm B. Seawell, Attorney General, to Luther H. Hodges, December 1, 1958, Box 312, Hodges Papers.

78. Correspondence Files A–Z, Box 312, Hodges Papers contain many letters taking Hodges to task for not uniting with Faubus and Virginia governor Lindsay Almond in support of segregation. See also Petition, postmarked October 13, 1958, Marshville, N.C., Box 312; and unsigned "Sympathy" card, Siler City, to Luther Hodges, September 22, 1957, Box 227, Hodges Papers.

79. REG [Robert E. Giles] to Governor Hodges, September 29, 1957, Box 522, Hodges Papers.

80. I. Beverly Lake, "Gradual Integration in N.C.," September 20, 1957, Box 227, Hodges Papers.

81. Ibid.

82. "Dr. Lake Hits NAACP Aims," Burlington, N.C., *Daily Times-News,* March 3, 1959.

83. Walter F. Anderson, Director, Bureau of Investigation, N.C. Dept. of Justice, to George B. Patton, Attorney General, and Robert Giles, Governor's Office, October 8, 1957, Box 227, Hodges Papers.

84. Powell, *North Carolina,* 188.

85. Memorandum: Regarding Telephone Conversation with Sheriff Malcolm McLeod of Robeson County, January 29, 1958, Box 313; Memorandum: Regarding Telephone Conversation with Mayor J. C. Oxendine of Pembroke, January 29, 1958, Box 313, Hodges Papers.

86. Statement by Gov. Luther H. Hodges, January 30, 1958, Box 312, Hodges Papers.

87. Agent L. E. Allen, State Bureau of Investigation, to the Director, January 27, 1958, Box 313, Hodges Papers.

88. Walter F. Anderson, Director, Bureau of Investigation, N.C. Dept. of Justice, to George B. Patton, Attorney General, and Robert Giles, Governor's Office, October 8, 1957, Box 227, Hodges Papers.

89. Ibid. Walter F. Anderson to Robert E. Giles, September 17, 1957, Box 227; A Very Concerned Citizen of Monroe, NC to Luther Hodges, October 7, 1957, Box 227; Agent L. E. Allen, State Bureau of Investigation, to the Director, June 29, 1958, Box 313; Agent J. N. Minter, State Bureau of Investigation, to the Director, August 18, 1958, Box 313, Hodges Papers.

90. Robert E. Giles to Governor Hodges, February 12, 1958, Box 313, Hodges Papers.

91. "Education, School Bombing—North Carolina," 3 Race Relations Law Reporter 464 (1958).

92. Ibid., 465–66.

93. *State v. Caldwell,* 105 S.E. 2d 189 (N.C. 1958). 3 Race Relations Law Reporter 1159 (Superior Court, Mecklenburg County 1958).

94. Agent L. E. Allen, State Bureau of Investigation, to the Director, April 15, June 1, June 8, June 29, 1958, Box 313, Hodges Papers.

95. "The North Carolina Ku Klux Klan Revival," no location given: North Carolina Office of the Anti-Defamation League of B'nai B'rith, n.d., context suggests fall 1958, Box 131, Folio 22, Frederick Alexander Papers.

96. Agent L. E. Allen, State Bureau of Investigation, to the Director, June 29, 1958, Box 313, Hodges Papers.

97. Agent J. N. Minter, State Bureau of Investigation, to the Director, August 18, 1958, Box 313, Hodges Papers.

98. Agent L. E. Allen, State Bureau of Investigation, to the Director, August 10, 1958, Box 313, Hodges Papers.

99. Chafe states that the threat from the Klan was "less than it might have appeared" (*Civilities and Civil Rights,* 194). This comment could apply only to events in Greensboro, not to the state as a whole. The individuals involved, however, are the same as those who appear on the state scene. Chafe points out, correctly, that the Klan had been infiltrated by law enforcement officers. My account of Klan activity is based on informant sources reported through the State Bureau of Investigation. The information these informers provided does not lead me to discount the level of threat that the Klan posed. On the contrary, the reports are alarming. They represent the information law enforcement officials had available at the time, which is much more important than hindsight.

100. "The North Carolina Ku Klux Klan Revival."

101. *Holt,* 164 F. Supp. (E.D.N.C. 1958), at 858, 859, 866–69. See also Ben Stocking, "Joseph Hiram Holt, Pioneer in School Desegregation, Dies at 88," Raleigh *News and Observer,* November 17, 1995.

102. 165 F. Supp. (M.D.N.C. 1958), at 952–953, 957.

103. 165 F. Supp. 957 (M.D.N.C. 1958).

104. *Covington,* 165 F. Supp. at 958, 959, 960.

105. *Covington v. Edwards,* 264 F. 2d 780 (4th Cir. 1959).

106. 265 F. 2d 95 (4th Cir. 1959).

107. *McKissick v. Durham City Board of Education,* 176 F. Supp. 3 (M.D.N.C. 1959). Family identification provided by Floyd McKissick III.

108. John D. Morris, "'Massive Resistance' Faces Critical Tests," *New York Times,* August 31, 1958, Box 312, Hodges Papers. "Human Relations Bulletin" (Charlotte: North Carolina Council on Human Relations, January 1960), Box 121, Folio 87, Frederick Alexander Papers.

109. "School Closing Plans," 3 Race Relations Law Reporter 807–40 (1958).

110. In Clinton, Tennessee, dynamite seriously damaged the local high school after blacks were admitted. See, for example, Claude Sitton, "Lines Hardening on Integration," *New York Times,* October 19, 1958, Box 312, Hodges Papers.

111. Robert E. Giles, telephone conversation with author, August 4, 1992.

112. A. T. Spaulding to Luther H. Hodges, October 4, 1957, Box 522, Hodges Papers. The letter bears Hodges's handwritten note, "Friday, 11th, 11:45 a.m."

113. Robert E. Giles, interview with author.

114. Qtd. in "Human Relations Bulletin" (Charlotte: North Carolina Council on Human Relations, November 1958), Box 121, Folio 87, Frederick Alexander Papers.

115. Dallas Herring, "Door of Education Must Remain Open," *Charlotte Observer,* June 24, 1960.

116. Dallas Herring, telephone conversation with author, August 4, 1992.

117. "Human Relations Bulletin" (Charlotte: North Carolina Council on Human Relations, May 1956), Box 121, Folio 86, Frederick Alexander Papers.

118. Ibid.

119. "Hodges Hits 'Appeasing' Minorities," *Charlotte Observer,* September 17, 1959.

120. Sitton, "Lines Hardening on Integration."

121. George Watts Hill to Luther Hodges, March 31, 1959; enclosure: "High Cost of 'Massive Resistance' Policy," *Durham Herald,* March 30, 1959, Box 421, Hodges Papers.

122. "Report of the Executive Director to Members and Friends of the Southern Regional Council," October 19, 1959, Box 114A, Folio 6, Frederick Alexander Papers.

123. 186 F. Supp. 511 (W.D.N.C. 1960).

124. *Griffith,* 186 F. Supp., 513–17.

125. 179 F. Supp. 745 (M.D.N.C. 1960).

126. *McCoy v. Greensboro City Board of Education,* 283 F. 2d 667 (4th Cir. 1960).

127. *McCoy,* 283 F. 2d at 670.

128. Alexander R. Stoeson, "A Celebration of Guilford County Since 1890," *History of Guilford County, N.C.* ([Greensboro, N.C.]: Guilford County Bicentennial Commission, 1971), 200.

129. "Lunch Counter Demonstrations" forms, Box 522, Hodges Papers. Powell, *North Carolina,* 189.

130. Thomas Wade Bruton, Attorney General, to Governor Luther H. Hodges, March 9, 1960, Box 522, Hodges Papers.

131. Conversation between Mr. Edward F. Harrington, Vice-President of F. W. Woolworth Company, and Governor Hodges, March 10, 1960; Telephone conversation between Governor Hodges and Mr. C. M. Purdy, District Manager of Woolworth's, Atlanta, March 10, 1960; Box 522, Hodges Papers.

132. Telephone conversation between Hodges and Purdy. Press Conference Statement by Governor Luther H. Hodges, March 10, 1960, Box 522, Hodges Papers.

133. Telephone conversations between Purdy, Harrigan, and Hodges, March 10, 1960, Box 522, Hodges Papers.

134. Governor Hodges to Robert Giles, March 9, 1960, Box 522, Hodges Papers.

135. Press Conference Statement by Governor Luther H. Hodges, March 10, 1960, Box 522, Hodges Papers.

136. Chafe, *Civilities and Civil Rights,* 78.

137. Qtd. in Michael S. Durham, *Powerful Days: The Civil Rights Photography of Charles Moore* (New York: Stewart, Tabori & Chang, 1991), 144.

CHAPTER FIVE

1. Graham Jones, "Sanford Officially Enters State's Gubernatorial Race," *Durham Morning Herald,* February 5, 1960.

2. Terry Sanford, letter to author, February 3, 1998.

3. Joseph C. Koenenn, "Gubernatorial Hopefuls Hit Home Stretch," *Durham Morning Herald,* May 22, 1960.

4. Charles Dunn, "Beverly Lake Enters Contest for Governor," *Durham Morning Herald,* March 2, 1960.

5. "Lake Urges Segregation School Policy," *Durham Morning Herald,* April 22, 1960.

6. "NAACP to Oppose Vigorously Lake's Bid," *Durham Morning Herald,* March 3, 1960. Charles Dunn, "Lake Dedicates Self to Defeat of NAACP Plans," *Durham Morning Herald,* May 1, 1960.

7. *North Carolina Manual,* 228.

8. "Lake Calls for Runoff Gubernatorial Contest," *Durham Morning Herald,* May 31, 1960.

9. "Lake Blasts NAACP in Mountain Talks," *Durham Morning Herald,* June 19, 1960.

10. "Sanford, Lake Aides Confer on Debate," *Durham Morning Herald,* June 4, 1960.

11. Sanford explained to me that he was using the term "integrationist" to mean "one agitating for extreme and immediate action." "My own play on words," Sanford stated. Terry Sanford, handwritten notes to author, February 3, 1998.

12. Dunn, "Lake Dedicates Self to Defeat of NAACP Plans." "Lake Expects Victory at Polls on Saturday," *Durham Morning Herald,* June 24, 1960.

13. "Lake Expects Victory at Polls on Saturday," *Durham Morning Herald,* June 24, 1960. "Pearsall Says Lake Willing to Gamble Schools for Gain," *Durham Morning Herald,* June 16, 1960.

14. "Lake Authorship Claim Supported," *Durham Morning Herald,* June 18, 1960.

15. "Pearsall Says Lake Draft of School Law Rewritten," *Durham Morning Herald,* June 19, 1960.

16. "Seawell Backs Sanford; Act Reveals Split," *Durham Morning Herald,* June 24, 1960.

17. Maupin, Taylor, and Ellis subsequently became law partners in one of the largest and most influential firms in the State.

18. "N.C. Race Foes Step Up Charges," *Durham Sun,* June 23, 1960.

19. *North Carolina Manual,* 229.

20. "Sanford's Lead Shown as 76,228," *Durham Morning Herald,* July 2, 1960.

21. Chafe, *Civilities and Civil Rights,* 51, 80–81, 94–97, 152.

22. *North Carolina Manual,* 232.

23. "Philpott Takes Wide Lead in Race for Lt. Governor," *Durham Morning Herald,* May 29, 1960.

24. Terry Sanford, handwritten notes to author, February 3, 1998.

25. uselectionatlas.org /RESULTS/.

26. Civil Rights Digital Library, crdl.usg.edu/events/civil_rights_act_1957/?Welcome.

27. North Carolina Advisory Committee [on Civil Rights], "Equal Protection of the Law in Education in North Carolina," October 1, 1960, Box 112, Terry Sanford Papers, State Archives, Raleigh.

28. Terry Sanford, handwritten notes to author, February 3, 1998.

29. "Brandis Throws Light on Meaning of Integration," *Chapel Hill Weekly,* March 2,

1959; "UNC Dean Protests School Board Ruling," unidentified clipping, n.d., in envelope postmarked August 5, 1959, Box 421, Hodges Papers.

30. Joseph C. Koenenn, "Token School Integration Reaches 8th Tarheel Town," *Durham Morning Herald,* July 3, 1960.

31. Alan K. Whiteleather, "Chapel Hill Body Opens Way for Elementary Integration," *Durham Morning Herald,* July 4, 1961.

32. Jim Shumaker, "For School Integration, a Geographic Plan," *Durham Morning Herald,* July 9, 1961.

33. "Judge Rules in Vickers' Favor," *Durham Morning Herald,* August 5, 1961.

34. Alan K. Whiteleather, "Integration Expanded in Chapel Hill Schools," *Durham Morning Herald,* July 10, 1962.

35. North Carolina Advisory Committee [on Civil Rights], "Equal Protection of the Law in Education in North Carolina."

36. "Duke Trustees Vote to End All Segregation Throughout University," *Durham Morning Herald,* June 3, 1962. See also *Legacy, 1963–1993: Thirty Years of African-American Students at Duke University* (Durham, N.C.: Duke University, Office of the University Vice President and Vice Provost, 1995), 13, 24; facesofcourage.wfu.edu. library.davidson.edu/archives/acs/integration/kates_page.htm.

37. A point made by Robert E. Giles, interview with author, April 20, 1992.

38. This discussion is based on Terry Sanford's telephone conversation with the author, August 5, 1992, with additional evidence from an internal memorandum, no author indicated, Notes for Governor Sanford, n.d., Box 111, Sanford Papers. Context clearly indicates the memo was prepared at the beginning of Sanford's term, in early 1961. Further confirmed by Terry Sanford, handwritten notes to author, February 3, 1998.

39. Notes for Governor Sanford, n.d., no author indicated, Box 111, Sanford Papers.

40. Sanford, Telephone conversation with author.

41. Ibid. Quotation from Terry Sanford, letter to author, February 3, 1998. Additional evidence from W. W. Finlator to Terry Sanford, February 2, 1961, Box 111; Rev. Thomas H. House, The Duplin Charge, to Terry Sanford, January 23, 1961, Box 112; Henry G. Ruark, Minister, First Methodist Church, Laurinburg, to Hugh Cannon, April 28, 1961, Box 112; Terry Sanford to Most Reverend Vincent S. Waters, May 15, 1963, Box 348; Terry Sanford to Right Reverend Thomas A. Fraser, May 15, 1963, Box 348; Mother M. Raphael, Mercy Hospital, to Terry Sanford, June 3, 1963, Box 347; Rev. Richard N. Ottaway, St. Paul's Episcopal Church, Greenville, to Terry Sanford, June 26, 1963, Box 347; George Walker Buckner, D.D., Lit.D., Chapel Hill, to Terry Sanford, July 4, 1963, Box 346; A. Walton Litz, Presbyterian Foundation, Charlotte, to Terry Sanford, July 9, 1963, Box 347; David G. Brown Jr., Minister, First Christian Church, Belhaven, to Terry Sanford, July 26, 1963, Box 346; Robert M. Cooper, St. David's Episcopal Church, Laurinburg, to Governor Sanford, Box 346; Collins Kilburn, Minister, United Church, Raleigh, to Terry Sanford, June 27, 1963, Box 347; Rev. Henry G. Ruark, First Methodist Church, Rocky Mount, to Terry Sanford, September 11, 1963, Box 347; W. W. Finlator, Pullen Memorial Baptist Church, to Terry Sanford, January 27, 1964, Box 450; Rev. A. T. Ayscue, Wise Baptist Church, Wise, to Terry Sanford, May 1, 1964, Box 450; Sanford Papers.

42. Sanford, telephone conversation with author. Additional evidence in Allyn S. Park Jr., Executive Director, Union County Industrial Development Commission, to Terry Sanford, August 30, 1961, Box 112, Sanford Papers.

43. Kelly M. Alexander, Discussion in Reference to Equality of Opportunity in State Government Employment, and a Request for Qualified Negroes to Be Employed in State

Governmental Agencies and Departments on an Equal Basis with Other Citizens, October 27, 1961, Box 111, Sanford Papers.

44. Sanford, telephone conversation with author.

45. Thomas J. Pearsall to Terry Sanford, May 29, 1961, Box 112, Sanford Papers.

46. David T. Lambert, Colonel, Commanding, State Highway Patrol, to Hugh Cannon, Administrative Assistant, Governor's Office, June 13, 1961, Box 111, Sanford Papers.

47. Maj. C. Raymond Williams, Director, Enforcement Division, State Highway Patrol, to Commissioner Edward Scheidt, Department of Motor Vehicles, August 28, 1961, Box 112, Sanford Papers.

48. "Police Dogs and Fire Hoses used in Birmingham Strife," *Durham Morning Herald*, May 4, 1963.

49. Robert F. Kennedy to Hon. Terry Sanford, May 21, 1961, Box 111, Sanford Papers.

50. Terry Sanford, "A Statement of Faith and Purpose in Education," November 21, 1960, in Memory F. Mitchell, ed., *Messages, Addresses, and Public Papers of Terry Sanford* (Raleigh: Council of State, 1966), 91.

51. Sanford, "Statement of Faith and Purpose in Education," 95, 97.

52. Terry Sanford, "Budget Message to the General Assembly," February 9, 1961, in Mitchell, ed., *Messages, Addresses and Public Papers of Terry Sanford*, 30.

53. Mitchell, ed., *Messages, Addresses and Public Papers of Terry Sanford*, 26, 114. Sanford, telephone conversation with author.

54. Sanford, telephone conversation with author.

55. Mitchell, ed., *Messages, Addresses and Public Papers of Terry Sanford*, xxvii, xxviii.

56. www.ncgovschool.org/overview/.

57. www.ncpublicschools.org/students/edhistory.

58. Sanford, Address to City-Wide PTA Rally, Fayetteville, February 28, 1961, in Mitchell, ed., *Messages, Addresses and Public Papers of Terry Sanford*, 114.

59. Sanford, telephone conversation with author.

60. North Carolina Citizens Committee for Better Schools, Minutes, February 22, 1962, 114.21/M11.31, Herring Papers.

61. Mitchell, ed., *Messages, Addresses and Public Papers of Terry Sanford*, xxxiv.

62. Statement by Governor Terry Sanford, "Observation for a Second Century," January 18, 1963, Box 281, Sanford Papers.

63. Statement by Governor Terry Sanford, The Good Neighbor Program, January 18, 1963, Box 281, Sanford Papers.

64. 195 F. Supp. 109 (W.D.N.C. 1961).

65. www.cms.k12.nc.us/mediaroom/aboutus/Pages/History.aspx.

66. *Morrow*, 195 F. Supp. at 112–14.

67. 196 F. Supp. 71 (M.D.N.C. 1961). It is noteworthy that one of the plaintiffs in *Wheeler* was C. C. Spaulding III, grandson of the founder of North Carolina Mutual Insurance, the largest black-owned firm in the United States. The elder Spaulding had opposed defying the white power structure, preferring to work slowly and quietly behind the scenes to improve racial conditions. See Ware, "*Hocutt*: Genesis of *Brown*," 227–33.

68. *Wheeler*, 196 F. Supp. at 81.

69. "7 More Negroes in White Schools," *Durham Morning Herald*, August 25, 1960.

70. *Wheeler*, 196 F. Supp. at 83.

71. "Durham to Integrate Elementary School," Raleigh *News and Observer*, August 22, 1961.

72. Jon Phelps, "Harris Hits School Board Method of Voting Down Requests," *Durham Morning Herald,* August 9, 1961.

73. Charles Barbour, "City School Board Hears 133 Appeal Reassignment Pleas," *Durham Morning Herald,* August 22, 1961.

74. Jon Phelps, "City Board of Education Rejects All 133 Appeals," *Durham Morning Herald,* August 24, 1961.

75. *Wheeler v. Durham City Board of Education,* 210 F. Supp. 839 (M.D.N.C. 1962).

76. *Wheeler v. Durham City Board of Education,* 309 F. 2d 630 (4th Cir. 1962).

77. Ibid., at 633.

78. Jon Phelps, "183 Negroes May Transfer to White Schools Jan. 22," *Durham Morning Herald,* January 4, 1963.

79. Jon Phelps, "46 Negroes Assigned in Integration Order," *Durham Morning Herald,* January 17, 1963. "Education Board Acts on Requests of Negro Pupils," *Durham Morning Herald,* January 22, 1963.

80. "Integration of New Semester Is Unmarred," *Durham Morning Herald,* January 23, 1963.

81. Charmaine McKissick-Melton, "Pain of First Students to Desegregate Durham Schools Endures," *The Durham News,* October 28, 2014, www.thedurhamnews.com/2014/10/28/4272312_charmaine-mckissick-melton-pain.html?rh=1.

82. "City School Integration Plan Given," *Durham Morning Herald,* April 20, 1963.

83. Jon Phelps, "Court Outlines 'Freedom of Choice' for Jr. High, Elementary Students," *Durham Morning Herald,* July 12, 1963.

84. "City Education Board Files Further Desegregation Plan," *Durham Morning Herald,* April 30, 1964.

85. 165 F. Supp. 951 (M.D.N.C. 1958).

86. *Jeffers v. Whitley,* 309 F. 2d (4th Cir. 1962) at 628.

87. Ibid., at 627.

88. "School Integration in Caswell Results in Shooting of Two," *Durham Morning Herald,* January 23, 1963.

89. C. O. Pearson, telegram to Terry Sanford, n.d., Box 347, Sanford Papers.

90. C. O. Pearson to Richard H. Chadwick, State Highway Patrol, March 7, 1963, Box 347, Sanford Papers.

91. The Director [State Bureau of Investigation] to the Files, Bureau of Investigation, May 16, 1963; Director to the Files, Bureau of Investigation, May 20, 1963; Director to the Files, Bureau of Investigation, May 21, 1963; Agent W. F. Anderson to the Files, Bureau of Investigation, May 29, 1963; Box 346; Director Walter F. Anderson to the Files, May 22, 1963, Box 450, Sanford Papers.

92. Boxes 347, 348, and 350 of Sanford Papers contain extensive memoranda from the State Highway Patrol to Governor Terry Sanford. These memoranda form the foundation for my narrative.

93. "White Man Killed, Another Hurt in N.C. Racial Violence," *Durham Morning Herald,* June 7, 1963.

94. Carl E. De Vane, Shaw University, to Terry Sanford, May 12, 1963, Box 346, Sanford Papers.

95. "Statement of North Carolina Demonstration Leaders Presented to Governor Terry Sanford at Conference in Raleigh, North Carolina," June 25, 1963, Box 527, Sanford Papers.

96. Terry Sanford, handwritten notes to author, February 3, 1998.

97. "N.C. Racial History Made During Week," *Durham Morning Herald,* June 9, 1963.

98. "Southern Regional Council Newsletter," May 1963, Box 114A, Folio 6, Frederick Alexander Papers.

99. L. M. Wright Jr., "Charlotte Has Built Its Integration Road," *Charlotte Observer,* July 14, 1963.

100. Agent L. M. Harton to the Director, Bureau of Investigation, Subject: Race Riots in Oxford, June 15, 1963, Box 347, Sanford Papers.

101. Golden A. Frinks, Field Secretary, Southern Christian Leadership Conference, to Terry Sanford, October 17, 1963, Box 346, Sanford Papers.

102. "Sanford Asks End of Discrimination," *Winston-Salem Journal,* July 11, 1963, Box 346, Sanford Papers.

103. Melvin G. Cording, Mayor of Wallace, to Terry Sanford, July 11, 1963, Box 346, Sanford Papers.

104. "Minutes of Organizational Meeting of N.C. Mayors Cooperating Committee," July 11, 1963, Box 527; "Extra Municipal Ordinances" File, Box 527, Sanford Papers.

105. Meeting of North Carolina Good Neighbor Council, April 28, 1964, Box 386, Sanford Papers.

106. W. O. Warner, Attorney, Rocky Mount, to Terry Sanford, September 20, 1963, Box 347, Sanford Papers.

107. Terry Sanford to George Birmingham Jr., Durham, April 13, 1964, Box 450, Sanford Papers.

108. Sam O. Worthington to David E. Reid, State YDC President, July 19, 1963, Box 348, Sanford Papers.

109. Charles A. Speed, Major, State Highway Patrol, to Colonel David T. Lambert, June 15, 1964, Box 450, Sanford Papers.

110. "Speakers at Klan Meeting Denounce U.S., N.C. Officials," *Durham Morning Herald,* August 9, 1964, Box 450, Sanford Papers.

111. "The Continuing Crisis" (Atlanta: Southern Regional Council, and New York: American Jewish Committee, May 1966), Box 114A, Folio 7A, Frederick Alexander Papers.

112. "Newsman at Scene of Blasts," *The Carolinian,* November 27, 1965. Roy Reed, "4 Negro Homes Hit by Bombs in South," *New York Times,* November 23, 1965, Box 128, Folio 4, Frederick Alexander Papers.

113. "120 Ministers Meet at Site of Bombings," *Charlotte Observer,* December 6, 1965, Box 132, Series 6, Folio 1, Frederick Alexander Papers.

114. "Operation Rebuilding Has $3,700 Left Over," *Charlotte News,* June 2, 1966; "Observer Is Returning Reward Fund Checks," *Charlotte Observer,* June 1, 1966; Box 132, Series 6, Folio 1, Frederick Alexander Papers. Julius Chambers, interview with author, August 14, 1997.

115. "Negro Home Bomb Case Is Unsolved," *Charlotte News,* November 22, 1968, Box 132, Series 6, Folio 2, Frederick Alexander Papers.

116. "Human Relations Bulletin" (Charlotte: N.C. Council on Human Relations, November 1960), Box 121, Folio 87, Frederick Alexander Papers.

117. The Pupil Assignment Act provided very broad authority to boards regarding assignment. Boards provided little, if any, rationale for their decisions, just as they provide little now. Reasons for the denials do not appear in case reports.

118. 224 F. Supp. 472 (E.D.N.C. 1963) at 475.

119. Taylor Branch, guest, "The Diane Rehm Show," PBS, January 17, 2013, radio.

120. Title IV, "A Summary of the Civil Rights Act of 1964," *Civil Rights Digest* (Washington: U.S. Commission on Civil Rights, 1964), Box 450, Sanford Papers.

121. 42 U.S.C. ss 2000c-(6)a.

122. Title VI, "A Summary of the Civil Rights Act of 1964."

123. Title VII, "A Summary of the Civil Rights Act of 1964."

124. James R. Dunn, "Title VI, the Guidelines, and School Desegregation in the South," *Virginia Law Review* 5 (1967): 49–52. *Simkins v. Moses Cone Memorial Hospital,* 323 F.2d 959 (4th Cir. 1963), *cert. denied,* 376 U.S. 938 (1964).

125. Terry Sanford to J. Boyd Burke, Burlington, August 19, 1964, Box 450, Sanford Papers.

126. Sanford, telephone conversation with author.

127. "Public Affairs Feature: Governor Sanford's Statement," Charlotte: Jefferson-Standard Broadcasting Company, July 14, 1964, Box 450, Sanford Papers.

128. Dallas Herring, telephone conversation with author, July 14, 1992.

129. Douglas, *Reading, Writing, and Race,* 114.

130. Kluger, *Simple Justice,* 755–60.

131. "Preyer, Moore to Meet in Runoff," *Durham Morning Herald,* May 31, 1964.

132. Charles Barbour, "Support for Beverly Lake Is Still Strong in Durham," *Durham Morning Herald,* April 10, 1964.

133. "Moore Says 'False' to Preyer Charges," *Durham Morning Herald,* April 13, 1964.

134. "Moore Says Sanford Named 3 Who Pushed Racial Strife," *Durham Morning Herald,* April 15, 1964. The individuals were Curtis Gans of the North Carolina Volunteers, plus Leon Rooke and William Darity, of the North Carolina Fund.

135. Barbour, "Support for Beverly Lake Is Still Strong in Durham."

136. Luebke, *Tar Heel Politics 2000,* 142–43.

137. Terry Sanford, handwritten notes to author, February 3, 1998.

138. "Preyer, Moore to Meet in Runoff," *Durham Morning Herald,* May 31, 1964. Additional confirmation regarding Moore's position appears in Dan K. Moore, Democratic Candidate for Governor, to John W. Green, East Lumberton, N.C., October 8, 1964, Box 72, Moore Papers.

139. Allen Macduff, "Lake Charges Preyer Statements Conflicting," *Durham Morning Herald,* April 22, 1964.

140. "How Tarheel Counties Voted for Governor," *Durham Morning Herald,* June 1, 1964.

141. *North Carolina Manual,* 261–62. Other voting data from same source.

142. "Lake Throws Support to Moore for Runoff," *Durham Morning Herald,* June 6, 1964.

143. "Lake Throws Support to Moore for Runoff."

144. *North Carolina Manual,* 550. Lake was to complete the term of Clifton L. Moore, deceased. Lake was elected to a full, eight-year term in 1970. *North Carolina Manual,* 677.

145. Herring, telephone conversation with author.

146. Dunn, "Daniel Killian Moore," in Mitchell, ed., *Messages, Addresses and Public Papers of Terry Sanford,* xxxii.

147. Mitchell, ed., *Messages, Addresses and Public Papers of Terry Sanford,* 733.

148. "Teachers Repudiate Trigg," *The Carolinian,* April 8, 1950; "Dr. Harold L. Trigg on Another Rampage in State," *The Carolina Times,* June 14, 1952; James A. Shephard, "Martin School Issue Has 'Another Side,'" *The Carolinian,* July 26, 1952; "President of Raleigh School Quits Under Fire From Trustees," *The Carolina Times,* January 15, 1955.

149. Mitchell, ed., *Messages, Addresses and Public Papers of Terry Sanford,* 183–84.

150. Ibid., 217–22.

151. Charles Dunn to R. C. Jervay, Editor, *Wilmington Journal,* April 22, 1968, Box 348, Moore Papers. P. C. Hill to Charles Dunn, April 1, 1968, Box 348, Moore Papers

152. Adrian King, "U.S. Law Orders Total, Complete School Integration in N.C.: Moody," Raleigh *News and Observer,* January 27, 1965, in *Negroes in North Carolina,* 898, North Carolina Collection.

153. H. P. Taylor Jr. to Messrs. John Webb & Russell Kirby, Wilson; Irvin B. Tucker, Sr., Raleigh; Robert R. Blackwell, Yanceyville; David M. Conner, Wilson; Thomas H. Morris, Kinston; W. P. Pearce, Franklinton; December 16, 1966, Box 269. George Ragsdale to Governor Moore, December 16, 1966, Box 269. Thomas H. Morris to H. P. Taylor Jr., December 20, 1966, Box 269. T. W. Bruton to H. P. Taylor Jr., December 21, 1966, Box 269. L. H. Fountain to Ralph Moody, December 29, 1966, Box 269. Thomas H. Morris to Ralph Moody, December 30, 1966, Box 269. Kirby and Webb to Ralph Moody, January 2, 1967, Box 269. George R. Ragsdale to H. P. Taylor Jr., January 6, 1967, Box 269. George R. Ragsdale to Messrs. John Webb and Russell Kirby and others, January 6, 1967, Box 269. Dan Moore to William A. Sutherland, January 6, 1967, Box 269. Loran A. Johnson to George R. Ragsdale, January 16, 1967, Box 269. George R. Ragsdale to H. P. Taylor Jr., January 26, 1967, Box 269. J. D. Williams (of Sutherland, Asbill and Brennan) to Ralph Moody, January 30, 1967, Box 269. J. D. Williams to Peter R. Goldschmidt, Department of Health, Education, and Welfare, February 2, 1967, Box 269. John Webb to Ralph Moody, February 6, 1967, Box 269. George Ragsdale to John Webb, February 8, 1967, Box 269. John Kirby to George Ragsdale, February 9, 1967, Box 269. J. D. Williams, of Sutherland, Asbill & Brennan, to John Webb, February 14, 1967, Box 269. George T. Davis, Swan Quarter, to Mr. J. D. Williams, of Sutherland, Asbill & Brennan, March 10, 1967, Box 269. Andrew A. Vanore Jr. to William A. Sutherland, April 3, 1967, Box 269. J. D. Williams, of Sutherland, Asbill & Brennan, to Andrew A. Vanore Jr., May 18, 1967, Box 269. Elbert S. Peel and William R. Peel to Andy Vanore, June 30, 1967, Box 269. All in Moore Papers.

154. United States Commission on Civil Rights, *Federal Rights under School Desegregation Law,* [Washington, DC, n.d.]: CCR Clearinghouse Publication 6 (June 1966). www.law.umaryland.edu/marshall/usccr/documents/cr1106.pdf. Dunn, "Title VI, The Guidelines, and School Desegregation in the South."

155. *Guidelines for School Desegregation* (Washington: U.S. Government Printing Office, 1966), 12, 14.

156. Kate Erwin, "'Guidelines'—Simple Word Becomes Bombshell," Raleigh *News and Observer,* May 29, 1966, in *Negroes in North Carolina,* 904.

157. Erwin, "'Guidelines'—Simple Word Becomes Bombshell."

158. "School Guidelines Come Under Fire," Raleigh *News and Observer,* April 8, 1966, in *Negroes in North Carolina,* 909.

159. Walter B. Jones, Alton Lennon, Harold Cooley, L. H. Fountain to Honorable Dan K. Moore, April 7, 1966, 114.52/1165, Herring Papers. Sam Ervin, "Department of Education's New Statement of Policies for Desegregation of Public Schools," *Congressional Record,* April 1, 1966.

160. "Senate Defeats Southerners' Bid for 'Choice' Plan," *The Asheville Citizen,* December 18, 1969, in *Negroes in North Carolina,* 912.

CHAPTER SIX

1. 11 Race Relations Law Reporter 748 (E.D.N.C. 1965).
2. Ibid., 740 (E.D.N.C. 1965).
3. 345 F. 2d 329 (4th Cir. 1965).
4. This is the same Julius Chambers who was graduated from UNC Law School.
5. *Bowditch,* 345 F. 2d at 331, 332.

6. *Nesbit v. Statesville City Board of Education,* 232 F. Supp. 288 (W.D.N.C. 1964).
7. Ibid., 345 F. 2d 333 (4th Cir. 1965).
8. Ibid., at 335, 336.
9. 349 F. 2d 366 (4th Cir. 1965).
10. *Felder,* 349 F. 2d at 367, 368.
11. 10 Race Relations Law Reporter 166 (M.D.N.C. 1965).
12. *Clayton v. Person County Board of Education,* 12 Race Relations Law Reporter 228 (M.D.N.C. 1966).
13. 10 Race Relations Law Reporter 167 (M.D.N.C. 1965); 12 Race Relations Law Reporter 233 (M.D.N.C. 1966).
14. 11 Race Relations Law Reporter (E.D.N.C. 1966) at 1788.
15. 22 Race Relations Law Reporter 1234 (1966).
16. *Wheeler and Spaulding v. Durham City Board of Education,* 249 F. Supp. 145 (M.D.N.C. 1966).
17. Ibid., 363 F. 2d 738 (4th Cir. 1966), 740–41.
18. 243 F. Supp. 667 (W.D.N.C. 1965). The *Swann* case has been the subject of book-length treatments (see Bibliography, Davison M. Douglas, Bernard Schwartz, and Frye Gaillard). I have sought to place the *Swann* case in a context that considers the litigation as part of a state and national trend in NAACP-backed lawsuits.
19. *Swann,* 243 F. Supp. at 668–71.
20. *Swann v. Charlotte-Mecklenburg Board of Education,* 369 F. 2d 29 (4th Cir. 1966).
21. Schwartz, *Swann's Way,* 12.
22. "First Test," Raleigh *News and Observer,* September 27, 1961, in *Negroes in North Carolina,* 992.
23. "Carrboro Couple Informed of Pearsall Grant Steps," Raleigh *News and Observer,* September 29, 1961, in *Negroes in North Carolina,* 992.
24. Alan K. Whiteleather, "Test of Tuition Grants Looming in Orange," Durham *Morning Herald,* September 27, 1961, in *Negroes in North Carolina,* 992.
25. "Grant Bid Is Seen Doomed," *Greensboro Daily News,* January 9, 1962, in *Negroes in North Carolina,* 993.
26. Robert Hummerstone, "Local Board Okays Tuition Grant Request," *Charlotte Observer,* n.d., in *Negroes in North Carolina,* 994.
27. Kate Erwin, "State Rejects First Request for Tuition," Raleigh *News and Observer,* November 5, 1965, in *Negroes in North Carolina,* 998.
28. Kate Erwin, "Private Tuition Authorized," Raleigh *News and Observer,* December 3, 1965, in *Negroes in North Carolina,* 996.
29. "Suit Challenges N.C. Tuition Law," Raleigh *News and Observer,* December 10, 1965, in *Negroes in North Carolina,* 996. *Hawkins v. North Carolina State Board of Education,* 11 Race Relations Law Reporter 745 (W.D.N.C. 1966).
30. Roy Parker Jr., "U.S. Challenges N.C.," Raleigh *News and Observer,* January 12, 1966, in *Negroes in North Carolina,* 998.
31. "Pearsall Plan Framer Charges It's Invalid," Raleigh *News and Observer,* February 24, 1966, in *Negroes in North Carolina,* 997.
32. Andrew Vanore Jr., telephone conversation with author, April 10, 1992.
33. *Hawkins v. North Carolina State Board of Education,* 11 Race Relations Law Reporter 745 (1966).
34. Kate Erwin, "State Not Appealing Pearsall Plan Ruling," Raleigh *News and Observer,* April 23, 1966, in *Negroes in North Carolina,* 999. Crow, Escott, and Hatley, in *History of African Americans in North Carolina,* 170, state that *Godwin v. Johnston County*

Board of Education 301 F. Supp. (E.D.N.C. 1969) ruled the Pearsall Plan unconstitutional. That is not correct. *Godwin,* discussed below, held that state officials had an affirmative duty to disestablish the dual, segregated educational system that existed in North Carolina, citing *Hawkins* as precedent.

35. G.S. 115-142.

36. Black educators belonged to the NCTA. White educators belonged to the N.C. Education Association. The two organizations subsequently merged into the N.C. Association of Educators in 1970. See Percy Murray, *History of the North Carolina Teachers Association,* ([Washington, D.C.:] National Education Association, n.d.), 131.

37. E. B. Palmer, qtd. in Murray, *History of the North Carolina Teachers Association,* 93, 94.

38. 242 F. Supp. 721 (E.D.N.C. 1965).

39. *Johnson v. Branch,* 242 F. Supp. at 722. The other attorneys representing Johnson were Samuel S. Mitchell of Raleigh and Philip J. Hirschkop of Alexandria, Virginia. The firm of Allsbrook, Benton, and Knott of Roanoke Rapids represented the defendant, Joseph Branch, attorney for the Halifax County Board of Education. Branch was later appointed to the North Carolina Supreme Court.

40. *Johnson v. Branch,* 242 F. Supp. at 728, 729, 730–31, 732.

41. Ibid., 364 F. 2d 177 (4th Cir. 1966) at 179, 182.

42. Murray, *History of the North Carolina Teachers Association,* 94. The amount stated is twenty thousand dollars, but Murray does not provide a source to support the assertion.

43. *Chambers,* 245 F. Supp. (W.D.N.C. 1965) at 760, 761, 762, 763, 764, 765. Scores on the National Teacher Examination were the subject of separate litigation in the mid-1970s. Edwin M. Speas Jr., North Carolina Attorney General's Office, telephone conversation with author, July 17, 1992.

44. *Chambers v. Hendersonville City Board of Education,* 364 F. 2d 189 (4th Cir. 1966) at 191, 192, 193.

45. 259 F. Supp. (M.D.N.C. 1966) at 256.

46. *Wall v. Stanly County Board of Education,* 378 F. 2d (4th Cir. 1967) at 276, 277.

47. *North Carolina Teachers Association v. Asheboro City Board of Education,* 393 F. 2d at 746.

48. Angela Davis, "N.C. School Integration: 20 Years Later," Raleigh *News and Observer,* May 12, 1974, in *Negroes in North Carolina,* 925. Murray's chart shows 226 black principals employed in 1963–64, followed by only 15 a decade later. The largest number of black principals was employed in union schools, which served all grades. Union schools were closed, however, so of course no black principals continued to administer union schools. Union schools were converted to elementary schools, which the chart omits (*History of the North Carolina Teachers Association,* 97–98).

49. A. C. Davis to Dr. Harold L. Trigg, September 8, 1972, 114.106/0432, Herring Papers.

50. This observation is based on numerous, but informal, conversations with superintendents more experienced than I, especially those who served during the 1960s and 1970s. Such conversations span a period of fifteen or more years during the 1980s and 1990s.

51. C. Raymond Williams, Major, State Highway Patrol, to Dan K. Moore, January 25, 1965, Box 73, Moore Papers. United States Department of Justice, Federal Bureau of Investigation, Charlotte, N.C., RE: Edward Earl Fillingame; Laurie Latham Fillingame; Raymond Duguid Mills; February 9, 1965, Box 73, Moore Papers.

52. Dunn, "Daniel Killian Moore," 621–22.

53. Klan activity is revealed in hundreds of memoranda found in Boxes 151, 174, and 274, Moore Papers. See also "The Continuing Crisis," Box 114A, Folio 7A, Frederick Alexander Papers.

54. Remarks by Governor Dan Moore at State-Wide Meeting on Law and Order in North Carolina, Raleigh, September 16, 1966, Box 151, Moore Papers. At that meeting, Governor Moore stated that Klan meetings had been held from Wilkesboro to New Bern. In addition to that generality, see the correspondence noted above.

55. Unsigned Memorandum, n.d. (context indicates June 1966 regarding events in May), Box 151, Moore Papers.

56. Memoranda, Highway Patrol to Governor Moore, Box 274, Moore Papers.

57. Charles Dunn, Administrative Assistant, to Wade Bruton, Attorney General, June 8, 1966, Box 151; Ralph Moody, Deputy Attorney General, to Dan K. Moore, June 23, 1966, Box 151; Statement by Governor Dan Moore, July 28, 1966, Box 151, Moore Papers.

58. Douglas, *Reading, Writing, and Race,* 90.

59. Dunn, "Daniel Killian Moore," xxxi.

60. William D. Snider, *Helms and Hunt: The North Carolina Senate Race, 1984* (Chapel Hill: University of North Carolina Press, 1985), 17.

61. "Firm Guard Grip, Curfews Dampen Tar Heel Violence," *Durham Morning Herald,* April 8, 1968.

62. From the Governor's Office, April 6, 1968, Box 348, Moore Papers.

63. "NAACP Leader Asks for Halt of Destruction," *Durham Morning Herald,* April 8, 1968.

64. "Guard Routs Students from Buildings at A&T," *Durham Morning Herald,* May 24, 1968.

65. "Trouble in Greensboro: A Report of an Open Meeting Concerning the Disturbances at Dudley High School and North Carolina A&T State University," North Carolina State Advisory Committee to the United States Commission on Civil Rights, March 1970, Box 121, Folio 88, Frederick Alexander Papers.

66. Hazen Schumacher, Hudson L. Barksdale, John Gieringer, Earl Jones, and Robert A. Pittillo Jr., *Hyde County, North Carolina: School Boycott and the Roots of Conflict* ([Washington, D.C.:] National Education Association, 1969), 5, 12–13. Murray, *History of the North Carolina Teachers Association,* 99–101. David S. Cecelski, *Along Freedom Road: Hyde County, North Carolina, and the Fate of Black Schools in the South* (Chapel Hill: University of North Carolina Press, 1994).

67. Schumacher, *Hyde County,* 25, 38.

68. Discussion is based on Bill McAlister, "The Changing of the Negro Guard," Raleigh *News and Observer,* August 19, 1962, in *Negroes in North Carolina,* 1108–9. See also Crow, Escott, and Hatley, *History of African Americans in North Carolina,* 192–99, 204–7.

69. James S. Coleman, *Equality of Educational Opportunity* (Washington, D.C.: U.S. Government Printing Office, 1966), 9–12, 20–22, 29.

70. 272 F. Supp. (E.D.N.C. 1967) at 706, 708.

71. 273 F. Supp. (E.D.N.C. 1967) at 295, 296, 299, 300.

72. 294 F. Supp. (E.D.N.C. 1968) at 181, 182, 183.

73. 293 F. Supp. (E.D.N.C. 1968) at 1278, 1283, 1284.

74. 301 F. Supp. (E.D.N.C. 1969) at 1341.

75. S.B. 3, "An Act to Provide a Limited Form of Continuing Contract for Principals and Teachers in the Public School System," *Session Laws 1967* (Winston-Salem: Winston Printing, 1967), 272.

76. John L. Sanders, "A Brief History of the Constitutions of North Carolina," in Cheney, ed., *North Carolina Government,* 802.

77. John Sanders, Institute of Government, telephone conversation with author, July 16, 1992. One member of the committee with whom I spoke did not remember the committee even discussing the Pearsall Plan. William Snider, telephone conversation with author, July 16, 1992.

78. Sanders, "Brief History of the Constitutions of North Carolina," 804–6.

79. *Public School Laws of North Carolina* (Charlottesville, Va.: Michie, 1969), 333, 343. *Public School Laws of North Carolina* (1971), 397. Speas, "Legal Principles of Desegregation," 17-3–17-6.

80. "For a Better Constitution," *The News and Observer,* November 2, 1970, 4. "Tools for Better Government," *The News and Observer,* November 5, 1970, 4. *Public School Laws of North Carolina* (1971), 397. Section 12, "Education expense grants and local option," of Article IX was repealed. Compare *Public School Laws of North Carolina* (1969), 333.

81. Robert W. Scott, telephone conversation with author, August 26, 1992.

82. *North Carolina Manual,* 272.

83. Rob Wood, "Scott to Gardner: 'Tell It Like It Is,'" *Durham Morning Herald,* November 1, 1968.

84. Robert W. Scott, telephone conversation with author, August 26, 1992.

85. *North Carolina Manual,* 272.

86. "Gardner and Scott Close Campaigns," *Durham Morning Herald,* November 3, 1968.

87. "Nixon's Gain in South Offset by Humphrey Strength in East," *New York Times,* November 6, 1968. "Nixon Wins Presidency by Margin Probably Smaller than That of Kennedy in '60," *New York Times,* November 7, 1968. William C. Berman, *America's Right Turn* (Baltimore: Johns Hopkins University Press, 1998), 10–11, 17.

88. Evan Thomas, "Divide and Conquer," *Newsweek,* May 19, 2008, 48.

89. *North Carolina Manual,* 270.

90. Craig Phillips, telephone conversation with author, April 29, 2000.

91. 391 U.S. (1968) at 430, 435, 439, 440.

92. Schwartz, *Swann's Way,* 63.

93. 396 U.S. 19 (1969) at 20.

94. Bob Woodward and Scott Armstrong, *The Brethren* (New York: Simon and Schuster, 1979), 55.

95. Schwartz, *Swann's Way,* 92.

96. G.S. 115-176 (1969).

CHAPTER SEVEN

1. Unless otherwise noted, judges' biographical information is from *History of the Federal Judiciary,* www.fjc.gov, website of the Federal Judicial Center, Washington, D.C.

2. www2.1ib.unc.edu/mss/inv/b/Butler,Algernon_Lee.html.

3. Wilmington *Star-News,* September 6, 1978, news.google.com/newspapers?nid=1454&dat=19780906&id=brssAAAAIBAJ&sjid=LRMEAAAAIBAJ&pg=6229,1090523.

4. digital.lib.ecu.edu/special/ead/findingaids/0078/.

5. ncpedia.org/biography/larkins-john-davis-jr.

6. bioguide.congress.gov/scripts/biodisplay.pl?index=J000263

7. Gaillard, *Dream Long Deferred,* 39–41, 50.

8. Ibid., 49. Schwartz, *Swann's Way,* 13.

9. Schwartz, *Swann's Way,* 13.

10. *Swann v. Charlotte-Mecklenburg Board of Education,* 300 F. Supp. (W.D.N.C. 1969) at 1360, 1372.

11. Ibid., 306 F. Supp. (W.D.N.C. 1969) at 1304, 1308, 1309.

12. Schwartz, *Swann's Way,* 9.

13. *Swann v. Charlotte-Mecklenburg Board of Education,* 311 F. Supp. (W.D.N.C. 1970) at 268–81.

14. Ibid., 431 F. 2d 138 (4th Cir. 1970). Judge J. Braxton Craven Jr. disqualified himself from hearing the appeal. *Swann v. Charlotte-Mecklenburg Board of Education,* 431 F. 2d 135 (4th Cir. 1970).

15. *Swann v. Charlotte-Mecklenburg Board of Education,* 397 U.S. 978 (1970) initially refused to disturb the Fourth Circuit's partial stay with regard to elementary redistricting and bussing.

16. Ibid., 399 U.S. 926 (1970).

17. Ibid., 318 F. Supp. at 791.

18. Gaillard, *Dream Long Deferred,* 59–60.

19. Schwartz, *Swann's Way,* 92.

20. *Swann v. Charlotte-Mecklenburg Board of Education, cert. granted,* 399 U.S. 926 (1970).

21. Schwartz, *Swann's Way,* 28–30, 38–41, 105–84.

22. *Swann,* 402 U.S. at 24, 27, 31, 32.

23. Schwartz, *Swann's Way,* 188, 191–92, 21.

24. Southern Regional Council, News Release, March 25, 1971, Box 114A, Folio B, Frederick Alexander Papers.

25. Gaillard, *Dream Long Deferred,* 53–55, 80–81, 84–85, 99, 108, 110, 143–44, 149–50.

26. *Swann v. Charlotte-Mecklenburg Board of Education,* 67 F.R.D. 648 (W.D.N.C. 1975).

27. Charlotte-Mecklenburg superintendent terms, as well as a good history of the school system, can be found on the district website: www.cms.k12.nc.us/mediaroom/aboutus/Pages/History.aspx.

28. Kate Erwin, "School Integration May Reach 40,000 in State This Fall," Raleigh *News and Observer,* September 2, 1964, in *Negroes in North Carolina,* 902.

29. "72 School Units Still to Be Heard," Raleigh *News and Observer,* July 20, 1965, in *Negroes in North Carolina,* 898.

30. Erwin, "School Integration May Reach 40,000 in State This Fall."

31. Edward Eugene Causby, interview with author, May 12, 2000.

32. These developments are narrated in Batchelor, *Guilford County Schools,* 144–50.

33. Roy Parker, "School Integration Shows 12.8 Per Cent N.C. Gain," Raleigh *News and Observer,* December 9, 1966, in *Negroes in North Carolina,* 907. The article's title is misleading; the actual level of desegregation is correctly stated in the text.

34. Roy Parker Jr., "Student Integration In NC Reaches 28%," Raleigh *News and Observer,* January 18, 1969, in *Negroes in North Carolina,* 914.

35. "N.C. Integration Shows Increase," Raleigh *News and Observer,* June 18, 1971, in *Negroes in North Carolina,* 901.

36. Phillips, telephone conversation with author.

37. The correct spelling is "Strother," not "Strothers," as appears in some works.

38. Causby, interview with author. Dudley Flood, interview with author, May 2, 2000.

39. Causby, interview with author.

40. Flood, interview with author.

41. Phillips, telephone conversation with author. A review of DPI files in the North Carolina Archives produced almost no information relevant to this study.

42. Flood, interview with author.

43. Causby, interview with author.

44. Flood, interview with author.

45. Al Lineberry Jr., interview with author, May 20, 2000.

46. Reverend Hairston recalled these experiences in a 1983 interview with Stephen Rummage, Mike Brady, Tom Pitchford, and Brian Lutness, a team of my eighth-grade students at Northeast Guilford Junior High in a Tar Heel Junior Historians project. Rummage arranged for Reverend Hairston to conduct services at his conservative, all-white Baptist church. Dr. Rummage is now a Baptist minister at a large church in Florida.

47. John Newsom, "Careful Planning Made School Busing a Success," *The News and Record,* August 16, 1999.

48. Lineberry, interview with author.

49. Flood, Interview with author.

50. Newsom, "Careful Planning Made School Busing a Success."

51. www.unctv.org/biocon/jholshouser/part2.html.

52. www.ncfundfilm.com/?page_id=5.

53. Memory F. Mitchell, ed., *Addresses and Public Papers of James Eubert Holshouser, Governor of North Carolina, 1973–1977* (Raleigh: Division of Archives and History, 1978), xx–xxi, xxvi.

54. www.time.com/time/magazine/article/0,9171,712192–2,00.html (November 20, 1972).

55. Mitchell, ed., *Addresses and Public Papers of James Eubert Holshouser,* 69–71, 117, 180.

56. eric.ed.gov/ERICDocs/data/ericdocs2sql/content_storage_01/0000019b/80/35/b4/05.pdf

57. Mitchell, ed., *Addresses and Public Papers of James Eubert Holshouser,* xix, 183.

58. Snider, *Helms and Hunt,* 27.

59. Rob Christensen, "Revered and Reviled, Senator Revived State's Republican Party," *News and Record,* July 5, 2008, A1, A4. Snider, *Helms and* Hunt, 8.

60. Luebke, *Tar Heel Politics 2000,* 143–44, 162–63, 173–75, 182–84, 189–92. Jesse Helms, *Here's Where I Stand: A Memoir* (New York: Random House, 2005), 95–96.

61. Christensen, "Revered and Reviled, Senator Revived State's Republican Party."

62. Helms, *Here's Where I Stand,* 158–59.

63. See Gary Orfield, Susan E. Eaton, and the Harvard Project on School Desegregation, *Dismantling Desegregation* (New York: New Press, 1996), 1–22. See also Luebke, *Tar Heel Politics 2000,* 141.

64. Berman, *America's Right Turn,* 79.

65. Helms, *Here's Where I Stand,* 176.

66. Balkin and Rodriguez, *Civil Rights Chronology,* 1973.

67. www.senate.gov/artandhistory/history/common/generic/VP_Spiro_Agnew.htm.

68. www.whitehouse.gov/history/presidents/rn37.html.

69. www.oyez.org/justices/abe_fortas/.

70. Balkin and Rodriguez, *Civil Rights Chronology,* 1968, 1971.

71. 411 U.S. 1 (1973).

72. Balkin and Rodriguez, *Civil Rights Chronology,* 1973.

73. 413 U.S. 189 (1973).

74. www.oyez.org/oyez/resource/case/200/.

75. Jane Wettach, www.law.duke.edu/curriculum/courseHomepages/Fa112002/329_01/syllabusReadings, Class12-Keyes.pdf (unnumbered).

76. 418 U.S. 717 (1974).

77. www.law.cornell.edu/supct/html/historics/USSC_CR_0418_0717_ZS.html.

78. Balkin and Rodriguez, *Civil Rights Chronology,* 1974.

79. Gene Marlow, "Private Schools Worry Officials," Raleigh *News and Observer,* September 6, 1970, in *Negroes in North Carolina,* 903.

80. Southern Regional Council, "The Continuing 'Segregation Academy' Movement," February 7, 1971; Southern Regional Council, News Release, March 25, 1971; Box 114A, Folio B, Frederick Alexander Papers. Kitty Terjen, "White Flight: The Segregation Academy Movement," in Southern Regional Council, *The South and Her Children: School Desegregation, 1970–1971* (Atlanta: Southern Regional Council, 1971), 71.

81. Marlow, "Private Schools Worry Officials."

82. Gene Marlow, "N.C. May Lead South in Integration," Raleigh *News and Observer,* August 29, 1971, in *Negroes in North Carolina,* 915.

83. Angela Davis, "N.C. School Integration: 20 Years Later," Raleigh *News and Observer,* May 12, 1974, in *Negroes in North Carolina,* 925.

84. Balkin and Rodriguez, *Civil Rights Chronology,* 1975, 1976.

85. Douglas, *Reading, Writing, and Race,* 48, 62, 253–54.

86. Friedland, *Lift Up Your Voice Like a Trumpet,* 145–46. See also Samuel DeWitt Proctor, *The Substance of Things Hoped For* (New York: G. P. Putnam's Sons, 1995).

87. Collins Kilburn, interview with author, November 7, 2002.

88. W. W. Finlator, interview with author, August 31, 2002.

89. Ibid.

90. Friedland, *Lift Up Your Voice Like a Trumpet,* 251–52.

91. Mark Newman, "The Baptist State Convention of North Carolina and Desegregation, 1945–1980," *North Carolina Historical Review* 75 (1998): 1–28.

92. Kilburn, interview with author.

93. "Southern Baptists' Slavery Resolution, Apology Sought," *Charlotte Observer,* May 26, 1995. Ken Garfield, "Baptist Convention Apologizes for Not Fighting Racism," *Charlotte Observer,* June 21, 1995.

94. Newman, "Baptist State Convention of North Carolina and Desegregation," 12.

95. Douglas, *Reading, Writing, and Race,* 65–66.

96. Newman, "Baptist State Convention of North Carolina and Desegregation," 12. Newman specifically mentions Methodists and Catholics; my comment about Quakers grows out of my undergraduate years at Guilford College in the late 1960s. The Episcopal Church has tended to be more liberal than other denominations in the South on most social issues, including race. See also Douglas, *Reading, Writing, and Race,* 66–68.

97. Kilburn, interview with author.

98. Douglas, *Reading, Writing, and Race,* 84–106.

EPILOGUE

1. Gerald W. Bracey, *Setting the Record Straight* (Alexandria, Va.: Association for Supervision and Curriculum Development, 1997), 1–3. David C. Berliner and Bruce J. Biddle, *The Manufactured Crisis* (New York: Addison-Wesley, 1995).

2. Improvements in academic achievement are documented in the following sources: David Grissmer, Ann Flanagan, Jennifer Kawata, and Stephanie Williamson, *Improving*

Student Achievement: What State NAEP Test Scores Tell Us (Arlington, Va.: RAND, 2000); David W. Grissmer, Stephanie Williamson, Sheila Nataraj Kirby, and Mark Berends, *Exploring the Rapid Rise in Black Achievement Scores in the United States, 1970–1990* (Santa Monica, Calif.: RAND, 1997), 1, 27–29 (a report presented to North Carolina superintendents in a meeting arranged by DPI); Suzanne E. Triplett, "A Preliminary Analysis of the 1996 National Assessment of Educational Progress" (Center for Research in Education, Research Triangle Institute, March 10, 1997). See also DPI sources: www.ncpublicschools.org/docs/data/reports/education-data/other/measure-up.pdf; www.dpi.state.nc.us/docs/accountability/reporting/sat/2012/;
satreport2012.pdf. www.ncpublicschools.org/docs/data/reports/education-data/other/measure-up.pdf.

3. www.ncpublicschools.org/docs/data/reports/education-data/other/measure-up.pdf.

4. Berman, *America's Right Turn,* 65, 82, 82–83, 115.

5. Charles T. Clotfelter, Helen F. Ladd, and Jacob L. Vigdor, "Racial and Economic Diversity in North Carolina's Schools: An Update," Durham, N.C.: Sanford Working Papers Series, SAN13–01, January 16, 2013. Richard M. Ingersoll, "Core Problems: Out-of-Field Teaching Persists in Key Academic Courses and High-Poverty Schools," Washington, D.C.: Education Trust, November 2008.

Select Bibliography

PRIMARY SOURCES, UNPUBLISHED

Interviews

Causby, Edward Eugene. Interview with author. Greensboro, N.C., May 12, 2000.
Chambers, Julius. Interview with author. Durham, N.C., August 14, 1997.
Crew, Lunsford. Telephone conversation with author. July 15, 1992.
Flood, Dudley. Interview with author. Greensboro, N.C., May 2, May 6, 2000.
Frierson, Dargan. Interview with author. Greensboro, N.C., February 3, 1983.
Giles, Robert E. Interview with author. Raleigh, April 20, 1992.
Hairston, Rev. Otis. Interview with Stephen Rummage, Mike Brady, Tom Pitchford, and Brian Lutness. Greensboro, N.C., Spring 1983.
Herring, William Dallas. Interviews with author. Rose Hill, N.C., July 5–6, 1979; October 4, 1982; March 8, 1983. Telephone conversations with author, April 28, July 14, 1992. Personal conversation with author, July 2, 2001.
Johnston, Paul. Telephone conversation with author. July 14, 1983.
Lake, I. Beverly. Telephone conversation with author. July 17, 1992.
Lineberry, Al, Jr. Interview with author. Greensboro, N.C., May 20, 2000.
Melvin, E. S., "Jim." Interview with Author. Greensboro, N.C., June 6, 2000.
Morris, W. I. Telephone conversation with author. July 15, 1992.
Phillips, A. Craig. Telephone conversations with author. April 28, 1992; April 29, 2000.
Rankin, Edwin L., Jr. Telephone conversation with author, July 13, 1983.
Sanders, John. Telephone conversations with author, July 16, 1992, August 5, 1992.
Scott, Robert W. Telephone conversation with author, August 26, 1992.
Smith, McNeill. Telephone conversation with author, July 13, 1992.

Snider, William D. Telephone conversation with author, July 16, 1992.
Speas, Edwin M., Jr. Telephone conversation with author, July 17, 1992.
Taylor, W. W. Interview with author. Raleigh, July 14, 1992.
Vanore, Andrew A., Jr. Telephone conversation with author, April 10, 1992.
Womble, William F. Telephone Conversation with author, May 21, 1992.

Manuscript Sources

Alexander, Frederick. Papers. J. Murrey Atkins Library, University of North Carolina at Charlotte.
Alexander, Kelly. Papers. J. Murrey Atkins Library, University of North Carolina at Charlotte.
Chambers, Julius L. Papers. J. Murrey Atkins Library, University of North Carolina at Charlotte.
Department of Public Instruction, Papers, MARS 104.320 (10 boxes), 104.321 (1 box), 104.322 (2 boxes), State Archives.
Freedmen's Bureau. Papers. RG 105, National Archives, Washington, D.C.
Herring, William Dallas. Letter to author. May 14, 1982.
———. MS. speeches, entitled, "Essays on Education." 2 vols., Photocopies. Loaned to author by William Dallas Herring.
———. Papers (microfilm). State Archives, Raleigh.
Hodges, Luther Hartwell. Papers. State Archives, Raleigh.
Moore, Daniel Killian. Papers. State Archives, Raleigh.
Pearsall, Thomas J. Papers. #4300, Southern Historical Collection. Wilson Library, University of North Carolina at Chapel Hill.
Sanford, Terry. Handwritten notes to author, February 3, 1998.
———. Letter to author. February 3, 1998.
———. Papers. State Archives, Raleigh.
Scott, Robert W. Papers. State Archives, Raleigh.
Umstead, William Brantley. Papers. State Archives, Raleigh.

PRIMARY SOURCES, PUBLISHED

Cases

Adkins v. School Board of Newport News, 148 F. Supp. 430 (E.D. Va. 1957), *aff'd,* 246 F. 2d 325 (4th Cir. 1957).
Alexander v. Holmes County Board of Education, 396 U.S. 19 (1969).
Atkins v. School Board of Newport News, 148 F. Supp. 430 (E.D. Va. 1957), *aff'd,* 246 F. 2d 325 (4th Cir. 1957).
Barksdale v. Commissioners of Sampson County, 93 N.C. 473 (1885).

Barrow v. Washington City Board of Education, 11 Race Relations Law Reporter 1787 (E.D.N.C. 1966).
Belton v. Gebhart, 87 A. 2d 862 (Del. Ch. 1952).
Berea College v. Kentucky, 211 U.S. 45 (1908).
Blue v. Durham Public School District 95 F. Supp. 441 (M.D.N.C. 1951).
Board of Education of Oklahoma v. Dowell, 498 U.S. 237 (1991).
Bolling v. Sharpe, cert. granted, 344 U.S. 873 (1952), 344 U.S. 873 (1952).
Boomer v. Beaufort County Board of Education, 294 F. Supp. 179 (E.D.N.C. 1968).
Bowditch v. Buncombe County Board of Education, 345 F. 2d 329 (4th Cir. 1965).
Briggs v. Elliott, 98 F. Supp. 529 (E.D.S.C. 1951), 132 F. Supp. 776 (E.D.S.C. 1955).
Brown v. Board of Education, 98 F. Supp. 797 (D. Kan. 1951), 347 U.S. 483 (1954), 349 U.S. 294 (1955).
Bryant v. Carteret County Board of Education, 11 Race Relations Law Reporter 740 (E.D.N.C. 1965).
Carmichael v. McKissick, 341 U.S. 951 (1950).
Carson v. Board of Education of McDowell County, 227 F. 2d 789 (4th Cir. 1955).
Carson v. Warlick, 238 F. 2d 724 (4th Cir. 1956), cert. denied, 353 U.S. 910 (1957).
Chambers v. Hendersonville City Board of Education, 245 F. Supp. 759 (W.D.N.C. 1965), *rev'd,* 364 F. 2d 189 (4th Cir. 1966).
Civil Rights Cases, 109 U.S. 3 (1883).
Clayton v. Person County Board of Education, 10 Race Relations Law Reporter 166 (M.D.N.C. 1965), 12 Race Relations Law Reporter 228 (M.D.N.C. 1966).
Collie v. Commissioners of Franklin County, 145 N.C. 170 (1907).
Constantian v. Anson County, 244 N.C. 221 (1956).
Cooper v. Aaron, 358 U.S. 1 (1958).
Coppedge v. Franklin County Board of Education, 273 F. Supp. 289 (E.D.N.C. 1967).
Covington v. Edwards, 165 F. Supp. 957 (M.D.N.C. 1958), 264 F. 2d 780 (4th Cir. 1959).
Covington v. Montgomery County School Board, 139 F. Supp. 161 (M.D.N.C. 1956).
Cumming v. Board of Education, 175 U.S. 528 (1899).
Davis v. County School Board, 103 F. Supp. 337 (E. D. Va. 1952).
Duke v. Brown, 96 N.C. 127 (1887).
Epps v. Carmichael, 93 F. Supp. 327 (M.D.N.C. 1950)

Faubus v. United States, 254 F. 2d 797 (8th Cir. 1957).
Felder v. Harnett County Board of Education, 349 F. 2d 366 (4th Cir. 1965).
Freeman v. Pitts, 503 U.S. 467 (1992).
Gill v. Concord City Board of Education, 10 Race Relations Law Reporter 167 (M.D.N.C. 1965), 12 Race Relations Law Reporter 233 (M.D.N.C. 1966).
Gilliland v. Board of Education, 141 N.C. 482 (1906).
Godwin v. Johnston County Board of Education 301 F. Supp. (E.D.N.C. 1969).
Green v. County School Board of New Kent County, 391 U.S. 430 (1968).
Griffith v. Board of Education of Yancey County, 186 F. Supp. 511 (W.D.N.C. 1960).
Hare v. Board of Education, 113 N.C. 10 (1893).
Hawkins v. North Carolina State Board of Education, 11 Race Relations Law Reporter 745 (W.D.N.C. 1966).
Henderson v. United States, 339 U.S. 816 (1950.
Holt v. Raleigh City Board of Education, 134 F. Supp. 853 (E.D.N.C. 1958), 265 F. 2d 95 (4th Cir. 1959).
Hooker v. Town of Greenville, 130 N.C. 472 (1902).
In Re: Applications for Reassignment, 247 N.C. 413 (1958).
In Re: Applications for Reassignment, 2 Race Relations Law Reporter 967 (Superior Court, Guilford County, N.C., September 4, 1957).
In the Matter of Assignment of the School Children in the Stella Community of Carteret County, 242 N.C. 500 (1955).
Jeffers v. Whitley, 165 F. Supp. 951 (M.D.N.C. 1958), 309 F. 2d 621 (4th Cir. 1962).
Johnson v. Board of Education, 166 N.C. 468 (1914).
Johnson v. Branch, 242 F. Supp. 721 (E.D.N.C. 1965), *rev'd,* F. 2d 177 (4th Cir. 1966).
Jones v. Pamlico County Board of Education, 11 Race Relations Law Reporter (E.D.N.C. 1965).
Joyner v. McDowell County Board of Education, 244 N.C. 164 (1956).
Keyes v. Denver School District No. 1, 413 U.S. 189 (1973).
Lane v. Stanley, 65 N.C. 153 (1871).
Lowery v. School Trustees of Kernersville, 140 N.C. 33 (1905).
McCoy v. Greensboro City Board of Education, 179 F. Supp.745 (M.D.N.C. 1960), *rev'd.,* 283 F. 2d 667 (4th Cir. 1960).
McKissick v. Carmichael, 187 F. 2d 949 (4th Cir. 1951).
McKissick v. Durham City Board of Education, 176 F. Supp. 3 (M.D.N.C. 1959).
McLaurin v. Oklahoma State Regents for Higher Education, 87 F. Supp. 526 (W.D. Okla. 1948).
McLaurin v. Oklahoma State Regents, 339 U.S. 637 (1950).

Medlin v. County Board of Education, 167 N.C. 239 (1914).
Milliken v. Bradley, 418 U.S. 717 (1974).
Milliken v. Bradley II, 433 U.S. 267 (1977).
Missouri ex. rel. Gaines v. Canada, 305 U.S. 337 (1938).
Morrow v. Mecklenburg County Board of Education, 195 F. Supp. 109 (W.D.N.C. 1961).
Nesbit v. Statesville City Board of Education, 232 F. Supp. 288 (W.D.N.C. 1964), 345 F. 2d 333 (4th Cir. 1965).
North Carolina State Board of Education v. Swann, 402 U.S. 43 (1971).
North Carolina Teachers Association v. Asheboro City Board of Education, 259 F. Supp. 238 (M.D.N.C. 1966), *rev'd,* 393 F. 2d 736 (4th Cir. 1968).
Plessy v. Ferguson, 163 U.S. 537 (1896).
Puitt v. Commissioners, 94 N.C. 709 (1886).
Riggsbee v. Town of Durham, 94 N.C. 800 (1886).
Simkins v. Moses Cone Memorial Hospital, 323 F.2d 959 (4th Cir. 1963), *cert. denied,* 376 U.S. 938 (1964).
Sipuel v. Board of Regents of University of Oklahoma, 180 P. 2d 135 (Okla. 1947).
Sipuel v. Board of Regents of University of Oklahoma, 332 U.S. 631 (1948).
Slaughter-House Cases, 16 Wallace 36 (1873).
State ex. rel. Gaines v. Canada, 113 S. W. 2d 783 (Mo. 1938).
State v. Caldwell, 105 S.E. 2d 189 (N.C. 1958).
Story v. Board of Commissioners of Alamance County, 184 N.C. 336 (1922).
Swann v. Charlotte-Mecklenburg Board of Education, 243 F. Supp. 667 (W.D.N.C. 1965), *aff'd,* 369 F. 2d 29 (4th Cir. 1966), 300 F. Supp. 1358 (W.D.N.C. 1969), 306 F. Supp. 1299 (W.D.N.C. 1969), *aff'd in part,* 431 F. 2d 138 (4th Cir. 1970), 431 F. 2d 135 (4th Cir. 1970), *aff'd,* 397 U.S. 978 (1970), *cert. granted,* 399 U.S. 926 (1970), *aff'd,* 402 U.S. 1 (1971), 67 F.R.D. 648 (W.D.N.C. 1975).
Sweatt v. Painter, 210 S. W. 2d 442 (Tex. Civ. App. 1948).
Sweatt v. Painter, 339 U.S. 629 (1950).
Teel v. Pitt County Board of Education, 272 F. Supp. 703 (E.D.N.C. 1967).
United States v. Bertie County Board of Education, 293 F. Supp. 1276 (E.D.N.C. 1968).
Wall v. Stanly County Board of Education, 259 F. Supp. 238 (M.D.N.C. 1966), *rev'd,* 378 F. 2d 275 (4th Cir. 1967).
Warlick v. White, 76 N.C. 166 (1877).
Wheeler and Spaulding v. Durham City Board of Education, 249 F. Supp. 145 (M.D.N.C. 1966), *rev'd,* 363 F. 2d 738 (4th Cir. 1966).
Wheeler v. Durham City Board of Education, 196 F. Supp. 71 (M.D.N.C. 1961).

Wheeler v. Durham City Board of Education, 210 F. Supp. 839 (M.D.N.C. 1962), *rev'd,* 309 F. 2d 630 (4th Cir. 1962).
Wichita Falls Junior College v. Battle, 347 U.S. 974 (1954).

Legal Brief

Brief of Harry McMullan, Attorney General of North Carolina, Amicus Curiae, *Brown v. Board of Education,* 349 U.S. 294 (1955). U.S. Supreme Court Records and Briefs. Microform, Inc.

Manuscript Sources

Corbitt, David Leroy, ed. *Public Addresses, Letters, and Papers of William Bradley Umstead.* Raleigh: Council of State, 1957.
———. *Public Addresses, Letters, and Papers of William Kerr Scott.* Raleigh: Council of State, 1957.
Mitchell, Memory F., ed. *Addresses and Public Papers of James Eubert Holshouser, Governor of North Carolina, 1973–1977.* Raleigh: Division of Archives and History, 1978.
———. *Addresses and Public Papers of Robert W. Scott.* Raleigh: Division of Archives and History, 1974.
———. *Messages, Addresses, and Public Papers of Terry Sanford.* Raleigh: Division of Archives and History, 1966.
Patton, James W., ed. *Messages, Addresses, and Public Papers of Luther Hartwell Hodges.* Raleigh: Council of State, 1960.

Memoirs

Helms, Jesse. *Here's Where I Stand: A Memoir.* New York: Random House, 2005.
Hodges, Luther H. *Businessman in the Statehouse.* Chapel Hill: University of North Carolina Press, 1962.

Newspapers

Ashe County News.
Asheville Citizen.
Asheville Citizen-Times.
The Daily Times-News, Burlington, N.C.
Carolina Times.
The Carolinian.
The Chapel Hill Weekly.

The Charlotte News.
The Charlotte Observer.
Durham Morning Herald.
Durham News.
Durham Sun.
Education Week.
Greensboro Daily News.
The News and Record, Greensboro, N.C.
Greensboro Record.
The New York Times.
The News and Observer, Raleigh.
USA Today.
Winston-Salem Journal.

Oral Argument

Lake, I. Beverly. Argument on Behalf of the State of North Carolina as the Friend of the Court of the United States: The Warren Court, 1953 Term—1968 Term, *Brown v. Board of Education,* 349 U.S. 294 (1955), Fiche 1, Case 1. University Publications of America.

Reports

Biennial Report of the Superintendent of Public Instruction. Raleigh: Edwards and Broughton; later editions published by Department of Public Instruction, 1902–52.

Bracey, Gerald W. "Overcoming Disinformation: What Do the Data Really Say about Schools?" Phi Delta Kappa Professional Development Seminar, Charlotte, N.C., October 10, 1995.

Civil Rights Digest. Washington, D.C.: U.S. Commission on Civil Rights, August 1964.

Coates, Albert, ed. *A Report to the Governor of North Carolina.* Chapel Hill, N.C.: Institute of Government, 1954.

———. *Some Background Material for the State School Finance Commission.* Chapel Hill, N.C.: Institute of Government, 1958.

Coleman, James S. *Equality of Educational Opportunity.* Washington, D.C.: U.S. Government Printing Office, 1966.

Cotton, Oscar. *Desegregation in Durham, North Carolina: A Case Study.* Washington, D.C.: National Institute of Education, 1970. ED 117 274.

Education in North Carolina Today. Raleigh: United Forces for Education, 1948.

Fancher, Betsy. *Voices from the South: Black Students Talk About Their Experiences in Desegregated Schools.* Atlanta: Southern Regional Council, 1970. ED 042 841.

Grissmer, David W., Stephanie Williamson, Sheila Nataraj Kirby, and Mark Berends. *Exploring the Rapid Rise in Black Achievement Scores in the United States, 1970–1990.* Santa Monica, Calif.: RAND, 1997.

Journal of the House of Representatives of the General Assembly of the State of North Carolina. Winston-Salem, N.C.: Winston Printing Co., published after each session of the General Assembly.

Journal of the Senate of the General Assembly of the State of North Carolina. Winston-Salem, N.C.: Winston Printing Co., published after each session of the General Assembly.

Lachat, Mary Ann. *Desegregation in Goldsboro, North Carolina: A Case Study.* Washington, D.C.: Office of Education, 1973. ED 117 278.

Proposed Constitutional Amendment and Implementing Acts Relating to Public Education. Raleigh: Secretary of State, 1956.

Public School Laws of North Carolina. Charlottesville, Va.: Michie, published biennially.

Session Laws of the State of North Carolina. Winston-Salem, N.C.: Winston Printing, published after each legislative session.

Rothstein, Richard. *What Do We Know About Declining (or Rising) Student Achievement?* Arlington, Va.: Educational Research Service, 1997.

Schumacher, Hazen, Hudson L. Barksdale, John Gieringer, Earl Jones, and Robert A. Pittillo Jr. *Hyde County, North Carolina: School Boycott and the Roots of Conflict.* [Washington, D.C.:] National Education Association, 1969.

Shannon, Barbara. "Title VI Issues regarding Assignment of Students to Classes and Programs." Raleigh: Department of Public Instruction, Conference on Equity Issues in Law, December 5, 1994.

Southern Regional Council. *The South and Her Children: School Desegregation, 1970–1971.* Atlanta: Southern Regional Council, 1971.

———. *Tension and Conciliation: A Report on Contributing Factors Causing Racial Disagreements and Conflicts within the Hickory, North Carolina, City Schools.* Atlanta: Southern Regional Council, 1977. ED 142 594.

Triplett, Suzanne E. "A Preliminary Analysis of the 1996 National Assessment of Educational Progress." Center for Research in Education, Research Triangle Institute, March 10, 1997.

U.S. Commission on Civil Rights. *Federal Rights under School Desegregation Law.* [Washington, DC:] CCR Clearinghouse Publication 6 (June 1966).

SECONDARY WORKS

Articles

Beezer, Bruce. "North Carolina's Rationale for Mandating Separate Schools: A Legal History." *Journal of Negro Education* 52 (1983): 213–26.

Black, Earl. "The Militant Segregationist Vote in the Post-Brown South: A Comparative Analysis." *Social Science Quarterly* (June 1973): 66–84.

Boger, John Charles. "Education's 'Perfect Storm?' Racial Resegregation, 'High Stakes' Testing, & School Inequities: The Case of North Carolina." Paper submitted for Conference on *The Resegregation of Southern Schools? A Crucial Moment In the History (and the Future) of Public Schooling in America,* 2002, Chapel Hill, North Carolina, August 30, 2002.

Bond, Horace Mann. "The Extent and Character of Separate Schools in the United States." *Journal of Negro Education* 4 (1935): 321–27.

Bunche, Ralph J. "A Critical Analysis of the Tactics and Programs of Minority Groups." *Journal of Negro Education* 4 (1935): 308–20.

Burns, Augustus M., III. "Graduate Education for Blacks in North Carolina, 1930–1951." *Journal of Southern History* 66 (1980): 195–218.

Campanella, Philip J. "Recent Legislation: Constitutional Law—Equal Protection—Pupil Placement Statutes." *Western Reserve Law Review* 16 (1965): 800–808.

Clark, Kenneth B. "The *Brown* Decision: Racism, Education, and Human Values." *Journal of Negro Education* 57 (1988): 125–32.

Clotfelter, Charles T., Helen F. Ladd, and Jacob L. Vigdor. "Racial and Economic Diversity in North Carolina's Schools: An Update." Durham, N.C.: Sanford Working Papers Series. SAN13-01, January 16, 2013.

Coon, Charles L. "The Beginnings of North Carolina City Schools, 1867–1887." *South Atlantic Quarterly* 12 (1913): 235–47.

———. "School Support and Our North Carolina Courts." *North Carolina Historical Review* 3 (1926). Rpt. Raleigh: Edwards and Broughton, 1926. In North Carolina Collection, Louis Round Wilson Library, University of North Carolina, Chapel Hill.

DuBois, W. E. Burghardt. "Does the Negro Need Separate Schools?" *Journal of Negro Education* 4 (1935): 328–35.

Dunn, James R. "Title VI, the Guidelines, and School Desegregation in the South," *Virginia Law Review* 53 (1967): 42–88.

Edmonds, Ronald. "Effective Schools for the Urban Poor," *Educational Leadership* (October 1979): 15–24.

Erskine, Hazel Gaudet. "The Polls: Race Relations." *Public Opinion Quarterly* 26 (Spring 1962): 137–48.

Ferguson, James S. "An Era of Educational Change." *North Carolina Historical Review* 66 (April 1969): 130–41.

Finkelman, Paul. "Exploring Southern Legal History." *North Carolina Law Review* 64 (1985): 77–116.

Fiss, Owen M. "Racial Imbalance in the Public Schools: The Constitutional Concepts." *Harvard Law Review* 78 (1965): 565–617.

Frankenberg, Erica, and Chungmei Lee. "Race in American Public Schools: Rapidly Resegregating School Districts." Cambridge, Mass.: Civil Rights Project, Harvard University. August 2002.

Goldsmith, Kory. "The Civil Rights Act of 1964 and School Desegregation." *School Law Bulletin* (Fall 1991): 17–24.

Greeley, Andrew M., and Paul B. Sheatsley. "Attitudes toward Racial Integration." *Scientific American* (December 1971): 13–19.

Hyman, Herbert H., and Paul B. Sheatsley. "Attitudes toward Desegregation." *Scientific American* (December 1956): 35–39; (July 1964): 16–23.

Jones, H. G. "In Light of History." *Eden Daily News,* February 17, 1986.

Long, Howard Hale. "Some Psychogenic Hazards of Segregated Education of Negroes." *Journal of Negro Education* 4 (1935): 336–50.

Meador, Daniel J. "The Constitution and the Assignment of Pupils to Public Schools." *Virginia Law Review* 45 (1959): 517–71.

Mickelson, Roslyn Arlin. "The Academic Consequences of Desegregation and Segregation: Evidence from the Charlotte-Mecklenburg Schools." Paper prepared for the Conference on the Resegregation of Southern Schools, Chapel Hill, North Carolina, August 29–30, 2002.

Nabrit, James M., Jr. "Resort to the Courts as a Means of Eliminating 'Legalized' Segregation." *Journal of Negro Education* 20 (1951): 460–74.

Newman, Mark. "The Baptist State Convention of North Carolina and Desegregation, 1945–1980." *North Carolina Historical Review* 75 (1998): 1–28.

Olson, Lynn. "The Common Good." *Education Week,* January 27, 1999.

Orfield, Gary. "Public School Desegregation in the United States, 1968–1980," Washington, DC: Joint Center for Political Studies, 1983. civilrightsproject.ucla.edu/.

Palmer, Charles L. "The Fourteenth Amendment: Some Reflections on Segregation in Schools." *American Bar Association Journal* 49 (1963): 645–51.

Peterson, Gladys Tignor. "The Present Status of the Negro Separate School as Defined by Court Decisions." *Journal of Negro Education* 4 (1935): 351–74.

Pleasants, Julian M. "'Call Your Next Case': H. F. 'Chub' Seawell Jr., the Gu-

bernatorial Election of 1952, and the Rise of the Republican Party in North Carolina." *North Carolina Historical Review* 76 (1999): 66–101.
Rutledge, Archibald. "The World's Largest Negro Business." *Reader's Digest.* June 1943.
Siegel-Hawley, Genevieve, and Erica Frankenberg. "Southern Slippage: Growing School Segregation in the Most Desegregated Region of the Country." Cambridge, Mass.: Civil Rights Project. September 2012.
Smith, Ralph Lee. "The South's Pupil Placement Laws: Newest Weapon against Integration." *Commentary* 30 (October 1960): 326–29.
Thompson, Charles H. "How Imminent Is the Outlawing of Segregation?" *Journal of Negro Education* 20 (1951): 495–98.
Ware, Gilbert. "*Hocutt*: Genesis of *Brown*." *Journal of Negro Education* 52 (1983): 227–33.
Webb, Robert G. "Constitutional Law—Little Rock School Litigation—Reexamination of North Carolina Laws," *North Carolina Law Review* 37 (1959): 177–84.

Articles, Unsigned

"Racial Imbalance in the Public Schools—Legislative Motive and the Constitution." *Virginia Law Review.* 50 (1964): 464–534.
"School Closing Plans." *Race Relations Law Reporter* 3 (August 1958): 807–40.
"A Survey of Statutory Changes." *North Carolina Law Review* 33 (1955): 552–55.

Books

Ames, Jesse Daniel. *The Changing Character of Lynching.* Atlanta: Commission on Interracial Cooperation, 1942.
Ashmore, Harry S. *The Negro and the Schools.* Chapel Hill: University of North Carolina Press, 1954.
Bardolph, Richard, ed. *The Civil Rights Record.* New York: Crowell, 1970.
Bartley, Numan V. *The Rise of Massive Resistance.* Baton Rouge: Louisiana State University Press, 1969.
Bass, Jack, and Walter DeVries. *The Transformation of Southern Politics.* New York: Basic Books, 1976.
Batchelor, John E. *The Guilford County Schools: A History.* Winston-Salem, N.C.: John F. Blair, 1991.
Berliner, David C., and Bruce J. Biddle. *The Manufactured Crisis.* New York: Addison-Wesley, 1995.
Berman, Daniel M. *It Is So Ordered.* New York: W. W. Norton & Co., 1966.

Berman, William C. *America's Right Turn: From Nixon to Clinton.* Baltimore: Johns Hopkins University Press, 1998.

Black, Earl. *Southern Governors and Civil Rights.* Cambridge, Mass.: Harvard University Press, 1976.

Blaustein, Albert P., and Clarence Clyde Ferguson Jr. *Desegregation and the Law.* New York: Random House, 1962.

——, and Robert L. Zangrando. *Civil Rights and the American Negro.* New York: Random House, 1962.

Bracey, Gerald W. *Setting the Record Straight.* Alexandria, Va.: Association for Supervision and Curriculum Development, 1997.

Brink, William, and Louis Harris. *Black and White.* New York: Simon and Schuster, 1967.

——. *Negro Revolution in America.* New York: Simon and Schuster, 1964.

Britt, Clarinda, and James E. Britt, eds. *So Proudly We Taught.* Charlotte: N.C. Retired School Personnel Division of N.C. Association of Educators, 1976.

Bullock, Henry Allen. *A History of Negro Education in the South.* Cambridge, Mass.: Harvard University Press, 1967.

Butler, Lindley S., and Alan D. Watson. *The North Carolina Experience.* Chapel Hill: University of North Carolina Press, 1984.

Campbell, Ernest Q. *When a City Closes Its Schools.* Chapel Hill: University of North Carolina Press, 1960.

Carolina Population Center. *County Population Trends, North Carolina, 1790–1960, State / Region / County / Residence / Color.* Chapel Hill: Carolina Population Center, University of North Carolina, and Dept. of Administration, State of North Carolina, March 1969.

Carter, Dan T. *The Politics of Rage: George Wallace, The Origins of the New Conservatism, and the Transformation of American Politics.* New York: Simon and Schuster, 1995.

Carter, W. Horace. *Virus of Fear.* Tabor City, N.C.: Atlantic Publishing, 1991.

Cecelski, David S. *Along Freedom Road: Hyde County, North Carolina, and the Fate of Black Schools in the South.* Chapel Hill: University of North Carolina Press, 1994.

Chadbourn, James Harmon. *Lynching and the Law.* Chapel Hill: University of North Carolina Press, 1933.

Chafe, William H. *Civilities and Civil Rights.* New York: Oxford University Press, 1980.

Cheney, John L., Jr., ed. *North Carolina Government, 1585–1974: A Narrative and Statistical History.* Raleigh: Secretary of State, 1975.

Chubb, John E. and Terry M. Moe. *Politics, Markets, and America's Schools.* Washington, D.C.: Brookings Institution, 1990.

Clabaugh, Gary K. *Thunder on the right; the Protestant Fundamentalists.* Chicago: Nelson-Hall, 1974.

Clark, Thomas D. *The Emerging South.* New York: Oxford University Press, 1968.

———, and Albert D. Kirwan. *The South Since Appomattox.* New York: Oxford University Press, 1967.

Clay, James W., Douglas M. Orr Jr., and Alfred W. Stuart, eds. *North Carolina Atlas.* Chapel Hill: University of North Carolina Press, 1975.

Coates, Albert. *Talks on the Rule of Law and the Role of State Government in the Cities, the Counties, and the State of North Carolina.* Chapel Hill, N.C.: Professor Emeritus Fund, n.d..

Cooke, Dennis Hargrove. *The White Superintendent and the Negro Schools in North Carolina.* Nashville: George Peabody College, 1930.

Coon, Charles L. *The Beginnings of Public Education in North Carolina: A Documentary History, 1790–1840.* Raleigh: Edwards and Broughton, 1908.

———. *A Statistical Record of the Progress of Public Education, 1870–1906.* Raleigh: State Superintendent of Public Instruction, 1907.

Crawford, Alan. *Thunder on the Right: the "New Right" and the Politics of Resentment.* New York: Pantheon Books, 1980.

Crow, Jeffrey J., Paul D. Escott, and Charles L. Flynn Jr., eds. *Race, Class, and Politics in Southern History.* Baton Rouge: Louisiana State University Press, 1989.

———, and Flora J. Hatley. *A History of African Americans in North Carolina.* Raleigh: Division of Archives and History, 1992.

Cutler, James Elbert. *Lynch-Law.* London: Longmans, Green, 1905.

Dabney, Virginius. *Virginia: The New Dominion.* Charlottesville: University Press of Virginia, 1971.

Douglas, Davison M. *Reading, Writing, and Race: The Desegregation of the Charlotte Schools.* Chapel Hill: University of North Carolina Press, 1995.

Durham, Michael S. *Powerful Days: The Civil Rights Photography of Charles Moore.* New York: Stewart, Tabori & Chang, 1991.

Egerton, John. *Speak Now Against the Day.* New York: Alfred A. Knopf, 1994.

Eure, Thad. *North Carolina Government.* Raleigh: Secretary of State, 1975.

Franklin, John Hope. *From Slavery to Freedom.* New York: Alfred A. Knopf, 1967.

———. *Race and History.* Baton Rouge: Louisiana State University Press, 1989.

Friedland, Michael B. *Lift Up Your Voice Like a Trumpet: White Clergy and the Civil Rights and Antiwar Movements, 1954–1973*. Chapel Hill: University of North Carolina Press, 1998.

Gaillard, Frye. *The Dream Long Deferred*. Chapel Hill: University of North Carolina Press, 1988.

Gates, Robbins L. *The Making of Massive Resistance*. Chapel Hill: University of North Carolina Press, 1964.

George, W. C. *The Race Problem from the Standpoint of One Who Is Concerned about the Evils of Miscegenation*. Birmingham, Ala.: American States Rights Association, 1955.

Golden, Harry. *Mr. Kennedy and the Negro*. Greenwich, Conn.: Fawcett, 1964.

Greenberg, Jack. *Race Relations and American Law*. New York: Columbia University Press, 1959.

Grissmer, David, Ann Flanagan, Jennifer Kawata, and Stephanie Williamson. *Improving Student Achievement: What State NAEP Test Scores Tell Us*. Arlington, Va.: RAND, 2000.

Hamby, Alonzo L. *Liberalism and Its Challengers*. New York: Oxford University Press, 1992.

Havard, William C., ed. *The Changing Politics of the South*. Baton Rouge: Louisiana State University Press, 1972.

Hicks, John D. *The Populist Revolt*. Minneapolis: The University of Minnesota Press, 1931.

Higginbotham, A. Leon, Jr. *Shades of Freedom*. New York: Oxford University Press, 1996.

Jackson, Walter A. *Gunnar Myrdal and America's Conscience*. Chapel Hill: University of North Carolina Press, 1990.

Key, V. O., Jr. *Public Opinion and American Democracy*. New York: Alfred A. Knopf, 1961.

———. *Southern Politics in State and Nation*. New York: Alfred A. Knopf, 1950.

Kluger, Richard. *Simple Justice*. New York: Alfred A. Knopf, 1976.

Ladd, Everett Carl, Jr. *Negro Political Leadership in the South*. Ithaca, New York: Cornell University Press, 1966.

Lefler, Hugh Talmage, and Albert Ray Newsome. *North Carolina: The History of a Southern State*. Chapel Hill: University of North Carolina Press, 1973.

Legacy, 1963–1993: Thirty Years of African-American Students at Duke University. Durham, N.C.: Duke University, Office of the University Vice President and Vice Provost, 1995.

Leloudis, James L. *Schooling the New South*. Chapel Hill: University of North Carolina Press, 1996.

Link, William. *William Friday: Power, Purpose, and American Higher Education.* Chapel Hill: University of North Carolina Press, 1995.

Long, Hollis Moody. *Public Secondary Education for Negroes in North Carolina.* New York: Teachers College, Columbia University, 1932.

Lubell, Samuel. *The Future of American Politics.* New York: Harper and Brothers, 1952.

Luebke, Paul. *Tar Heel Politics: Myths and Realities.* Chapel Hill: University of North Carolina Press, 1990.

———. *Tar Heel Politics 2000.* Chapel Hill: University of North Carolina Press, 1998.

Matthews, Donald R., and James W. Prothro. *Negroes and the New Southern Politics.* New York: Harcourt, Brace & World, Inc., 1966.

Mays, David J. *A Question of Intent: The States, Their Schools and the 14th Amendment.* Statement before a U.S. Senate subcommittee, May 14, 1959.

Miller, Arthur S. *Racial Discrimination and Private Education.* Chapel Hill: University of North Carolina Press, 1957.

Murray, Percy. *History of the North Carolina Teachers Association.* [Washington, D.C.:] National Education Association, n.d.

Muse, Benjamin. *Ten Years of Prelude.* New York: Viking Press, 1964.

———. *Virginia's Massive Resistance.* Bloomington: Indiana University Press, 1961.

Noble, M. C. S. *A History of the Public Schools of North Carolina.* Chapel Hill: University of North Carolina Press, 1930.

North Carolina Advisory Committee on Civil Rights. *Equal Protection of the Laws in North Carolina.* Washington, D.C.: U.S. Government Printing Office, [1962].

O'Brien, Gail Williams. *The Color of the Law: Race, Violence, and Justice in the Post-World War II South.* Chapel Hill: University of North Carolina Press, 1999.

Orfield, Gary, Susan E. Eaton, and the Harvard Project on School Desegregation. *Dismantling Desegregation.* New York: New Press, 1996.

Peltason, J. W. *Fifty-Eight Lonely Men.* New York: Harcourt, Brace & World, 1961.

Phay, Robert E., and Janine M. Murphy, eds. *Education Law in North Carolina.* Chapel Hill, N.C.: Institute of Government, 1991.

Pierce, Truman, James B. Kincheloe, R. Edgar Moore, Galen N. Drewry, and Bennie E. Carmichael. *White and Negro Schools in the South: An Analysis of Biracial Education.* Englewood Cliffs, New Jersey: Prentice-Hall, 1955.

Pleasants, Julian M., and Augustus M. Burns III. *Frank Porter Graham and the 1950 Senate Race in North Carolina.* Chapel Hill: University of North Carolina Press, 1990.

Powell, William S., ed. *Dictionary of North Carolina Biography.* Chapel Hill: University of North Carolina Press, 1979.

———. *The First State University.* Chapel Hill: University of North Carolina Press, 1992.

———. *North Carolina: A History.* New York: W. W. Norton, 1977.

Proctor, Samuel DeWitt. *The Substance of Things Hoped For.* New York: G. P. Putnam's Sons, 1995.

Raper, Arthur F. *The Tragedy of Lynching.* Chapel Hill: University of North Carolina Press, 1933.

Ross, Irwin. *The Loneliest Campaign.* New York: Signet Books, 1968.

Sanford, Terry. *But What About the People?* New York: Harper & Row, 1966.

Sarratt, Reed. *The Ordeal of Desegregation.* New York: Harper & Row, 1966.

Schwartz, Bernard. *Swann's Way.* New York: Oxford University Press, 1986.

Schwartz, Mildred A. *Trends in White Attitudes toward Negroes.* Chicago: University of Chicago Press, 1967.

Shoemaker, Don, ed. *With All Deliberate Speed.* New York: Harper & Brothers, 1957.

Smith, Bob. *They Closed Their Schools.* Chapel Hill: University of North Carolina Press, 1965.

Smith, Charles Lee. *The History of Education in North Carolina.* Washington: Government Printing Office, 1888.

Snider, William D. *Helms and Hunt: The North Carolina Senate Race, 1984.* Chapel Hill: University of North Carolina Press, 1985.

Southern Commission on the Study of Lynching. *Lynchings and What They Mean.* Atlanta: The Commission, n.d..

Southern Education Reporting Service. *Status of School Segregation—Desegregation in the Southern and Border States.* Nashville: Southern Education Reporting Service, 1957.

———. *Statistical Summary: Segregation-Desegregation in the Southern and Border States.* Nashville: Southern Education Reporting Service, 1967.

Southern Regional Council. *The Schools and the Courts.* Atlanta: Southern Regional Council, 1953.

State Education Commission. *Education in North Carolina Today and Tomorrow.* Raleigh: United Forces for Education, 1948.

Steahr, Thomas E. *North Carolina's Changing Population.* Chapel Hill, N.C.: Carolina Population Center, 1973.

Stoeson, Alexander R. *History of Guilford County, N.C.* [Greensboro, N.C.:] Guilford County Bicentennial Commission, 1971.

Tindall, George Brown. *The Emergence of the New South, 1913–1945.* Baton Rouge: Louisiana State University Press, 1967.

Tumin, Melvin M. *Desegregation: Resistance and Readiness.* Princeton, N.J.: Princeton University Press, 1958.

Tushnet, Mark V. *The NAACP's Legal Strategy against Segregated Education, 1925–1950.* Chapel Hill: University of North Carolina Press, 1987.

Tyack, David, and Larry Cuban. *Tinkering Toward Utopia: A Century of Public School Reform.* Cambridge, Mass.: Harvard University Press, 1995.

U.S. Commission on Civil Rights. *Public Education.* Washington: United States Commission on Civil Rights, 1964.

Virginia Commission on Constitutional Government. *Did the Court Interpret or Amend?* [Richmond:] Virginia Commission on Constitutional Government, 1960.

Walker, Vanessa Siddle. *Their Highest Potential.* Chapel Hill: University of North Carolina Press, 1996.

Waynick, Capus; Brooks, John C.; and Pitts, Elsie W. *North Carolina and the Negro.* Raleigh: Mayors' Cooperating Committee, 1964.

White, G. Edward. *Patterns of American Legal Thought.* New York: Bobbs-Merrill, 1978.

White, Walter. *Rope and Faggot.* 1929. Rpt. New York: Arno Press and New York Times, 1969.

Wilkinson, J. Harvie, III. *From Brown to Bakke.* New York: Oxford University Press, 1979.

Woodward, Bob, and Scott Armstrong. *The Brethren.* New York: Simon and Schuster, 1979.

Woodward, C. Vann. *Origins of the New South, 1877–1913.* Baton Rouge: Louisiana State University Press, 1951.

Zangrando, Robert L. *The NAACP Crusade against Lynching.* Philadelphia: Temple University Press, 1980.

Zopf, Paul E., Jr. *North Carolina: A Demographic Profile.* Chapel Hill: Carolina Population Center, n.d., ca. 1968.

Broadcast Media

Branch, Taylor. Guest. "The Diane Rehm Show." NPR. January 17, 2013. Radio.

Dissertations and Theses

Batchelor, John Ellsworth. "Rule of Law: North Carolina School Desegregation from *Brown* to *Swann,* 1954–1974." Raleigh: North Carolina State University, 1992.

Calaway, Jacqueline G. "The Pearsall Program—1954–1956 in North Carolina." MA thesis. Wake Forest University, 1972.

Godwin, John Lochlan. "Wilmington and the North Carolina Way: Race, Culture, and Economy through the Civil Rights Years." Columbia: University of South Carolina, 1994.

Huff, H. H. "Negro Education in North Carolina." Chapel Hill: University of North Carolina, 1925.

Long, Joseph Kindred. "Trends in the Equalization of Educational Opportunity in North Carolina." Nashville: George Peabody College, 1936.

O'Quinn, Marion Nolan. "Carpetbagger Samuel S. Ashley and His Role in North Carolina Education, 1865–1871." MA thesis. North Carolina State University, 1975.

Raynor, William Reed. "Educational Discriminations Between Whites and Negroes in the South." Chapel Hill: University of North Carolina, 1940.

Shaffer, Albert. "The Social Organization of a Rural Community in Transition." Chapel Hill: The University of North Carolina, 1957.

Reference Books

Martindale-Hubbell Law Directory. Summit, N.J.: Martindale-Hubbell, 1990, 1992.

North Carolina Manual. Raleigh: Secretary of State, published biennially.

Videotapes

Wilson, John B., Jr. and Martin Clark. *Dr. Frank: The Life and Times of Frank Porter Graham*. Chapel Hill: UNC Arts and Sciences Foundation and UNC Center for Public Television, 1994.

Sanford: A Life of Service. Durham, N.C.: WTVD NewsChannel 11/ABC, Inc., 1998.

WEBSITES

Balkin, Jack M., and Cristina M. Rodriguez. *Civil Rights Chronology*. www.yale.edu/lawweb/jbalkin/brown/1903.html.

bioguide.congress.gov.

Civil Rights Greensboro, library.uncg.edu/dp/crg/topicalessays/schooldeseginteg.aspx.ncpedia.org/category/subjects/biography.

facesofcourage.wfu.edu. library.davidson.edu/archives/acs/integration/kates_page.htm.

History of the Federal Judiciary. www.fjc.gov.

stateboard.ncpublicschools.gov/about-sbe/history/history-of-sbe.

uselectionatlas.org.
www.cms.k12.nc.us/mediaroom/aboutus/Pages/CMSTimeline.aspx.
www.cms.k12.nc.us/mediaroom/aboutus/Pages/History.aspx.
www.cs.duke.edu.
www.ncleg.net/.
www.supremecourt.gov.
www.wmich.edu/politics/mlk/.

Index